BEHAVIORAL PROCEDURES FOR A PSYCHIATRIC UNIT AND HALFWAY HOUSE

BEHAVIORAL PROCEDURES FOR A PSYCHIATRIC UNIT AND HALFWAY HOUSE

Frederick J. Fuoco, Ph.D.
Broughton Hospital
Morganton, North Carolina

Barry J. Naster, Ph.D.
Florida Mental Health Institute
Tampa, Florida

Janice B. Vernon, M.A.
Robert T. Morley, M.A.
John F. Middleton, M.A.
Broughton Hospital
Morganton, North Carolina

VAN NOSTRAND REINHOLD COMPANY
——————————— New York

Copyright © 1985 by Van Nostrand Reinhold Company Inc.

Library of Congress Catalog Card Number: 85-3285
ISBN: 0-442-22491-5

All rights reserved. No part of this work covered by the copyright hereon may be reproduced or used in any form or by any means—graphic, electronic, or mechanical, including photocopying, recording, taping, or information storage and retrieval systems—without permission of the publisher.

Manufactured in the United States of America

Published by Van Nostrand Reinhold Company Inc.
135 West 50th Street
New York, New York 10020

Van Nostrand Reinhold Company Limited
Molly Millars Lane
Wokingham, Berkshire RG11 2PY, England

Van Nostrand Reinhold
480 Latrobe Street
Melbourne, Victoria 3000, Australia

Macmillan of Canada
Division of Gage Publishing Limited
164 Commander Boulevard
Agincourt, Ontario M1S 3C7, Canada

15 14 13 12 11 10 9 8 7 6 5 4 3 2 1

Library of Congress Cataloging in Publication Data
  Main entry under title:
Behavioral procedures for a psychiatric unit and halfway
  house.

  Includes index.
  1. Mentally ill—Rehabilitation—Life skills guides—
Handbooks, manuals, etc. 2. Behavior modification—
Handbooks, manuals, etc. I. Fuoco, Frederick J. [DNLM:
1. Behavior Therapy—handbooks. 2. Halfway Houses—
handbooks. 3. Hospitals, Psychiatric—handbooks.
4. Residential Treatment—handbooks. WM 39 B419]
RC439.5.B44 1985   616.89   85-3285
ISBN 0-442-22491-5

To
The Residents of the Behavior Therapy Unit
and the Project Reentry Halfway House
Past, Present, and Future

PREFACE

Presented in this book are program-wide behavioral treatment procedures developed for chronic residents in a residential psychiatric treatment unit and in a halfway house. These procedures have been developed over a period of several years and have been effectively used in a variety of settings.

The first section of the book includes general information regarding the treatment setting, population, purpose, and goals. Program-wide treatment procedures for the psychiatric unit are presented in the second section. The third section contains the treatment procedures for the halfway house.

This book is directed primarily to clinical staff working in psychiatric treatment facilities, and secondly, to clinical staff employed in other types of residential treatment facilities. The procedures presented in this book provide clinicians with a proven and refined treatment package that can be used as a model when developing behavioral treatment procedures for residential treatment populations.

Even though the treatment package is primarily intended for use as a deinstitutionalization program for psychiatric residents, other applications are possible. The procedures can be used for research and evaluation, and staff training. In addition, portions may be used with clinical populations other than chronic psychiatric residents.

The procedures presented in this book may be reproduced for clinical practice. Reproduction for resale or general distribution without written permission of the publisher is prohibited and is unlawful. Material which is reproduced for clinical practice must contain the following statement:

Reproduced from: Fuoco, Frederick J., Naster, Barry J., Kirk, Janice B., Morley, Robert T., and Middleton, John F. (1985). *Behavioral Procedures for a Psychiatric Unit and Halfway House.* New York: Van Nostrand Reinhold.

ACKNOWLEDGMENTS

Numerous individuals have contributed in various ways to the development of this procedure manual. First, appreciation is extended to Broughton Hospital administrative and clinical staff, who have been directly or indirectly involved in the development of the treatment package presented in this volume. Mr. William Lowrance, Director, Broughton Hospital has provided substantial administrative support. Drs. James Johnson, Clinical Director, William Moody, Associate Clinical Director, Louis Stein, Assistant Clinical Director, and Alexander Manning, Psychology Department Director, have provided both administrative and clinical support that is greatly appreciated.

Special appreciation is extended to staff members of the Behavior Therapy Unit (B.T.U.) and the Project Reentry Halfway House (H.W.H.) who have contributed significantly. Specifically, we gratefully acknowledge Mrs. Frances Drum, R.N., B.T.U. Head Nurse, Mrs. Betty Smith, R.N., B.T.U. Nurse Supervisor I, Mrs. Mae Hardin, B.T.U. Health Care Technician Supervisor, Mrs. Sybil Rice, R.N., B.T.U. Nurse Supervisor I, Mr. Rod Birdsong, H.W.H. Co-Manager, Ms. Vicki Nelson, H.W.H. Co-Manager, and Mr. Dick Helms, H.W.H. Assistant Manager. These individuals have provided excellent administrative and clinical services to the B.T.U. or H.W.H. and have contributed in various ways to the development of the procedures presented in this book. Appreciation is also expressed to the Direct-Care staff, nurses, and other staff of the B.T.U. and H.W.H. Without their conscientious and dedicated work, treatment delivery would not be possible.

Special appreciation is extended to Mrs. Debbie Wilson and Ms. Karen St. Louis for their excellent clerical services. Mrs. Wilson typed numerous revisions of the procedures for implementation in the B.T.U. and the Project Reentry Halfway House. Ms. St. Louis was responsible for typing the final procedures for this book.

Several organizations were involved in the early stages of the development of the treatment package presented in this book. In this regard, appreciation is extended to (1) the North Carolina Division of Community Colleges and Western Piedmont Community College (Morganton, N.C.) for professional services and funds; (2) the North Carolina Division of Vocational Rehabilitation and the Vocational Rehabilitation Facility in Morganton, N.C. for clinical services and funds; and (3) Foothills Area Mental Health Programs (Morganton, N.C.) for clinical and administrative services. Special gratitude is extended to Dr. Walter Stelle, Director, Foothills Area Mental Health Programs for his crucial involvement in the establishment and development of Project Reentry and for his continued support, encouragement, and advice.

Appreciation is also extended to Ms. Susan Munger of Van Nostrand Reinhold Publishing Company for her assistance and support throughout the preparation of this book.

The B.T.U. and H.W.H. have been supported in part by (1) federal categorical 314-D funds (1976-77, 1977-78, 1978-79, 1979-80) awarded to Foothills Area Mental Health Programs; and (2) U.S. Department of Health, Education, and Welfare funds (1977-78, 1978-79) awarded to Western Piedmont Community College.

CONTENTS

Preface / vii
Introduction / 1

    Treatment Levels / 1
        Behavior Therapy Unit / 1
            Physical setting / 2
            Resident referrals / 2
            Staffing pattern / 2
            Treatment Level 1 / 3
            Treatment Level 2 / 3
            Treatment Level 3 / 3
        Halfway House / 4
            Physical setting / 4
            Resident referrals / 4
            Staffing pattern / 4

Psychiatric Unit Procedures / 5

    Behavior Therapy Facility Regulations / 5
    Interdisciplinary Treatment Team Conferences Procedure / 12
    Individual Program Book Procedure / 19
    Token Economy Program / 23
    Canteen Procedure / 38
    Self-Care Skills / 41
        Bedroom Area Preparation Procedure / 55
        Wake-up Procedure / 61
        Dental Hygiene Procedure / 67
        Shower Procedure / 71
        Locker Maintenance Procedure / 75
        Medication Procedure / 79
        Meal Procedure / 86
        Dressing Procedure / 91
    Communication Skills Program / 96
    Problem-Solving Skills (Daily Diary) Program / 118
    Goal Orientation Procedure (Daily Living Schedule) / 134
    Household Financial Management Program / 151
    Recreational-Leisure Activities Program / 179
    Job Assignment Procedure / 182
    Outside (On-Campus) Privileges Procedure / 191
    Weekend Visits Procedure / 198
    Agitation Procedure / 206
    Smoking Policy / 213
    Elopement Policy / 215
    Discharge Preparation Group / 218

Halfway House Procedures / 222

    Halfway House Policies / 222
    Interdisciplinary Treatment Team Conferences Procedure / 225
    Individual Program Book Procedure / 230
    Self-Care Skills Maintenance Procedure / 234
    Meals Procedure / 241
    Therapeutic Community / 253
    Resident Payments and Rent Program / 259
    Worksharing Program / 263
    Agitation / 270
    Elopement Procedure / 273

Index / 275

BEHAVIORAL PROCEDURES FOR A PSYCHIATRIC UNIT AND HALFWAY HOUSE

INTRODUCTION

The primary goal of the procedures presented in this book is the deinstitutionalization of chronic residents in a psychiatric hospital and in a halfway house. These procedures were developed for use in the Behavior Therapy Unit (B.T.U.) of Broughton Hospital, and the Project Reentry Halfway House, both located in Morganton, North Carolina.

The dominant treatment used in the B.T.U. and the Halfway House is behavior therapy. In addition to the procedures presented in this book, individualized behavioral treatment programs—tailored to the specific treatment demands and needs of individual residents—are developed and implemented as needed. These individualized treatment programs consist of modified program-wide procedures and/or other treatment procedures for target behaviors not addressed in the general procedures.

There are three treatment levels (Levels 1, 2, and 3) in the B.T.U. The specific level to which a resident is admitted is determined by the resident's demonstrated level of functioning, presenting problem areas, and treatment goals. Treatment begins with the self-care skills program followed by treatment that addresses more complex behavior (e.g., communication skills, money management). The rate and extent of advancement is determined by criteria-based performance, and the needs, capabilities, and treatment goals of each resident. Upon meeting specified treatment criteria for a given treatment level an individual may advance to a higher treatment level within the unit or be placed in the community. Community placement is selected if it is determined that an individual has reached his/her maximum level of self-sufficiency and is capable of living in the community. Selection of a specific setting in the community (i.e., halfway house, group home, rest home, independent living, etc.) is based upon a resident's overall level of functioning.

The Halfway House procedures were developed to facilitate deinstitutionalization and to ensure continuity of care between the B.T.U. and the community. For the purpose of ensuring the maintenance of skills, several of the Halfway House treatment procedures (e.g., Self-Care Skills, Problem Solving Skills) briefly address behavior previously treated in the B.T.U. In addition, in order to facilitate a successful transition from the unit to the Halfway House, programming parameters are such that they enable B.T.U. residents to receive treatment in the Halfway House during the day before actual admission to the facility. Similarly, subsequent to admission to the Halfway House, residents may temporarily continue receiving limited treatment services (e.g., Communication Skills Program) in the B.T.U.

TREATMENT LEVELS

Behavior Therapy Unit

A key feature of the psychiatric unit behavioral treatment procedures described in the following section is the division of the procedures into three treatment levels (Levels 1, 2, and 3). As stated earlier, this approach is based upon the program developed in the Bahvior Therapy Unit (B.T.U.) of Broughton Hospital, Morganton, North Carolina. In adapting these procedures to other treatment settings it may be useful to understand the main elements of the B.T.U., particularly the physical layout, the resident characteristics, and the staffing patterns of each level.

Physical setting. The B.T.U. has a maximum resident capacity of 107. Levels 1 and 2 contain 37 and 40 beds, respectively, and Level 3 has 30 beds. The building in which the unit is located is four stories, thus allowing the physical separation of each program level. Each level is divided into one male and one female ward. Nearly all the residents have single bedrooms, although each level has a few two-bed and four-bed rooms. Level 2 and 3 are "open" wards, which means that the outside doors remain unlocked during the day. Level 1 is "closed," allowing entry and exit only by key.

Each of the three levels has one or more activity rooms where residents may meet for social activities, recreation, or therapy groups. Other rooms on each level are designated for staff offices, time-out/seclusion (one per ward), and the physician's examination room.

The furnishings on each of the levels are arranged to give a "homelike" atmosphere—comfortable upholstered furniture, table lamps, attractive pictures, draperies, and plants all help to dispel the "institutional" atmosphere. The atmosphere, however, varies across the three levels; that is, Level 1 has fewer decorative features owing to the greater frequency of aggressive or self-abusive behavior among the residents. In addition, sofas are not found on Level 1 because the more withdrawn and apathetic residents use them for sleeping during the day. The relative attractiveness of the wards increases from Level 1 to Level 3, and is due largely to the increasing ability of the residents to improve their living area, and also to their desire for amenities. As one might predict, the increasing attractiveness of each level provides an incentive for the residents to move upward to a more comfortable and visually pleasing living area.

Meals are served in a central cafeteria. All levels dine at the same time but residents from each level sit together. Four residents are seated at each table and seating arrangements are left to the residents' discretion, unless otherwise determined for programmatic reasons (e.g., placing food-stealing residents separately to help decrease this behavior).

Resident referrals. Residents entering the B.T.U. are typically referred from the acute treatment units within the hospital, although residents from the long-term treatment units are occasionally referred. Referrals from the community may be accepted, depending upon the needs and overall census of the hospital. A Referral Evaluation Committee, comprised of the unit's head nurse, the supervisor of the direct-care staff, one of the unit's three psychologists, and one of the two social workers, interviews each prospective resident. The interview is conducted to assess the potential for treatment success, and to determine the optimum program level for admission. The final decision concerning admission and treatment level assignment rests with the Unit Director. Criteria for admission to each level have been established and are outlined below. It should be noted, however, that these criteria serve as guidelines rather than strict parameters and may be waived in specific cases.

Staffing pattern. Throughout the unit, the typical staffing pattern for each of the six wards includes one registered nurse and three or four direct-care staff. On 2d and 3d shifts, one registered nurse may cover one or two wards. One clinical psychologist (M.A. level) is assigned to each treatment level and is responsible for the overall management of the behavior programs. He/she also serves as the leader of the Interdisciplinary Treatment Team at that level. Two social workers are assigned to the unit, each providing services to 1.5 treatment levels. Medical/psychiatric service is provided by a half-time psychiatrist, a half-time physician, and a full-time physician's assistant. Other full-time clinical staff include five licensed practical nurses, two recreational therapists, one direct-care supervisor, one head nurse (registered nurse), and one unit director (Ph.D. level clinical psychologist). The unit is also served by an array of support services from the hospital at large (e.g., vocational rehabilitation counselor, music therapist). Overall clinical and administrative management of the unit is provided by the head nurse, the direct-care staff supervisor, and ultimately by the unit director.

All clinical staff assigned to the unit on a full-time basis receive extensive training in the implementation of behavioral treatment procedures.

Treatment Level 1. Admission to Level 1 is generally based upon the following criteria:

1. Current hospitalization of less than two years
2. A minimum of 120 days hospitalization during the preceding 12 months
3. Eighteen years of age or older
4. Absence of severe organic brain syndrome
5. Basic understanding of the goals and objectives of the program
6. Stabilization of psychotropic medication (if prescribed)
7. Potential for community placement
8. Absence of frequent physical aggression during the preceding 30 days

As stated earlier, these criteria offer general guidelines in the assessment of referred residents and exceptions are occasionally made.

Residents of Level 1 are typically low-functioning with significant psychological and/or intellectual impairment. The majority of residents exhibit psychotic behavior and modal diagnoses include both schizophrenic and affective disorders. Less frequent diagnoses include severe personality disorders. Mentally retarded residents in this level have substantial behavior disturbances.

Treatment in Level 1 addresses very basic survival skills, such as self-care, control of aggression, and basic interpersonal skills. The primary objective of treatment is to help residents acquire the appropriate skills needed to function in a residential care facility in the community (e.g., group home, nursing home), or to prepare them for advancement to a higher level within the unit (if this is deemed appropriate by the resident's Interdisciplinary Treatment Team). The expected duration of treatment in Level 1 is nine to twelve months.

Treatment Level 2. Criteria for admission to Level 2 are the same as those for Level 1. Resident characteristics reflect less debility than those in Level 1, with less overt psychotic behavior, higher social skills, and a lower frequency of aggression displayed by the Level 2 residents. Diagnoses, while still including schizophrenic and affective disorders, more often include personality disorders and mild mental retardation with behavior problems. Treatment in Level 2 addresses self-care skills and basic interpersonal skills, as in Level 1; however, the treatment criteria are higher. Level 2 provides an increasing degree of independence and responsibility, with more emphasis on rudimentary work skills and independent functioning without continuous direct supervision. The majority of the residents in this level are eventually discharged to more independent settings in the community (e.g., halfway houses, supervised apartments, their families), although a substantial percentage move to Level 3. The expected duration of treatment in Level 2 is nine to twelve months.

Treatment Level 3. The admission criteria for admission to Level 3 are as follows:

1. Eighteen to 65 years of age
2. Absence of severe organic brain syndrome
3. I.Q. of 70 or above
4. Stabilization on psychotropic medication (if prescribed)
5. Absence of frequent physical aggression during the preceding 30 days
6. Potential for community placement
7. Basic understanding of the goals and objectives of the program

Residents in Level 3 generally demonstrate little overt psychotic behavior. Residents with schizophrenic diagnoses are generally in remission and more specific behavioral problems (e.g., assertiveness problems, impulse control deficits, social skill deficits) are the focus of treatment. Therapeutic efforts address specific skill deficits with the goal of preparing each resident for independent living in the community. Placement goals typically consist of independent living, a return to the family or spouse, or temporary residency in an intermediary care facility in the community (e.g., halfway house). Treatment in Level 3 is generally more complex, more individualized, and more demanding than in Levels 1 and 2. The expected duration of treatment in Level 3 is six to nine months.

HALFWAY HOUSE

As stated earlier, the Project Reentry Halfway House procedures were developed to ensure continuity of treatment between the B.T.U. and the community, and to facilitate deinstitutionalization of chronic psychiatric residents. The design of the procedures enables the continuation, the advancement, and the completion of residential treatment initiated in the hospital. Concomitant with, and following, a brief period of treatment for basic skills (e.g., self-care skills) to ensure maintenance of skills acquired in the hospital, treatment addresses behaviors more appropriately treated in a halfway house setting. For example, procedures exist for meal preparation and planning, household management, and paying rent.

Physical setting. The Halfway House program is temporarily not in effect due to legislative cutbacks in federal funding. However, when in effect, the program was located in a one-story house approximately 4.5 miles from the hospital. The maximum resident capacity of the house was ten. Residents had single bedrooms of varying sizes. The larger bedrooms were given to residents who displayed exceptional progress in treatment. There was a living room, dining room, and kitchen in the house. Also, there was a self-contained apartment for live-in staff and a staff office.

Resident referrals. The majority of the residents in the Halfway House were graduates of the B.T.U. Referrals were also made, however, by other units in Broughton Hospital, and by other residential and non-residential treatment programs in North Carolina. Prospective residents were interviewed by the Halfway House staff. Admission was granted if there was an apparent need for the services provided in the program and if the individual displayed an adequate level of motivation to enter the program. Motivational level was determined by statements made by the individual during the interview concerning treatment needs and goals, and his/her level of understanding and interest in the program. Also, the individual was asked to contact a Halfway House staff member within two to three days following the interview to inform a staff member of his/her decision concerning admission, and to inquire about the decision made by the staff. If the resident did not contact the staff by the end of this three-day period, it was assumed that there was insufficient motivation and/or stabilization for admission to the program.

Staffing pattern. Three full-time and one part-time staff were employed in the Halfway House. The three full-time staff consisted of a live-in married couple who served as *house facilitators (house managers)*. The third full-time staff member (assistant house manager) served as a house facilitator during the day when the house managers were working, and served as a live-in house facilitator on weekends and when the couple was on vacation leave. The part-time employee was a clinical psychologist who served as the Halfway House director. Vocational rehabilitation, and community mental health employees also provided services to Halfway House residents on a limited basis.

PSYCHIATRIC UNIT PROCEDURES

BEHAVIOR THERAPY FACILITY REGULATIONS

I. Introduction
   A. Purpose
       The following regulations have been established for the purpose of regulating the framework and the general operating procedures of behavior therapy units and behavior therapy treatment in the facility. These regulations shall serve as a general guide to clinical practice, within the legal and ethical constraints relating to clients' (patients') rights and accepted professional practice.
   B. Definition of Behavior Therapy
       Behavior Therapy is herein defined as the systematic application of principles of conditioning and learning for the purpose of changing or remediating human behavior. It is assumed that learning plays a major role in the development of both appropriate and inappropriate behavior. The recipient of treatment should always know for what he/she is being treated and what the treatment procedure is. Whenever possible, he/she should play a role in deciding what direction treatment is to take, thus encouraging personal responsibility in his/her treatment. Because treatment effects are observable and measureable, procedures are open to change if desirable results are not forthcoming, and there are objective, often quantifiable data on which to base that change. The very nature of behavior therapy allows for greater public scrutiny than does any other therapeutic approach to behavior change.
       The goal of behavior therapy is to learn new, more appropriate and useful behaviors and to unlearn (extinguish) those behaviors that have resulted in poor personal adjustment. The emphasis is on learning.
   C. Identification of Behavior Therapy Units
       For the purposes of this document, a behavior therapy unit is a treatment unit which utilizes behavior therapy as the primary treatment approach.
       The director of the facility shall be responsible for the identification of treatment units in the hospital that qualify as behavior therapy units according to the definition of behavior therapy given in this document.
II. Clinical, Ethical, and Legal Considerations
   A. General
       Treatment plans should be developed and implemented with consideration given to the individuality of each client. As required by the facility for all treatment plans, these plans should include at a minimum: (1) objectively defined problem behaviors; (2) objective criteria; (3) objective short-term and long-term goals; (4) estimated length of time to achieve each short-term and long-term goal; (5) methods and procedures for implementation, data collection, and record keeping; (6) specification of responsible staff members; (7) implementation date; (8) estimated completion date; and (9) the approximate date the interdisciplinary team will review the treatment plan.
       A client participating in a behavior therapy unit or his/her legal guardian (if the client is legally incompetent) must be aware of the problems for which he/she is being treated, and must also be aware of the procedures to be utilized. Prior to admission to a behavior therapy unit, a client (guardian) must understand, agree with, and be given a description of the basic objectives, the treatment modalities/techniques, and the philosophy of the unit.
       Behavior therapy units and behavior therapy treatment plans in the facility shall conform to the regulations contained in the present document, to the laws on human rights as contained in North Carolina state statutes; and to the guidelines

for ethical practices as set forth by the American Psychological Association and the American Psychiatric Association.
   B. Informed Consent for Aversive/Intrusive Procedures
   Written consent shall be obtained prior to the initiation of an aversive/intrusive behavioral treatment procedure. Each consent form must include at least the following information: (1) an objective description of the problem behavior(s); (2) a concise description of procedure; (3) a description of any discomforts and/or risks that may result from the procedure; (4) the expected benefits or outcome; (5) a beginning date; (6) a statement of agreement/approval by the client (guardian); (7) a statement regarding the client's (guardian's) right to withdraw consent and discontinue participation in the procedure at anytime other than when the procedure is actually being implemented; and (8) a time limit on the consent (maximum 6 months).

   When consent for an aversive/intrusive procedure is withdrawn by a client (guardian), *or* when the client (guardian) refuses to give consent, the objection(s) to the procedure is to be submitted to the client's Interdisciplinary Treatment Team (I.T.T.). The I.T.T. is to assess the client's (guardian's) objections and the client's treatment needs and presenting problem(s), to decide whether to revise the client's treatment plan or to recommend the implementation of the procedure without consent. Before the I.T.T. can recommend implementation of the procedure without consent (1) the criteria specified in these regulations for aversive/intrusive procedures must be met (see Section V Aversive/Intrusive Procedures, p. 8); (2) the I.T.T. must determine that revision of the client's treatment plan is not indicated; *and* (3) the I.T.T. must determine that the behavior for which the procedure is prescribed poses a risk of bodily harm to the client or others. A recommendation by the I.T.T. to implement the procedure without client (guardian) consent is to be submitted by the Unit Director to the Behavior Therapy Oversight Committee, Human Rights Committee, and Clinical Director for review. Approval of these committees and the Clinical Director is required before the aversive/intrusive procedure may be implemented.
   C. Prohibited Procedures
   The following procedures are specifically prohibited from use under any circumstances:

   1. Contingent or noncontingent emetics for anything other than medical purposes
   2. Contingent or noncontingent application of cold showers
   3. Contingent or noncontingent physical contact punishment
   4. Contingent or noncontingent electrical shock
   5. Shouting or using a loud, sharp, harsh voice to frighten or threaten
   6. Contingent or noncontingent use of noxious chemicals or substances (e.g., lemon juice)
   7. Behavioral procedures that involve the restriction of a client's nonrestrictable legal rights as contained in North Carolina Patient's Rights (G.S. 122-55.1 through 122-55.7, 122-55.13, and 122-55.14 and 10 NCAC 14C .0200 PATIENTS RIGHTS)
   8. Withholding and/or denial of meals or other basic necessities of life (e.g., clothing) as a part of a contingency management, restrictive, and/or behavior therapy procedure

III. Records and Documentation
   A. General
   A significant component of behavior therapy is the documentation and evaluation of treatment interventions and behavior change through the development and

implementation of highly structured data collection and evaluation procedures. These procedures should include clear definitions of problem behaviors, performance criteria, short-term and long-term treatment goals, and methods for data collection, evaluation, and review. Structured data collection and evaluation procedures should be developed and implemented for both unit-wide behavioral procedures and individualized behavioral procedures.

B. Client Record/Chart

Each client shall have a program record which contains the following:

1. Data, reports, and forms routinely required by the facility (i.e., evaluations, history, doctors' orders, nursing plan, problem list, etc.)
2. Objective definition of each problem behavior
3. Objective short-term and long-term goals which are measurable and stated in measurable terms
4. Estimated length of time to achieve each short-term and long-term goal
5. Treatment plan to be implemented for each problem behavior to achieve each short-term and long-term goal
6. Staff member(s) who is responsible for implementation of each treatment program
7. Signatures of responsible staff member(s)
8. Behavioral contract/consent forms
9. Data collection procedure for each treatment plan
10. Assessment methods (including time-scheduled review procedure) for each treatment plan
11. Implementation date of each treatment plan
12. Estimated completion date of each treatment plan
13. Required documentation for implementation of aversive or intrusive procedures (see Section V: *Aversive/Intrusive Procedures*)

IV. Planning, Evaluation, and Review Committees and Procedures

A. Interdisciplinary Treatment Team

An Interdisciplinary Treatment Team (I.T.T.) shall be established in each unit to evaluate each client's needs, to develop individualized treatment plans to meet identified needs, and to periodically review each client's response to treatment plans and review the plans as needed.

The composition, duties, and responsibilities of the I.T.T. are as prescribed by the facility and the North Carolina Division of Mental Health, Mental Retardation and Substance Abuse Services.

B. Facility Behavior Therapy Oversight Committee

1. Purpose

The Behavior Therapy Oversight Committee shall review and evaluate all applications of behavior therapy in the facility and provide consultation to facility personnel regarding behavior therapy procedures and regulations

2. Composition

a. At least six persons, the majority of whom are well-qualified professionals by training and experience in the field of behavior therapy
b. At least one representative of the Human Rights Committee
c. At least one psychiatrist, psychologist, and nurse

NOTE: All committee members, with the exception of the representative of the Human Rights Committee, shall be Division employees unless the facility director requests from the division director, the appointment of a member outside the Division (G.S. 1438-147 (7) (a)).

3. Duties

a. Review and evaluate, at least annually, existing behavior therapy units

b. Investigate, review, and/or evaluate an established behavior therapy unit at the request of the facility director
c. Review, evaluate, and/or monitor individual applications of behavior therapy treatment plans at the request of the facility director or clinician who developed the behavior therapy treatment plan(s)
d. Review, evaluate, and monitor aversive/intrusive behavioral procedures as defined in this document (see Section V: *Aversive/Intrusive Procedures*)
e. Approve or reject behavior therapy unit procedures, individual applications of behavior therapy, and aversive/intrusive behavioral procedures as submitted, or modify the procedures to ensure compliance with these regulations, with accepted clinical practice, and with other federal, state, division, and facility regulations/guidelines. (Decisions of the committee shall be made by majority vote.)
f. Provide consultation to facility personnel regarding behavior therapy procedures and regulations

4. Frequency of Meetings
The Oversight Committee shall meet quarterly and as deemed necessary by the chairperson

V. Aversive/Intrusive Procedures
A. Purpose

Every effort is exerted to utilize positive treatment approaches; however, it may at times be necessary to develop and implement moderately aversive or intrusive procedures to weaken or eliminate inappropriate or dangerous behavior. The purpose of this section of the Behavior Therapy Regulations is to provide regulations for the use of such procedures.

B. Definition
1. *Aversive or intrusive procedure* herein refers to, but is not limited to, any *behavioral* procedure that
   a. Involves the use of physical restraint by a staff member(s) and/or mechanical devices to restrict or prevent a client's motor movement (excluding the use of restraints, seclusion, and time-out for agitated or destructive behavior and/or for the protection of self and/or others).
   b. Forces a client to engage in behavior that may be against his/her will.
   c. Involves the use of contingent or noncontingent confinement to a seclusion room (locked room) or time-out room (unlocked room) for other than agitated or destructive behavior and/or the protection of self and/or others.
   d. Involves the use of any negative or restrictive behavioral procedure which is not a commonly accepted behavioral treatment technique and/or accepted clinical practice at the facility.

2. Prohibited Aversive or Intrusive Procedures
The aversive or intrusive procedures specified in Section II-C. *Prohibited Procedures* (p. 6) are prohibited from use under any circumstances.

C. Procedure
1. General Information
   a. All aversive/intrusive procedures, as defined in Section V. B. *must* be reviewed and approved both by the Oversight Committee and Human Rights Committee prior to implementation.
   b. Generally, aversive/intrusive procedures are to be implemented after positive procedures have been systematically attempted and found to be ineffective. However, when it is determined that positive procedures are not appropriate for a given problem behavior, aversive/intrusive procedures may be implemented without first implementing positive procedures. This

determination must be based on clinical judgement, the interests of the client, *and* current behavior therapy literature.

c. When positive treatment procedures have been attempted and found to be ineffective, there must be clear documentation of the attempt and outcomes in the client's record before an aversive/intrusive procedure can be implemented.

d. When an aversive/intrusive procedure is to be implemented without first implementing positive procedures, there must be clear documentation of the justification for the aversive/intrusive procedure in the client's record before the procedure can be implemented. This justification must include: (1) the rationale for implementation of an aversive or intrusive procedure; and (2) supportive behavior therapy literature.

e. Aversive/intrusive procedures are to be designed and implemented only for the clinical benefit of the client and not for the convenience of the staff or as a substitute for a positive procedure.

f. In all cases, efforts are to be made to develop the least aversive/intrusive procedure(s) possible.

g. Aversive/intrusive procedures are to be assessed in terms of their effectiveness, their potential side effects, their public acceptability, and their potential for abuse.

h. Aversive/intrusive procedures *must* be amenable to monitoring and evaluation.

i. The implementation of aversive/intrusive procedures must be under the direct supervision of a psychologist, a physician, or a nurse. (Direct supervision may be provided by other specified professionals, if approved by the Oversight Committee.)

j. Before a professional may supervise the implementation of an aversive/intrusive procedure he/she must have received appropriate training in the theory and implementation of the procedure, as determined by the Oversight Committee.

k. Prior to the implementation of an aversive/intrusive procedure, written informed consent must be obtained from the client if he/she is legally competent, or from his/her legal guardian if the client is legally incompetent. (See p. 6.)

l. The Oversight Committee is to receive written monthly reports from the unit director regarding aversive/intrusive procedures in effect. These reports are to be reviewed by the committee at least quarterly and should include at a minimum: (1) number of days procedure was in effect, (2) frequency of implementation, (3) longest duration and mean duration of implementation, (4) summary of pertinent outcome data collected, and (5) any problems encountered and/or unexpected effects/responses.

m. Aversive/intrusive procedures must adhere to all of the regulations contained in this document.

2. External Review and Evaluation Procedure

Unit Directors who desire to implement an aversive/intrusive procedure are to submit a written proposal to the Oversight Committee for review, evaluation, and subsequent submission to the Human Rights Committee. Proposals are to include the following:

a. General Information
   (1) Identification of unit
   (2) Identification and signature of Unit Director
   (3) Identification and signature(s) of proponent(s)
   (4) Date of proposal

(5) Description of client (e.g., age, sex, diagnosis, history)
(6) Description of problem behavior(s)
(7) Documentation of positive procedures already attempted and their outcomes, *or* justification for the use of an aversive or intrusive procedure without first implementing positive procedures
(8) Justification for aversive/intrusive procedure

b. Proposed Treatment Plan
(1) Objective definition of problem behavior(s)
(2) Description of aversive/intrusive technique(s) to be implemented
(3) Description of positive technique(s) to be implemented
(4) Objective contingencies
(5) Objective criteria
(6) Objective short-term and long-term goals which are measurable and stated in behavioral terms
(7) Estimated length of time to achieve each short-term and long-term goal
(8) Method and procedure for implementation
(9) Method and procedure for data collection and assessment
(10) Staff who will implement procedure(s)
(11) Staff member who will supervise implementation of procedure(s)
(12) Estimated implementation date
(13) Estimated termination date
(14) Frequency and approximate dates of review by Interdisciplinary Treatment Team
(15) Signatures of unit director, physician, proponent(s), and staff member who will supervise the implementation of the procedure

c. Proposed consent form (See Section V.C.1.k., p. 9, and Section II.B., p. 6)
d. Description of potential risks and/or discomfort that may result from the procedure, and the precautions and procedures to be observed to minimize risks and to respond to injuries or negative side effects
e. Description of behavior, negative side effects, injuries, etc., that may lead to early termination
f. Description of information and data to be included in written monthly reports to the Oversight Committee

VI. Required Qualifications and Training of Behavior Therapy Unit Staff
   A. Qualifications
      1. Behavior Therapy Unit Director (Clinical Psychologist *or* Psychiatrist)
         a. Responsibilities
         This individual is responsible for the overall integrated implementation and administration of all clinical and administrative components of the unit. Primary duties include program development and implementation, administration, staff supervision, staff training, treatment delivery, and research and evaluation.
         b. Minimum Education and Experience
            (1) Clinical Psychologist
               (a) Doctoral degree in clinical psychology and possession of a current and valid permanent license issued by the North Carolina State Board of Practicing Psychologists
               (b) Extensive academic training in the theory, the methods, and the application of behavior therapy

(c) Two years of extensive experience in the application of behavior therapy
(d) Other experience, knowledge, skills, and abilities required by the North Carolina Office of State Personnel for a Psychologist II

(2) Psychiatrist
  (a) Graduation from an accredited school of medicine
  (b) Eligible for licensure to practice medicine in North Carolina and so licensed before permanent appointment
  (c) Extensive academic training in the theory, the methods, and the application of behavior therapy
  (d) Two years of extensive experience in the application of behavior therapy
  (e) Other experience, knowledge, skills, and abilities required by the North Carolina Office of State Personnel for a Physician I.

2. Direct-Care Staff/Behavior Technicians
  a. Responsibilities
  These individuals serve as direct-care staff and directly provide treatment to the clients. Responsibilities include the implementation of an array of behavioral programs and the completion of ward, medical, and office duties.
  b. Minimum Education and Experience
    (1) High school diploma
    (2) Formal training and experience in behavior therapy techniques is/are preferred
    (3) In-service training on behavior therapy techniques
    (4) Knowledge of the principles and practice of health care and the techniques of practical nursing, knowledge of sanitation, personal hygiene, and common health and safety techniques; ability to identify the physical and emotional needs of clients, and make written and oral reports
    (5) Other experience, knowledge, skills, and abilities required by the North Carolina Office of State Personnel for a Health Care Technician I

3. Additional staff are required as specified by the North Carolina State Statutes (e.g., physician, nurse, social worker); however, the training, experience, and qualifications needed for employment in behavior therapy units are not delineated here inasmuch as the requirements do *not* deviate from those normally required for employment in North Carolina psychiatric facilities. With all clinical positions, experience and/or training in the application of behavior therapy is preferred.

B. Training

Each individual employed in a behavior therapy unit who provides clinical care/services is to receive continuing in-service training in behavior therapy commensurate with the level and extent of his/her clinical responsibilities. This training is to include instruction in (1) behavioral procedures and techniques utilized in the unit, (2) clinical behavioral theories and methodology, (3) behavioral assessment and data collection techniques, and (4) ethical and legal issues regarding behavior therapy. In-service training can include classes, lectures, workshops, symposia, and in-vivo supervision.

LEVEL 1, LEVEL 2, AND LEVEL 3
INTERDISCIPLINARY TREATMENT TEAM CONFERENCES PROCEDURE

GENERAL STATEMENT

These policies and procedures have been formulated to specify the responsibility for constructing, monitoring, implementing, and updating individualized treatment plans for residents. Treatment plans are combinations of therapies and programs designed by the treatment team to ensure progress in areas of skill deficits, and reduce behavior problems.

An Interdisciplinary Team shall be established to evaluate each resident's needs, plan an individualized treatment plan to meet identified needs, and to periodically review the resident's response to his/her treatment plan and revise the plan accordingly.

This plan shall be based on an interdisciplinary evaluation of the needs of the individual resident. The objectives shall be described in behavioral terms that permit progress to be assessed. The plan shall provide for implementation, continuing assessment, and revisions as necessary.

The Interdisciplinary Team provides an array of services designed to enable residents to develop to their maximum potential. The regular review process ensures the appropriate modification of the treatment plan so that the resident may move from one level of achievement to another within the program and possibly within the unit, and out of the facility when he/she is ready.

Members of the team shall be selected from the following areas, as appropriate to the resident's needs. This includes those staff persons providing on-going services to the residents, as well as staff utilized on a consultant, or as-needed basis.

A. Staff persons utilized on an on-going basis include:
   1. Psychologist (Treatment Team Leader)
   2. Nurse
   3. Social Worker
   4. Activity Therapist (Representing Occupational Therapy, Recreational Therapy, Industrial Therapy, & Music Therapy)
   5. Direct-Care Staff (Health Care Technician)
   6. Director
   7. Chief Nurse
   8. Psychiatrist
   9. Physician's Assistant
B. Staff persons utilized on a consultant, or as-needed basis include:
   1. Physician
   2. Audiologist
   3. Dentist
   4. Dietitian or Dietary Representative
   5. Librarian
   6. Chaplain
   7. Family members (by permission of resident)
   8. Community liasons
   9. Appropriate staff of the unit from which the resident was referred
   10. Activity Therapists directly involved with resident

The personnel selected shall include those persons who work most directly with the resident, regardless of their profession, discipline, or service area. Ordinarily, this team will include the Treatment Team Leader, Director, Social Worker, Nurse, Activity Therapist, Physician's Assistant, and Direct-Care Staff. Other personnel shall be selected by the Treatment Team Leader, or other psychology staff, with consultation from other team members as needed.

The psychologist shall serve as team facilitator to implement the resident's treatment plan between regularly scheduled re-evaluation sessions by the team. The Director shall approve the treatment plan (and any revisions) in writing, and shall be responsible for the overall adequacy of the plan. Members of the team shall share their specialized professional skills and release their intervention role in the coordination of the treatment plan to the Director.

Duties of the Interdisciplinary Treatment Team

Members of the Interdisciplinary Treatment Team shall be responsible for

1. Comprehensive diagnosis and evaluation of each resident as a basis for planning, programming, and management upon admission to the program
2. Design and implementation of an individualized treatment plan to effectively meet the needs of the resident
3. Regular review, evaluation, and revision, if necessary, of the resident's treatment plan
4. Assuring movement of the resident from one level of achievement to another within the program through training, rehabilitation, and placement
5. Providing an array of those services that will enable the resident to develop to his/her maximum potential
6. Assuring that the resident's rights are protected

The Pre-Admission Evaluation

This evaluation shall be conducted to determine whether the individual should be accepted into the program and shall include:

1. A preliminary review of the individual's relevant histories, and an assessment of current needs, including skill deficits and specific maladaptive behavior which necessitates individual programming
2. Determination of admission criteria fulfillment
3. Recommendations for admission or refusal based on specific information
4. The names, titles, functions, and facility of all professional staff involved in this review.

A written and oral summary of pre-admission evaluation is to be presented to the Director

Attendance at the Pre-Admission Evaluation shall include the following staff:

1. Chief Nurse
2. Psychologist
3. Social Worker
4. Direct-Care Staff (DCS) Supervisor
5. Staff member from the referring unit/facility (optional)

Admissions

Individuals accepted into the program typically enter the program on Mondays or Tuesdays. At this time a DCS is to be assigned to the resident.

The Initial Treatment Plan Review

Within 96 hours of the resident's admission to the Program, the Interdisciplinary Team shall meet to determine the resident's needs for further testing and evaluation. The written results of the meeting, to be entered into the resident's record, shall include:

1. A brief summary of the resident's social, educational, psychological, medical, and other pertinent histories
2. Current psychological and physical strengths
3. A listing of the resident's personal strengths
4. An indication of what resources, such as family, guardians, or other contacts from the resident's usual environment will participate in treatment or continue to be involved with the resident
5. Initial goals for treatment and preliminary anticipated outcomes
6. Discussion of any individual problems and additional baselines needed
7. The names, titles, and functions of all persons participating in the treatment (interdisciplinary team present), and the signature of the Director, the Psychiatrist, and the Psychologist

The Revised Treatment Plan

Within 14 days of the initial treatment plan, the Interdisciplinary Treatment Team shall meet to devise a written, detailed treatment plan to be entered in the resident's record. The plan shall be based upon observations, diagnosis, and evaluation of the resident's behavior. The plan must provide for the resident's attainment of maximum independence in areas of skill deficits; a plan to minimize significant inappropriate behavior problems; and provisions to deal with any problems the resident may have with his/her family, or with the community (when possible). The plan shall include:

1. A detailed description of the resident's intellectual and emotional state, including a description of his/her behavior at the time the plan is prepared, along with a statement of the specific treatment or rehabilitation needs
2. A detailed description of the nature of the recommended individual counseling, behavior therapy, behavior modification, family counseling, or any other form of treatment constituting part of the treatment plan
3. The names and titles of persons who will be responsible for furnishing any of these forms of treatment or rehabilitation
4. A clear, concise statement of the elements of behavior which have been defined as problems, and which the plan is designed to treat; the short-term and long-term treatment goals, with a projected time table for their attainment
5. The names, titles, and functions of all members of the Treatment Team present, and the signature of the Director, the Psychiatrist, and the Psychologist

Additionally, the Revised Treatment Plan shall be directed at reviewing and updating the Pre-admission Evaluation and determining a prognosis that can be used to determine the appropriateness of the resident's placement into the program.

Prior to the meeting of the Interdisciplinary Team, all medical, vocational, psychological, social, educational, and other necessary evaluations shall be completed. The results of these evaluations are to be in the resident's ward chart. On the basis of these evaluations, the Interdisciplinary Team shall establish priorities for meeting the resident's rehabilitation needs. These priorities shall be stated in writing, as a part of the Treatment Plan, along with short and long-term goals and criteria for release from the facility.

When any staff member designated to attend this review cannot attend, he/she is to summarize in writing, any evaluations, comments, or other pertinent information, and give this summary to the psychologist prior to the review.

The resident shall always attend the Revised Treatment Plan Review. Attendance of the resident's family or surrogates, and other persons designated as necessary contributors to the Treatment Plan, shall be considered when appropriate. Permission for these people to attend must first be obtained from the resident.

DCS members on all three shifts shall be given the written Treatment Plan and required to read and study its contents.

Treatment Plan Reviews

Within eight weeks from the date of the Revised Treatment Plan, and once every eight weeks thereafter, unless otherwise indicated in the resident's individual program, the Treatment Plan shall be reviewed by the resident's Interdisciplinary Team to appraise his/her progress toward achieving the objectives specified by the plan and to update the plan if necessary. Residents who have been in the facility during their current admission for less than three months shall be reviewed every month following the Revised plan for the first three months of their current admission. Progress shall be assessed on the basis of program data as interpreted by the Interdisciplinary Team. The meeting shall include:

1. Assessment of the resident's progress
2. Necessary changes, additions, or deletions in the resident's treatment plan
3. Changes, additions, or deletions shall include procedures and goals
4. A detailed description of the nature of the changes and/or additions to the resident's treatment plan
5. The names and titles of persons who will be responsible for furnishing any of these additional forms of treatment or rehabilitation
6. A clear, concise statement of the elements of behavior which have been defined as additional problems and which the revised treatment plan is designed to address along with the short-term and long-term treatment goals for each problem
7. The names, titles, and functions of all members of the Treatment Team present, and the signature of the Director, the Psychologist, and the Psychiatrist

Members of the Interdisciplinary Team who are not able to attend these reviews are to summarize in writing any evaluations, comments, or other pertinent information, and give this summary to the psychologist prior to the review.

The resident shall always attend these reviews. Attendance of the resident's family or surrogates, and other persons designated as necessary contributors to the Treatment Plan, shall be considered when appropriate, provided prior consent is obtained from the resident.

DCS members on all three shifts shall be given the revised Treatment Plan and required to familiarize themselves with its contents.

Special Reviews

When needed, a member of the staff may request a special review of particular components of the resident's treatment program. Special reviews shall be conducted immediately following the occurrences of potentially harmful behaviors which have no programs, individual or ward-wide, which adequately address the behavior. Attendance at Special Reviews shall include:

1. Psychology staff member(s) (Treatment Team Leader)
2. DCS assigned to the resident, or his/her alternate
3. Any staff members who observed the occurrence of the target behavior, and/or who can contribute information concerning the behavior
4. Any staff member(s) who possess specific skills or knowledge that may be useful in the review (e.g., nurse, physician, psychologist, etc.)

Discharge Conferences

These conferences are to take place prior to transfer to another ward or community placement, when indicated. They should include consideration of the following:

1. Overall progress of the resident toward treatment goals
2. The current needs of the resident, including services and therapies currently required
3. The suitability of the proposed placement for providing these services and therapies
4. The suitability of the placement from the perspective of the resident, the resident's family, and/or the surrogate
5. Plans for follow-up with the resident and the family
6. The names, the titles, and the functions of the persons participating in this staffing, and the signature of the Director, the Psychologist, and the Psychiatrist

Staff participation in this review shall consist of the resident's Interdisciplinary Team.

Members of the Interdisciplinary Team who are not able to attend these reviews shall summarize in writing, any evaluations, comments, or other pertinent information, and give this summary to the psychologist prior to the review. The resident is to attend this review. Attendance of the resident's family or surrogates, and other persons designated as necessary contributors to this review, shall be considered when appropriate, provided that prior consent is obtained from the resident.

DOCUMENTATION OF DISSEMINATION OF TREATMENT PLAN REVIEW RESULTS

The resident's chart shall be used to document the results of the evaluations on which the Treatment Plan is based; specify the components of the Treatment Plan with the program goals stated in behavioral terms; report the progress of the resident toward goals as progress is assessed at Treatment Plan Reviews; document review proceedings, and modify the Treatment Plan and goals in light of the resident's response; and provide a means of communication among all persons contributing to the resident's Treatment Plan.

Individual program procedures and data sheets shall be placed in the resident's Individual Program Book and Individual Program Chart.

All components of the Initial Treatment Plan and the Revised Treatment Plan, including the review and updating of the Pre-Admission Evaluation and statement of the resident's prognosis, must be entered in the resident's record within 30 days of admission. In addition, a comprehensive evaluation and a psychological diagnosis shall also be entered within 30 days of admission. Thereafter, progress notes on the resident's response to his/her program shall be recorded in the medical chart with sufficient frequency to enable an evaluation of its efficiency. At least once a week, the DCS member assigned to the resident shall record a progress note in his or her chart describing therapeutic outcomes for the week. Progress notes must be made whenever a resident engages in any behavior that requires the special attention of the staff (e.g., elopement, aggression).

Reports of Treatment Plan Reviews which evaluate the program, the progress, and the status of the resident shall also be entered. The results of all evaluations and reviews shall be interpreted in action terms to the direct-care staff and special services staff responsible for implementing the resident's program; and to parents or their surrogates when prior written consent is obtained from the resident. Also, the results of reviews shall be interpreted to the resident. They are to receive copies of any new treatment plans formulated during the reviews. Data on individual programs and daily observations shall be recorded on the appropriate sheets in the resident's Individual Program Book and/or Individual Program Chart.

PROCEDURE

I. Scheduling of Reviews
   A. Pre-admission Evaluations
      1. Pre-admission evaluations shall be coordinated by the Referral Evaluation Committee.
      2. These evaluations shall be scheduled by the Referral Evaluation Committee.

3. Individuals accepted into the program typically enter the program on Mondays or Tuesdays.
   B. Initial Treatment Plans, Revised Treatment Plans, Treatment Plan Reviews, or any reviews for the purposes of developing special programs shall be conducted on Tuesdays.
      1. The Treatment Team leader (Psychologist) shall
         a. Submit for distribution, a schedule of reviews on a weekly basis. This schedule shall be submitted by Thursday of the preceding week
         b. Submit any revisions of this schedule to the Treatment Team as they are necessary
         c. Ensure that for each resident, the Initial Treatment Plan is formulated within approximately three days of admission; that the revised Treatment Plan is formulated within 14 days of the Initial Treatment Plan and that each resident's plan is reviewed monthly, and as needed. (NOTE: Every month during the first three months of the current admission and then every eight weeks thereafter.)
      2. The Social Worker shall
         a. Provide for notification of family members or other persons, as designated by the resident, of Initial, Revised, and Treatment Plan Reviews at least 48 hours prior to these reviews. (Prior written consent must be obtained from the resident)
         b. This notification is required only when requested by the resident, his/her family, or the Treatment Team Leader
      3. The secretary shall
         a. Deliver the schedule of residents who are to have an Interdisciplinary Treatment Team Conference during the coming week. This schedule is to be posted in a conspicuous place in the DCS offices
         b. Send copies of the schedule to all other members of the Treatment Team
         c. Send copies of the schedule to other professional staff as designated by the Treatment Team Leader or Director
II. Assignment of Direct-Care Staff (DCS) members to individual residents
   A. Assignments of DCS members to individual residents shall be made by the nursing staff immediately upon admission of the resident to the program.
   B. DCS assignments shall be made to individual residents. There are to be alternate DCSs assigned to residents to cover for DCSs when they are off duty.
   C. DCS assignments are to change every three months or as determined by the nursing staff and the psychologist on an individual basis.
   D. The responsibilities of the DCSs assigned shall be
      1. Recording all data during their shift for assigned residents
      2. Ensuring that all aspects of programs for their assigned residents are implemented by others
      3. Making prior arrangements with DCSs not on leave to assume duties for their assigned residents, when on scheduled leave. (When on unscheduled leave, assigned residents are to be assigned by the nursing staff, to DCSs not on leave. If an alternate is on duty, then he/she is to assume responsibility for residents assigned to DCSs on scheduled or unscheduled leave.)
III. Provisions for appropriate Clinical Staff attendance at Case Reviews
   A. The Treatment Team leader, with input from the other clinical staff members, is responsible for ensuring the presence of Interdisciplinary Team members as prescribed by policy, or as needed, at the formulation of Initial and Revised Treatment Plans, Recurrent Treatment Plan Reviews, Discharge Conferences, and other reviews.
   B. When the necessary clinical staff is not available for the proper conduction of

reviews, or when consultation is necessary, the following procedure shall be employed:
1. The Treatment Team Leader shall be informed that consultation from outside the program is necessary.
2. The Treatment Leader shall be responsible for requesting the attendance of the needed consultant.

IV. Entry of results of reviews into the resident's chart, the Individual Program Book, and the Individual Program Chart
   A. Preparation of the written report of the review shall be the responsibility of the psychologist and the Social Worker. The Director, the Psychologist and the Psychiatrist must sign the report.
   B. The report must be written, typed, and placed in the resident's chart. The Psychologist is to compose the *Assessment* and *Plan* sections of the report, and the Social Worker is to compose the *Subjective and Objective* section of the report.
   C. Results of reviews shall be approved and entered into the resident's chart within one week of the review.
   D. Any individual programs resulting from reviews shall be written, along with the necessary data sheets, and any other forms, by the psychologist within one week of the review.
   E. The resident's assigned/alternate 1st shift DCS shall place these individual programs in the resident's Individual Program Book and Individual Program Chart.
   F. Results of emergency or special meetings and resulting programs shall be written, approved, and placed in the appropriate locations within three days of the review.

LEVEL 1, LEVEL 2, AND LEVEL 3
INDIVIDUAL PROGRAM BOOK PROCEDURE

GENERAL STATEMENT

Each resident in the program has his/her own idiosyncracies, strengths, weaknesses, and individuality. Accordingly, the development of individual treatment programs is necessary in order to implement a workable treatment package. The Individual Program Book has been developed for the purpose of having an organized record of the treatment programs, contracts, data, and other materials and information pertinent to the treatment of each resident in the program.

PURPOSE

1. To develop individualized programs for specified individual problems
2. To encourage each resident to participate in the development of his/her treatment plan
3. To develop a reciprocal relationship
4. To foster a sense of responsibility
5. To recognize the person as an individual
6. To clearly state the responsibilities of the staff and the resident concerned

PROCEDURE

I. General Policies
   A. Each resident is to have his/her own Individual Program Book.
   B. Materials pertaining to a resident's treatment are to be kept in his/her Individual Program Book.
   C. Each resident, prior to entering the program is to read, or have explained to him/her, the program's policies and procedures.
II. Contents of the Individual Program Book
   A. Individual Treatment Agreement (See Figure 2-1, p. 22)
   B. Treatment Programs
   C. Contractual Agreements
   D. Data and Graphs
      1. Self-Care skills summary data and graphs
      2. Educational summary data and graphs
      3. Social and interpersonal skills summary data and graphs
      4. Recreational/interpersonal skills summary data and graphs
      5. Individualized data sheets
III. Individual Programs
   A. General information and policies
      1. All programs *must* be agreed upon by the staff and the resident in his/her Interdisciplinary Treatment Team Conference. (See Interdisciplinary Treatment Team Conference Procedure p. 12)
      2. All programs *must* be written.
      3. Before a program can be started, steps one and two above must be completed.
      4. A copy of each program is to be
         a. Given to the resident
         b. Given to the resident's psychologist
         c. Placed in the resident's Individual Program Book
      5. Any program may be negotiated, renegotiated, or cancelled at any time by an agreement between the resident and the resident's Interdisciplinary Treatment Team.

6. If a resident wishes to cancel or renegotiate a treatment program, the staff may decide that the program is necessary for the resident's rehabilitation and prescribe the continuation of the program, *or* the staff may develop an alternate program.
7. Programs are to be determined during
   a. Interdisciplinary Team Treatment Conferences
   b. Special (emergency) Reviews

IV. Specific Information and Policies
   A. All individual programs are to be developed with the resident present.
   B. Each behavior is to be operationally defined.
   C. When possible, baseline data are to be collected prior to the initiation of a treatment program.
   D. Each problem behavior is to be numerically coded, beginning with 1, 2, 3, ...*N*.
   E. Each program developed for each behavior is to be given a number 1, 2, 3, ...*N*.
   F. When a program is developed, an Individual Treatment Agreement is to be completed before the program is begun. (See Figure 2-1, p. 22) The agreement is to include the
      1. Resident's name
      2. Problem number
      3. Target behavior
      4. Behavioral definition
      5. Beginning date
      6. Resident's signature
      7. Direct-Care Staff (DCS) member's signature
      8. Psychologist's signature
      9. Physician's signature
   G. New or modified programs for the same behavior
      1. New or modified programs for the same behavior are to receive a new program number.
      2. New or modified programs are to be recorded on the same Individual Treatment Agreement.
      3. Any components of the previous program that are still in effect are to be transferred to the new program.
      4. Once a new or modified program has been written, all previous programs for that behavior are to be canceled.
   H. All staff members are to read all programs.
      1. DCS members are to know programs developed for residents assigned to them.
      2. Staff members are to initial each program after reading it.
   I. Programs are to begin on Mondays.

V. Example of the Individual Treatment Agreement and the Individual Program:
   A. John Doe has not been interacting with other residents in the program. John has stated that he would like to talk to other people more often, but he is uncomfortable around people.
   B. During an Interdisciplinary Treatment Team Conference a decision was made to begin a baseline on John Doe's verbal interactions with others.
      1. Verbal interaction is defined as any time he is observed talking to another individual.
      2. The behavior is to be observed on a 30 minute variable-interval (VI 30′) observation schedule.
   C. Verbal interaction is the target behavior. Since it is the sixth target behavior for John Doe it has been numerically coded as Problem Number 6.
   D. All programs relating to Verbal Interactions are to be assigned a Program Number.
      1. The first program is to be Program Number 1.
      2. The last program is to be Program Number *N*.

E. Treatment Program 1
   1. Name: John Doe
   2. Problem Number: 6
   3. Target Behavior: Verbal Interactions
   4. Program Number: 1
   5. Beginning Date: 7/13/83
   6. Program:
      a. Pay 1¢ in token money every time resident is observed engaging in verbal interactions with another individual during a variable-interval observation.
      b. Give verbal praise every time resident is observed engaging in verbal interactions with another individual during a variable-interval observation.
F. Individual Treatment Agreement is completed before the implementation of the program. The agreement includes:
   1. Name: John Doe
   2. Problem Number: 6
   3. Target Behavior: Verbal Interactions
   4. Behavioral Definition: Anytime he is observed talking to another individual during a variable-interval observation
   5. Program Number: 1
   6. Beginning date: 7/13/83
   7. Resident's Signature: John Doe
   8. DCS Member's Signature: Tom Smith
   9. Psychologist's Signature: William Jones, Ph.D.
   10. Physician's Signature: Mary Brown, M.D.

INDIVIDUAL TREATMENT AGREEMENT

I, _____ , have read or have had read to me the treatment program(s) specifically designed for me. I do agree to comply with the program(s) as specified. However, I reserve the right to cancel or renegotiate my agreement at any time. I further understand that the staff also reserves the right to alter my contract as long as it is in writing and I agree to the changes.

PROBLEM NUMBER: _____   TARGET BEHAV(S): _____

BEHAV. DEFINITION: _____

Program 1

Beginning Date _____   Ending Date _____

Resident: _____

DCS: _____

Psychologist: _____

Physician: _____

Program 4

Date: _____

Resident: _____

DCS: _____

Psychologist: _____

Physician: _____

Program 2

Date: _____

Resident: _____

DCS: _____

Psychologist: _____

Physician: _____

Program 5

Date: _____

Resident: _____

DCS: _____

Psychologist: _____

Physician: _____

Program 3

Date: _____

Resident: _____

DCS: _____

Psychologist: _____

Physician: _____

Program 6

Date: _____

Resident: _____

DCS: _____

Psychologist: _____

Physician: _____

Figure 2-1

LEVEL 1, LEVEL 2, AND LEVEL 3 TOKEN ECONOMY PROGRAM

GENERAL STATEMENT

The purpose of the Token Economy Program is to help to motivate residents to engage in a variety of specified target behaviors. The program is intended to serve as a catalyst, which eventually allows the natural environment to maintain these target behaviors.

The use of tokens provides a means of managing behavior through external incentives. The delivery of token payment contingent upon the performance of specified behaviors, along with the opportunity to exchange the tokens for desired activities or items, provides the basis for the external incentives. Since the environment outside the hospital does not provide these types of external incentives, it is necessary to systematically replace the external incentives with internal reinforcement and control. Gradually increasing the time between the performance of the target behavior and the consequent payment, is an effective means of facilitating the desired internal control.

PURPOSE

1. To increase self-esteem
2. To increase self-reliance
3. To increase motivation and participate in treatment
4. To increase appropriate behavior
5. To decrease inappropriate behavior
6. To increase intrinsic motivation to maintain target behaviors

TERMINAL OBJECTIVE

The terminal objective is to have residents maintain the behaviors acquired or developed while in the token economy program, after the elimination of token reinforcement.

PROCEDURE

I. General Policies
   A. Placement in Token Economy
      1. Initial placement
         a. Determined on an individual basis
         b. Determined during Revised Treatment Plan Review (See Interdisciplinary Treatment Team Conferences Procedure, p. 12)
         c. Decision based upon performance and general motivation during initial two-week baseline period
      2. Subsequent placement
         a. Determined on an individual basis
         b. Determined during Interdisciplinary Treatment Team Conference
         c. Decision based upon performance deterioration in specific behaviors (e.g., Self-Care Skills, work performance, activity attendance)
   B. Management of Tokens
      1. Token denominations
         a. Penny (small wooden cylinder—red)
         b. Nickel (medium wooden cylinder—yellow)
         c. Quarter (large wooden cylinder—silver)
         d. One dollar bill (Paper rectangles—$1)
         e. Five dollar bill (Paper rectangles—$5)

2. Contingent token payment given for
   a. Self-Care Skills (S.C.S.) (schedule of payments specified in program-wide S.C.S. Procedures)
   b. Job assignments (schedule of payments specified in program-wide Job Assignment Procedures)
   c. Other program-wide programs as determined on an individual basis by the resident's Interdisciplinary Treatment Team
   d. Other specific behaviors as determined on an individual basis by the resident's Interdisciplinary Treatment Team
3. Token payments are to be given to the resident by assigned/alternate direct-care staff (DCS) member.
4. Time of payment
   a. Payment time varies according to the progress of the resident in the Token Economy Program.
   b. Refer to Section II: Steps of Token Economy Program for a detailed description
5. Token charges and fines:
   a. Token charges and fines are specified in program-wide treatment procedures (e.g., Weekend Visits Procedure, Outside Privileges Procedure).
   b. Other token charges and fines are determined on an individual basis by the resident's Interdisciplinary Treatment Team.
   c. Token charges for activities (e.g., weekend visits) are to be paid by the resident prior to engagement in the activity.
   d. Token fines are to be paid by the resident immediately following observation of the inappropriate behavior.
   e. Resident is to be placed on ward restriction whenever he/she has an insufficient amount of token money to pay a token fine, whenever he/she refuses to pay a token fine, *and* whenever he/she refuses to pay for an activity which he/she has engaged in. The duration of the restriction is to be determined by the program psychologist. If the resident pays the fine (or charge) prior to the completion of the restriction period, the restriction is to be discontinued.

C. Token Elimination
1. All residents in the Token Economy Program are to undergo token elimination.
2. Token elimination is to be made in a series of gradual steps (See Section II: Steps of Token Economy Program).
3. Movement to each successive step is to be based upon
   a. Established criteria (e.g., Self-Care Skills)
   b. Decision of resident's Interdisciplinary Treatment Team on an individual basis.

II. Steps of Token Economy Program[1]
A. Step I
1. When a resident is placed in the Token Economy Program, Step 1, the assigned/alternate 1st shift DCS is to give him/her $2.00 in token money at 8 A.M. on the first morning of program participation.
2. Token payment for appropriate behavior is to be given by the assigned/alternate DCS *immediately* following the target behavior.
3. Token charges for activities are to be paid by the resident prior to engaging in the desired activity.
4. Movement to Step II is to occur when

---

[1] This section is, in part, based upon a token economy elimination program developed by Naster and Hindrichs (1983). (Naster, B. J. & Hindrichs, S. H. (1983). *Comprehensive token economy system.* Unpublished manuscript, University of South Florida, Florida Mental Health Institute, Tampa.)

a. Resident meets established Self-Care Skills criteria (See Self-Care Skills Program) for four consecutive weeks
b. Resident meets all other criteria established on an individual basis by his/her Interdisciplinary Treatment Team

B. Step II
1. Token payment for appropriate behavior is to be given to the resident by the assigned/alternate 1st shift DCS each morning (by 8:00 A.M.) for all tokens earned the previous day.
2. All token charges for activities are to be paid prior to engaging in the desired activity.
3. Movement to Step III is to occur when
   a. Resident meets Self-Care Skills Program criteria for two consecutive weeks (See Self-Care Skills Program)
   b. Resident meets all other criteria established on an individual basis by his/her Interdisciplinary Treatment Team
4. Regression to a lower step is to occur when
   a. Resident fails to meet Self-Care Skills Program criteria for two consecutive weeks
   b. Resident fails to meet any of the other criteria established by the Interdisciplinary Treatment Team for two consecutive weeks

C. Step III
1. Token payment is to be given to the resident by the assigned/alternate 1st shift DCS each Monday and Friday mornings (by 8:00 A.M.) for all tokens earned since the preceding payment.
2. All token charges for activities are to be paid by the resident prior to engaging in the desired activity.
3. Movement to Step IV is to occur when
   a. Resident meets Self-Care Skills Program criteria for two consecutive weeks (See Self-Care Skills Program)
   b. Resident meets all other criteria established on an individual basis by his/her Treatment Team
4. Regression to a lower step is to occur when
   a. Resident fails to meet Self-Care Skills Program criteria for two consecutive weeks
   b. Resident fails to meet any of the other criteria established by the Interdisciplinary Treatment Team for two consecutive weeks
5. Step to which resident regresses is to be determined by the program psychologist

D. Step IV
1. Token payment is to be given to the resident by the assigned/alternate 1st shift DCS each Monday morning (by 8:00 A.M.) for all tokens earned since the previous payment.
2. All token charges for activities are to be paid by the resident prior to engagement in the desired activity.
3. Movement to Step V is to occur when
   a. Resident meets established Self-Care Skills Program criteria for two consecutive weeks
   b. Resident meets all other criteria as established by his/her Interdisciplinary Treatment Team
4. Regression to a lower step is to occur when
   a. Resident fails to meet Self-Care Skills Program criteria for two consecutive weeks
   b. Resident fails to meet any of the other criteria established by the Treatment Team for two consecutive weeks
5. Step to which resident regresses is to be determined by program psychologist

E. Step V
1. No token payment is to be given to the resident for appropriate behavior.
2. No token charges are to be required to engage in activities.
3. Removal from the Token Economy is to occur when
   a. Resident meets Self-Care Skills Program criteria for two consecutive weeks
   b. Resident meets all other criteria established by his/her Interdisciplinary Treatment Team
4. Regression to a lower level is to occur when
   a. Resident fails to meet Self-Care Skills Program criteria for two consecutive weeks
   b. Resident fails to meet any of the other established criteria for two consecutive weeks
5. Step to which resident regresses is to be determined by program psychologist.

III. Token Economy Program Data Collection Procedure
  A. Token Economy Program Resident Step Sheet (See Figure 2-2, p. 30.)
    1. There is to be one Token Economy Program Resident Step Sheet displayed in each DCS office.
    2. On Sunday morning third shift DCSs are to indicate the Token Economy Program step each resident is to be in during the week (Monday through Sunday) by recording
       a. Name: Each resident's name
       b. Date: The date on which the resident is to begin a given step (i.e., Step I (SI), Step II (SII), Step III (SIII), Step IV (SIV), or Token Economy Elimination (T.E.E.))
          (Note: (1) If a resident is to remain in the same step for two consecutive weeks, it is not necessary to record a new date on the Token Economy Program Resident Step Sheet; (2) following the week during which a resident is removed from the Token Economy Program, it is no longer necessary to record his/her name, etc., on the Token Economy Program Resident Step Sheet.)
       c. When a resident is moved from one step to another a single line is to be drawn through the date recorded for the step from which he/she is to be moved.
  B. Daily Token Economy Program Work Sheet (See Figure 2-3, p. 31.)
    1. Each resident participating in the Token Economy Program is to have a Daily Token Economy Program Work Sheet.
    2. The Daily Token Economy Program Work Sheet is to be located in a program chart titled "Token Economy."
    3. Assigned/alternate 1st, 2d, and 3d shift DCSs are responsible for recording data on the data sheet on an on-going basis.
    4. The following data are to be recorded on the Daily Token Economy Program Work Sheet:
       a. Date
       b. TE Step: Record the Token Economy Program step the resident is currently in.
          SI: Record "SI" if the resident is in Step I.
          SII: Record "SII" if the resident is in Step II.
          SIII: Record "SIII" if the resident is in Step III.
          SIV: Record "SIV" if the resident is in Step IV.
       c. Tokens earned: Amount of tokens earned by the resident.
       d. Tokens pd to res.: Amount of tokens paid to resident.
       e. Tokens spent: Amount of tokens spent by resident.
       f. Token fines: Amount of tokens resident is fined.
       g. Token fines pd: Amount of tokens paid by resident for fines.

h. Token fines owed: Amount of tokens owed by resident for fines. (Token fines—Token fines pd)
   i. DCS: Initials of DCS recording data.
C. Token Economy Program Summary Data Sheet
   1. Each resident participating in the Token Economy Program is to have a Token Economy Program Summary Data Sheet.
   2. The data sheet is to be located in the resident's Individual Program Chart.
   3. Assigned/alternate 1st, 2d, and 3d shift DCSs are responsible for recording data on this data sheet at the end of each of their shifts.
   4. There is a different Token Economy Program Summary Data Sheet for each of the three Token Economy Program steps.
   5. Token Economy Program Summary Data Sheet—Step I (See Figure 2-4, p. 32.)
      a. Assigned/alternate 1st, 2d, and 3d shift DCSs are to record data at the end of each of their shifts.
      b. The following data are to be recorded:
         (1) Date: Record the current date.
         (2) Tot. Tokens Earned: Record the total amount of tokens earned by resident during respective shift.
         (3) Tot. Tokens Pd. to Res.: Record the total amount of tokens paid to resident during respective shift.
         (4) Tot. Tokens Spent: Record the total amount of tokens spent by resident during respective shift.
         (5) Tot. Token Fines: Record the total amount of tokens resident is fined during respective shift.
         (6) Tot. Token Fines Pd: Record the total amount of tokens paid by resident for fines.
         (7) Tot Token Fines Owed: Record the total amount of tokens owed by resident for fines at the end of respective shift. (Tot Token Fines—Tot. Token Fines pd. = Total Token Fines Owed)
         (8) DCS: Record the initials of DCS recording data.
   6. Token Economy Program Summary Data Sheet—Step II (See Figure 2-5, p. 33.)
      a. Assigned/alternate 1st, 2d, and 3d shift DCSs are to record data at the end of each of their shifts.
      b. The following data are to be recorded:
         (1) Date: Record the current date.
         (2) Tot. Tokens Earned: Record the total amount of tokens earned by the resident during respective shift.
         (3) Tot. Tokens Spent: Record the total amount of tokens spent by resident during respective shift.
         (4) Tot. Token Fines: Record the total amount of tokens resident is fined during respective shift.
         (5) Tot. Token Fines Pd.: Record the total amount of tokens paid by resident for fines during respective shift.
         (6) Tot. Token Fines Owed: Record the total amount of tokens owed by resident for fines at the end of respective shift.
         (7) D.T.T.E.: Record the daily total amount of tokens earned by resident that day. To be completed each night by 3d shift. (Tot. tokens earned 1st shift + Tot. tokens earned 2d shift + Tot. tokens earned 3d shift = D.T.T.E.)
         (8) DCS: Record the initials of DCS recording data.
         (9) D.T.T.P.: Record the daily total amount of tokens paid to resident (to be completed by 1st shift DCS each morning by 8:00 A.M.)

28 PSYCHIATRIC UNIT PROCEDURES

7. Token Economy Program Summary Data Sheet—Step III (See Figure 2-6, p. 34.)
   a. Assigned/alternate 1st, 2d, and 3d shift DCSs are to record data at the end of each of their shifts.
   b. The following data are to be recorded:
      (1) Date: Record the current date.
      (2) Tot. Tokens Earned: Record the total amount of tokens earned by resident during respective shift.
      (3) Tot. Tokens spent: Record the total amount of tokens spent by resident during respective shift.
      (4) Tot. Token Fines: Record the total amount of tokens resident is fined during respective shift.
      (5) Tot. Token Fines Pd.: Record the total amount of tokens paid by resident for fines during respective shift.
      (6) Tot. Token Fines Owed: Record the total amount of tokens owed by resident for fines at the end of respective shift.
      (7) D.T.T.E.: Record daily total amount of tokens earned by resident that day. To be completed each night by 3rd shift. (Tot. tokens earned 1st shift + Tot tokens earned 2d shift + Tot tokens earned 3d shift = D.T.T.E.)
      (8) G.T.T.E.: Record the grand total amount of tokens earned by the resident from
         (a) Monday to Thursday
            i. To be recorded by 3d shift DCSs at the end of the shift on Friday morning.
            ii. G.T.T.E. = D.T.T.E. (Mon.) + D.T.T.E. (Tues.) + D.T.T.E. (Wed.) + D.T.T.E. (Thurs.)
         (b) Friday to Sunday
            i. To be recorded by 3d shift DCSs at the end of the shift on Monday morning.
            ii. G.T.T.E. = D.T.T.E. (Fri.) + D.T.T.E. (Sat.) + D.T.T.E. (Sun.)
      (9) G.T.T.P.: Record the grand total amount of tokens paid to resident on
         (a) Monday (1st shift DCSs by 8:00 A.M.)
         (b) Friday (1st shift DCSs by 8:00 A.M.)
8. Token Economy Program Summary Data Sheet—Step IV (See Figure 2-7, p. 36.)
   a. Assigned/alternate 1st, 2d, and 3d shift DCS are to record data at the end of each of their shifts.
   b. The following data are to be recorded:
      (1) Date: Record the current date.
      (2) Tot. Tokens Earned: Record the total amount of tokens earned by resident during respective shift.
      (3) Tot. Tokens Spent: Record the total amount of tokens spent by resident during respective shift.
      (4) Tot. Token Fines: Record the total amount of tokens resident is fined during respective shift.
      (5) Tot. Token Fines Pd.: Record the total amount of tokens paid by resident for fines during respective shift.
      (6) Tot. Token Fines Owed: Record the total amount of tokens owed by resident for fines at the end of respective shift.
      (7) D.T.T.E.: Record daily total of tokens earned by resident for day. To be completed each night by 3d shift (Tot. tokens earned 1st shift + Tot. tokens earned 2d shift + Tot. tokens earned 3d shift = D.T.T.E.)

(8) DCS: Record the initials of DCS recording data.
(9) W.T.E.: Record the weekly total amount of tokens earned by the resident.
   (a) To be recorded by 3d shift DCSs at the end of the shift on Monday morning.
   (b) W.T.T.E. = D.T.T.E. (Mon.) + D.T.T.E. (Tues.) + D.T.T.E. (Wed.) + D.T.T.E. (Thurs.) + D.T.T.E. (Fri.) + D.T.T.E. (Sat.) + D.T.T.E. (Sun.)
(10) W.T.T.P.: Record the weekly total amount of tokens paid to the resident. (To be recorded by 1st shift DCSs on Monday morning by 8:00 A.M.)
(11) DCS: Record the initials of the DCS recording data.

TOKEN ECONOMY PROGRAM RESIDENT STEP SHEET

NAME	STEP I (IMMEDIATE TOK. REINF.)	STEP II (TOK. REINF. ONCE PER DAY)	STEP III (TOK. REINF. MON. & FRI.)	STEP IV (TOK. REINF. MON.)	T.E.E. (NO TOK. REINF.)

Figure 2-2

DAILY TOKEN ECONOMY PROGRAM WORK SHEET

DATE	T.E. STEP	TOKENS EARNED	TOKENS PD. TO RES.	TOKENS SPENT	TOKEN FINE	TOKEN FINES PD.	TOKEN FINES OWED	DCS

Figure 2-3

TOKEN ECONOMY PROGRAM SUMMARY DATA SHEET
(STEP I)

DATE	TOT. TOKENS EARNED	TOT. TOKENS PD. TO RES.	TOT. TOKENS SPENT	TOT. TOKEN FINES	TOT. TOKEN FINES PD.	TOT. TOKEN FINES OWED	DCS

Figure 2-4

TOKEN ECONOMY PROGRAM SUMMARY DATA SHEET
(STEP II)

DATE	TOT. TOKENS EARNED		TOT. TOKENS SPENT	TOT. TOKEN FINES	TOT. TOKEN FINES PD.	TOT. TOKEN FINES OWED	DCS
			DCS				
D.T.T.E.							
D.T.T.P.							
Date							
		DCS					
D.T.T.E.							
D.T.T.P.							
Date							
		DCS					
D.T.T.E.							
D.T.T.P.							

Figure 2-5

TOKEN ECONOMY PROGRAM SUMMARY DATA SHEET
(STEP III)

DATE	TOT. TOKENS EARNED	D.T.T.E.	TOT. TOKENS SPENT	TOT. TOKEN FINES	TOT. TOKEN FINES PD.	TOT. TOKEN FINES OWED	DCS
Mon.							
Tues.							
Wed.							
Thurs.							
G.T.T.E.							
G.T.T.P.							

Figure 2-6

TOKEN ECONOMY PROGRAM SUMMARY DATA SHEET
(STEP III) (CONTINUED)

DATE	TOT. TOKENS EARNED	D.T.T.E.	TOT. TOKENS SPENT	TOT. TOKEN FINES	TOT. TOKEN FINES PD.	TOT. TOKEN FINES OWED	DCS
Fri.							
Sat.							
Sun.							
G.T.T.E.							
G.T.T.P.							

TOKEN ECONOMY PROGRAM SUMMARY DATA SHEET
(STEP IV)

DATE	TOT. TOKENS EARNED	D.T.T.E.	TOT. TOKENS SPENT	TOT. TOKEN FINES	TOT. TOKEN FINES PD.	TOT. TOKEN FINES OWED	DCS
Mon.							
Tues.							
Wed.							
Thurs.							
Fri.							

Figure 2-7

TOKEN ECONOMY PROGRAM SUMMARY DATA SHEET
(STEP IV) (CONTINUED)

DATE	TOT. TOKENS EARNED	D.T.T.E.	TOT. TOKENS SPENT	TOT. TOKEN FINES	TOT. TOKEN FINES PD.	TOT. TOKEN FINES OWED	DCS
Sat.							
Sun.							
W.T.T.E.							
W.T.T.P.							

LEVEL 1, LEVEL 2, AND LEVEL 3 CANTEEN PROCEDURE

GENERAL STATEMENT

Purchasing desired and/or needed items in stores is often a source of personal satisfaction. Several skills are required to complete a purchase; first, is the ability to read labels, advertisements, etc. Next, is the ability to read numbers and manipulate these numbers (e.g., add, subtract, count change, recognize various sizes of merchandise). Third, the individual must be able to make decisions regarding purchases (e.g., which of several similar items should be purchased; which size article should be purchased; how many pieces of an item should be purchased; the cost of items purchased in relationship to the amount of money available). Finally, the individual needs to be able to appropriately interact with store personnel when paying for items, returning items, asking questions, etc. The institutionalized individual typically needs training to either learn or redevelop the skills required for appropriate shopping. The canteen serves the functions of education, practical experience, and motivation.

PURPOSE

1. To help develop self-sufficiency
2. To help create appropriate money management skills
3. To help increase motivational levels
4. To help develop interpersonal skills

PROCEDURE

I. General Policies
   A. All residents are to have the opportunity to use the canteen.
   B. The canteen is to be open seven days per week during the following periods:
      1. 8:00–8:30 A.M.
      2. 1:00–1:30 P.M.
      3. 6:30–7:00 P.M.
      4. 9:00–9:30 P.M.
   D. The operation of the canteen is to be by direct-care staff (DCS) members
   E. All purchases are to be made with token money. Token money represents real money in the resident's Canteen account (See Section VIII: Resident Canteen Account).
   F. DCS members are not permitted to purchase items from the canteen.
II. Behavioral Requirements For Participation
   A. Daily self-care skills criterion is to be met for the current day (See Self-Care Skills Procedure, p. 41.)
   B. There is to be an absence of any restrictions in effect that would preclude use of the canteen (e.g., ward restriction).
III. Financial Responsibilities
   A. The resident is to have token money to exchange for real money.
   B. The resident is to have "real" money in his/her canteen account.
IV. Canteen Ledger
   A. Each resident is to have a canteen ledger.
   B. The canteen is to retain an exact copy of the resident's ledger.
   C. All transactions are to be recorded in each ledger book.
      1. The resident is to record in his/her ledger.
      2. The DCS is to assist the resident only when necessary and as little as possible.
      3. The DCS is to ensure the accuracy of the resident's entries and calculations.
      4. The DCS is to initial each entry.

5. The resident is to be required to determine if enough money is in his/her account and if he/she has a sufficient amount of token money.
6. The DCS is to record all transactions in the copy of the resident's canteen ledger.
7. After all entries are completed in both ledgers, the resident is to initial the copy of the resident's ledger.
  D. Before any merchandise is given to the resident, the DCS is to ensure that the ledgers are complete and correct.
  E. The resident is to be charged $2.00 in token money to replace a lost canteen ledger.
  F. No resident is to be allowed to purchase from the canteen without his/her ledger.
  G. Each entry into the ledger is to consist of
    1. The date of the purchase
    2. The total cost of purchase
    3. The total tax levied on the purchase
    4. The amount of any deposits
    5. Balance
V. Canteen Inventory Ledger
  A. All merchandise purchased from the Canteen is to be recorded in the Canteen Inventory Ledger.
  B. On the first of each month, a complete inventory of the canteen is to be conducted and the results recorded in the Canteen Inventory Ledger.
  C. Each item purchased by a resident is to be recorded at the time of the purchase, in the Canteen Inventory Ledger.
  D. Once each month, calculate and record the following in the Canteen Inventory Ledger:
    1. Total number of sales
    2. Total profit
    3. Actual inventory
    4. Monthly inventory
    5. Inventory difference
    6. Inventory loss or gain
  E. At the end of each month, the total amount of sales for the month plus inventory is to be calculated. The resulting figure is to be submitted to the facility business office.
VI. Daily Item Inventory Ledger
  A. Each day the canteen is open, a daily inventory is to be completed on each item.
  B. Each time an item is purchased by a resident, the sale is to be recorded in the Daily Item Inventory Ledger.
  C. At the end of each operation period, the totals of each inventory (for each item) are to be transferred to the Canteen Inventory Ledger.
  D. After each operation period, five randomly selected items are to be counted. The resulting figure is to be recorded in the Canteen Inventory Ledger.
VII. Canteen Purchasing
  A. The selection of items by a resident is to be on a self-serve basis.
  B. Only one resident is to be allowed in the canteen at a time.
  C. Payment of purchases is to occur upon leaving the canteen.
  D. The resident is to be allowed to purchase any item(s) available (given the availability of real money and tokens).
  E. When purchases are made, the resident is to count aloud, the amount of token money given to the DCS and count aloud, any change received.
VIII. Resident Canteen Account
  A. A resident must have real money in his/her Canteen Account to purchase items from the canteen.
  B. A resident may have as little or as much real money placed into his/her Canteen Account as he/she has available and is willing to place into the account.

C. Each resident is to inform a DCS of the amount of real money to be deposited in his/her Canteen Account.
D. The DCS is to notify the unit clerk of the real money deposit.
E. Deposits in a resident's Canteen Account are to be recorded in his/her Canteen Ledger and in the copy of his/her Canteen Ledger, after the unit clerk provides official notification of the deposit.
F. A resident who is *not* in the token economy program is to be given an amount of token money equal to the amount of real money deposited in his/her Canteen Account. This token money is to be used to purchase items in the canteen.

LEVEL 1, LEVEL 2, AND LEVEL 3 SELF CARE SKILLS GENERAL PROCEDURE

GENERAL STATEMENT

In order to survive and become a successful member of today's society, a person must be able to care for his/her physical being and living quarters. The self-care skills program is the initial step in helping a resident become self sufficient. This program is the first of a series of structured procedures dealing with education, recreation, interpersonal skills, and vocational interests.

PURPOSE

1. To help develop awareness of one's appearance
2. To help develop socially acceptable meal behavior
3. To help increase a positive self-concept
4. To help develop socially acceptable skills
5. To help create proper hygiene
6. To help develop self-sufficiency

TERMINAL OBJECTIVE

The terminal objective is to have the resident meet the self-care skills criteria specified for each skill without the use of an extrinsic motivation program (e.g., token economy program).

GENERAL PROCEDURE—LEVELS 1, 2, AND 3

I. Self-Care Skill Behaviors
   A. Bedroom Area Preparation
   B. Wake-up Procedure
   C. Dental Hygiene
   D. Shower
   E. Locker Preparation
   F. Medication
   G. Meals
   H. Dressing (Level 3 only)
   I. For definitions and procedures for each self-care skill refer to the procedure that addresses the specific skill.
II. Baseline Period
   A. Baseline data are to be collected on all residents during their first two weeks in the program.
   B. The resident is to be given the opportunity to participate in all programs and activities (e.g., Self-Care Skills, Recreational-Leisure Activities, Communication Skills).
   C. The resident is not to receive any token payments for participating in programs.
   D. Prompt participation is desired but *not* required.
III. Baseline Assessment
   A. Following the two-week baseline period, the resident's behavior is to be evaluated in an Interdisciplinary Treatment Team Conference.
   B. If the resident has met the specified criteria for all the self-care skills and generally shows a high level of motivation, he/she is not to be placed in the token economy system (See Section IV).
   C. If the resident has not met the specified criteria for all the self-care skills and/or generally does not show a high level of motivation, he/she is to be placed in the token economy system.
   D. Placement into the token economy system may also be determined on an individual basis in staffing when such placement seems therapeutically appropriate.

E. Evaluation of the resident's behavior within specific self-care skills is also to be completed. When necessary, individualized programs may be developed for specific self-care skills in order to meet the needs and capabilities of the resident.

IV. Placement (Token Economy or No Token Economy)
   A. The self-care skills procedures are to be followed for both the residents placed into the token economy system *and* those residents not in the token economy system.
   B. Residents not in the token economy system are *not* to receive any token reinforcement for skills.
   C. Residents not in the token economy system and residents in the token economy system are both to receive verbal praise when prescribed in the procedures.
   D. A resident not in the token economy system may be placed into that system if he/she falls below the specified weekly criteria for two consecutive weeks.

V. When a Self-Care Skill is not completed or not completed appropriately
   A. Always prompt or request the resident to engage in the task; *never* tell him/her to do so
   B. Prompt the resident; then walk away for 15 minutes before prompting again.
   C. Always use a positive approach.

VI. Data Recording
   A. Each resident is to have one data sheet for each of the eight self-care skills (Bedroom Area Preparation, Wake-up Procedure, Dental Hygiene, Shower, Locker, Medication, Meals, and Dressing).
   B. The Self-Care Skills Data Sheets are to be located in the Resident's Program Chart.
   C. The Self-Care Skills Weekly Criteria Data Sheets are to be located in the resident's Individual Program Book.
   D. Data recorders are specified in each Self-Care Skill procedure

PROCEDURE—LEVEL 1

I. Self-Care Skills Treatment Phases and Criteria
   A. General
      1. The Daily and Weekly Self-Care Skills criteria consist of meeting the requirements specified below (See I.C. and I.D.).
      2. The resident is to meet the skill criterion in Treatment Phase I for four consecutive weeks in order to move to Treatment Phase II.
      3. Once the criterion for Phase II has been met for four consecutive weeks, the resident may be removed from token reinforcement (upon review by psychologist).
      4. For the purpose of facilitating a gradual shaping process toward mastery of self-care skills, individualized criteria may be used which take into account the resident's base rate skills and skill advancement.
      5. Possible scores for Level 1 Self-Care Skills are 1, 2, 3, 4, and 5.
   B. Direct-Care Staff (DCS) Responsibilities
      1. 2d shift DCSs:
         a. Review each resident's self-care skill performance before bedtime.
         b. If resident met daily criterion, give a 10¢ (token) bonus (if in token economy) and verbal praise.
         c. If resident did *not* meet the daily criterion, the DCS is to explain the deficiencies, give verbal praise for those skills performed correctly, and explain the deficiencies in the other skills.
      2. 3rd Shift DCSs are to initiate movement from Treatment Phase I to Treatment Phase 2.
   C. Criteria—Treatment Phase I
      1. Daily Criterion
         a. Medication: No scores greater than 2 for the day (possible scores for medication are 1, 2, or 5)
         b. All other Self-Care Skills: No more than one score of 5 for the day

2. Weekly Criterion
    a. Medication: No scores greater than 2 (possible scores for medication are 1, 2, or 5)
    b. All other Self-Care Skills: No more than one score of 5 for each Self-Care Skill (during the current week or current and preceding seven days).
D. Criteria—Treatment Phase 2
  1. Daily Criterion
     a. Medication: No score greater than 2 for the day (possible scores for medication are 1, 2, or 5)
     b. All other Self-Care Skills: No more than one score of 5 and no more than one score of 4 for the day
  2. Weekly Criterion
     a. Medication: No scores greater than 2 (possible scores for medication are 1, 2, or 5)
     b. All other Self-Care Skills: No more than one score of 5 and no more than one score of 4 for each Self-Care Skill (during the current week *or* current and preceding seven days)

II. Privileges
  A. Daily Criterion
    1. When the self-care skills criterion is met on a given day (given that there are no conflicting restrictions in effect as a function of other programs and/or inappropriate behavior such as stealing, sexual inappropriateness, and/or aggression), allow the resident (if he/she desires)
       a. Off-ward activities (group activities)
       b. Single privileges (if granted)
       c. Token earning power
    2. When the self-care skills criterion is *not* met on a given day
       a. Restrict the resident to the ward that day from the point in time at which the criterion is not met (This restriction is to the exclusion of the resident's daily outside time as required by Clients' Rights.) (Note: Resident will still be allowed to attend regularly scheduled therapeutic activities (e.g., Recreation Therapy, Music Therapy, etc.)
       b. Do *not* allow resident to purchase consumables (e.g., soft drinks, candies, food)
  B. Weekly Criterion
    1. When the weekly self-care skills criterion is met (given that there are no conflicting restrictions in effect as a function of other programs and/or inappropriate behavior such as stealing, sexual inappropriateness, and/or severe agitation) allow the resident (if he/she desires)
       a. All of the privileges allowed when the Daily Criterion is met (see II A. 1. above)
       b. Off-campus activities, if resident is eligible
    2. When the weekly self-care skills criterion is *not* met
       a. Do *not* allow the resident to engage in any off-campus activities (excluding week-end visits)
       b. Impose other restrictions as specified in the resident's Individual Treatment plan

PROCEDURE—LEVEL 2

I. Self-Care Skills Treatment Phases and Criteria
  A. General
    1. The resident is to meet the weekly criteria specified for Phase I for at least four consecutive weeks in order to progress to Phase II.
    2. For the pupose of facilitating a gradual shaping process toward the eventual

mastery of appropriate self-care skills, individualized self-care skills criteria may be formulated which take into consideration the individual's base rate skills and skill advancements.
3. Token payments for self-care skills are to be eliminated after the resident meets the weekly criteria specified for Phase II for four consecutive weeks.
4. Possible scores for Level 2 Self-Care Skills are 1, 2, 3, 4, and 5.

B. Direct-Care Staff (DCS) Responsibilities
1. 2d shift DCSs:
   a. Review each resident's self-care skill performance before bedtime.
   b. If the resident *met* the specified daily criterion for the treatment phase he/she is currently in, the DCS is to give him/her a 10¢ (tokens) bonus (if in the token economy system) and verbal praise.
   c. If the resident did *not* meet the specified daily criterion, the DCS is to explain the deficiencies and give him/her verbal praise for those skills performed appropriately.
2. 3d shift DCSs are to initiate movement from Treatment Phase I to Treatment Phase 2.

C. Criteria—Treatment Phase 1
1. Daily Criterion
   a. A score of 1 or 2 in medication for the day. (NOTE: Possible scores for medication are 1, 2, or 5)
   b. No more than one score of 5 for the day
   c. No more than three scores of 4 for the day
2. Weekly Criterion
   a. Medication: No scores greater than 2 (NOTE: Possible scores for medication are 1, 2, or 5)
   b. All other self-care skills: No more than one score of 5 and no more than three scores of 4 for the week for each self-care skill (during the current week *or* current and preceding seven days)

D. Criteria—Treatment Phase 2
1. Daily Criterion
   a. A score of 1 or 2 in medication for the day (NOTE: Possible scores for medication are 1, 2, or 5)
   b. No scores of 4 or 5 for the day
   c. No more than two scores of 3 for the day
2. Weekly Criterion
   a. Medication: No scores greater than 2 (NOTE: Possible scores for medication are 1, 2, and 5)
   b. All other self-care skills: No scores of 4 or 5 and no more than one score of 3 for the week for each self-care skill (during the current week *or* current and preceding seven days)

II. Privileges
A. Daily Criterion
1. When the self-care skills criterion is met on a given day (given that there are no conflicting restrictions in effect as a function of inappropriate behavior such as stealing, sexual inappropriateness and/or severe agitation), allow the resident (if he/she desires)
   a. Off-ward activities (if applicable)
   b. Use of the I.B.P. Canteen
   c. Token earning power
   d. Group activities (if applicable)
2. When the self-care skills criterion is *not* met on a given day
   a. Restrict the resident to the ward that day from the point of time at which the criterion is not met (this restriction is to the exclusion of the resident's daily

outside time as required by Clients' Rights and individualized programs, i.e., Industrial Therapy, Music Therapy, etc.)
        b. Do not allow the resident to use the canteen that day
        c. Do not allow the resident to purchase consumable items via other resident or staff
   B. Weekly Criterion
      1. When the weekly self-care skills criterion is met (given that there are no conflicting restrictions in effect as a function of other programs and/or inappropriate behavior such as stealing, sexual inappropriateness, and/or severe agitation), allow the resident (if he/she desires)
        a. All of the privileges allowed when the Daily Criterion is met (see II A. 1. Above)
        b. Weekend visit (as specified in the Level 2 Weekend Visit Procedure)
        c. Off-campus activities, if resident is eligible
      2. When the weekly self-care skills criterion is not met
        a. Do *not* allow the resident to engage in any off-campus activities
        b. Impose other restrictions as specified in the resident's Treatment Plan

PROCEDURE—LEVEL 3

I. Self-Care Skills Phases and Criteria
   A. General
      1. The resident is to meet the weekly criteria specified for each self-care skill for at least four consecutive weeks in order to meet the overall self-care skills criteria.
      2. For the purpose of facilitating a gradual shaping process toward the eventual mastery of appropriate self-care skills, individualized self-care skills criteria may be formulated which take into consideration the resident's base rate skills and skill advancements.
      3. Possible scores for Level 3 Self-Care Skills are 1, 2, and 3.
      4. Token payments for Self-Care Skills are to be eliminated after the resident meets the weekly criteria specified for each skill for four consecutive weeks (the resident must be in the last step of the medication program and receiving all scores of 1), and after the resident has been involved in other programs for two of those four weeks, or as determined on an individual basis in staffing.
   B. Direct-Care Staff (DCS) Responsibilities
      1. 2d Shift DCS:
        a. Review each resident's self-care skills performance before bedtime.
        b. If the resident met the specified daily criterion, the DCS is to give him/her a 10¢ (tokens) bonus (if in the token economy) and verbal praise.
        c. If the resident did *not* meet the specified daily criterion, the DCS is to explain the deficiencies and give him/her verbal praise for those skills performed appropriately.
      2. 3d Shift DCSs are to initiate the Self-Care Skills Evaluation Elimination Program (See Section IV: Elimination of Self-Care Skills Evaluations).
   C. Criteria
      1. Daily Criterion
        a. Medication: All scores of 1 for the day
        b. All other Self-Care Skills: No more than two scores of 2 and no scores of 3 for the day
      2. Weekly Criterion
        a. Medication: All scores of 1 for the week
        b. All other Self-Care Skills: No more than one score of 2 and no scores of 3 for each Self-Care Skill (during the current week or current and preceding seven days)

II. Privileges
   A. Daily Criterion
      1. When the self-care skills criterion is met on a given day (given that there are no conflicting restrictions in effect as a function of other programs and/or inappropriate behavior such as stealing, sexual inappropriateness, and/or aggression), allow the resident (if he/she desires)
         a. Off-ward activities
         b. Token earning power
      2. When the self-care skills criterion is *not* met on a given day
         a. Restrict the resident to the ward that day (this restriction is to the exclusion of the resident's daily outside time as required by Clients' Rights)
         b. Do *not* allow the resident to use the canteen that day
         c. Allow the resident to do ward jobs if he/she desires; but the resident is to receive token payments for only those jobs completed as part of the Goal Orientation Program (See Goal Orientation Program, p. 134.)
         d. Allow the resident to spend already earned tokens if he/she desires; but the resident is *not* to have token earning power that day except for self-care skills and for ward jobs as specified in II. A. 2. c. above
   B. Weekly Criterion
      1. When the weekly self-care skills criterion is met (given that there are no conflicting restrictions in effect as a function of other programs and/or inappropriate behavior such as stealing, sexual inappropriateness, and/or aggression), allow the resident (if he/she desires)
         a. All of the privileges allowed when the Daily Criterion is met (see II A. 1. above)
         b. Weekend visit (as specified in the Level 3 Weekend Visit Procedure
         c. Off-campus activities
      2. When the weekly self-care skills criterion is *not* met
         a. Do *not* allow the resident to engage in a weekend visit (as specified in the Level 3 Weekend Visit Procedure)
         b. Do *not* allow the resident to engage in any off-campus activities
IV. Elimination of Self-Care Skills Evaluations
   A. Elimination Steps
      1. Elimination Step 1 (E1): After the resident has met the specified criteria for each self-care skill for one month, eliminate daily evaluations of all self-care skills (for the Medication Procedure the resident must be in the last step and receiving all scores of 1)
         a. Begin evaluating five times per week
         b. Continue this procedure until the resident has met all criteria for two consecutive weeks
      2. Elimination Step 2 (E2): After the resident has met the specified criteria for each self-care skill for two consecutive weeks of five evaluations per week (for the Medication Procedure the resident must be in the last step and receiving all scores of 1)
         a. Begin evaluating three times per week
         b. Continue this procedure until the resident has met all criteria for two consecutive weeks
      3. Elimination Step 3 (E3): After the resident has met the specified criteria for each self-care skill for two consecutive weeks of three evaluations per week (for the Medication Procedure the resident must be in the last step of the procedure and receiving all scores of 1)
         a. Begin evaluating one time per week
         b. Continue this procedure until the resident has met all criteria for two consecutive weeks

4. Elimination Step 4 (E4): After the resident has met the criteria for each self-care skill for two consecutive weeks of one evaluation per week (For the Medication Procedure the resident must be in the last step of the procedure and receiving all scores of 1)
   a. Begin evaluating twice per month (These two days cannot be in the same week)
   b. Continue this procedure until the resident leaves Level 3
B. Procedure
   1. Whenever a resident in one of the elimination steps does not meet the daily criterion and/or the weekly criterion, he/she is to be evaluated daily as of the next day.
   2. Daily evaluations are to continue for the remainder of the current Self-Care Skills week and the following Self-Care Skills week (Note: Level 3 Self-Care Skills week begins on Tuesday and ends on Monday).
   3. If the resident meets the weekly criterion during the entire period of daily evaluations specified in #2 above, he/she is to be placed in the elimination step preceding the one that he/she was in prior to the initiation of daily evaluations (Example: If a resident was in Elimination Step 3 (E3) prior to *not* meeting criterion, and subsequently meets the weekly criterion during the entire period of daily evaluations, then he/she is to be placed in Elimination Step 2 (E2)).
   4. If the resident does *not* meet the *weekly* criterion during the entire period of daily evaluations specified in #2 above, he/she is to be placed in the elimination step that is two steps below the step that he/she was in prior to initiation of daily evaluations (Example: If a resident was in Elimination Step 3 (E3) prior to *not* meeting criterion, and he/she does *not* meet the weekly criterion during the entire period of daily evaluations, then he/she is to be placed on Elimination Step I (E1)).
   5. Elimination Step changes are to occur on Tuesday.
   6. Whenever a resident is moved back from Elimination Step 1 (E1) or Elimination Step 2 (E2) to the Self-Care Skills treatment period (T) (evaluations seven days per week), he/she is only required to meet the Self-Care Skills weekly criterion for two consecutive weeks in order to return to Elimination Step 1 (E1).
   7. Whenever a resident in one of the elimination steps meet the weekly criterion for two consecutive weeks, he/she is to be advanced to the next elimination phase.
C. Daily Evaluations Schedule Sheet (See Figure 2-8, p. 51)
   1. There is to be one Daily Evaluations Schedule Sheet displayed in each DCS office.
   2. Whenever a resident begins daily evaluations because he/she has missed the daily criterion and/or weekly criterion, the data specified below are to be recorded on the Daily Evaluation Schedule Sheet by the second shift DCS, who summarizes the daily Self-Care Skills data on the day the resident misses the criterion:
      a. Name: Record the name of the individual.
      b. Beginning Date: Record the date on which daily evaluations are to begin.
      c. Termination Date: Record the date on which daily evaluations are to end.
D. Level 3 Self-Care Skills Evaluations Schedule Sheet (See Figure 2-9, p. 52.)
   1. There is to be one Self-Care Skills Evaluation Schedule Sheet displayed in each DCS office.
   2. On Monday evening, the third shift DCS, who summarizes the weekly Self-Care Skills data on each ward, is to indicate the phase each resident is to be in during the next Self-Care Skills week (beginning on Tuesday) by recording:
      a. Name: Each resident's name
      b. Date: The date on which the resident is to begin a given phase (i.e., Baseline

48 PSYCHIATRIC UNIT PROCEDURES

(B), Treatment (T), Elimination Step 1 (E1), Elimination Step 2 (E2), Elimination Step 3 (E3), or Elimination Step 4 (E4).

(Note: If a resident is to remain in the same phase for two consecutive weeks, it is not necessary to record a new date on the Evaluation Schedule Sheet).

c. When a resident is moved from one phase to another, draw a single line through the date recorded for the phase from which he/she is moved.

DATA COLLECTION AND GRAPHING PROCEDURE - LEVELS 1, 2, AND 3

V. Self-Care Skills Data Sheet *and* Self-Care Skills Weekly Criterion Data Sheet
  A. Self-Care Skills Data Sheet (See Figure 2-10, p. 52.)
    1. There is to be one Self-Care Skills Data Sheet per resident.
    2. The Self-Care Skills Data Sheet is to be located in the resident's Individual Program Book.
    3. Data are to be recorded each evening by the second Shift assigned/alternate DCS:
      a. Date—Record the date for that day.
      b. Sleeping Area; Wake-up; Dental Hygiene; Shower; Locker; Medication; Meals; Dressing—For each skill, record the highest single score the resident obtained for that day (Levels 1 and 2—Either a 1, 2, 3, 4, or 5 score; Level 3—Either a 1, 2, or 3 score) from the score obtained on each Self-Care Skills data sheet (for Medication, also record the step of the Medication procedure that the individual is currently in. Step 1 = A; Step 2 = B; Step 3 = C; Step 4 = D. For example, if an individual is in Step 1 and receives a score of 1, record 1/A).
      c. Daily freq. of 1, 2, 3, 4, and 5—Record the frequency of 1, 2, 3, 4, and 5 scores for the day (across all self-care skills).
      d. DCS—Record the initials of the DCS making the daily recordings on the Self-Care Skills Data Sheet.
      e. Bonus payment—Place a check mark (✓) if the resident received the 10¢ bonus payment that day *or* and X if the resident did not receive the bonus payment.
    4. Each Monday evening, the third shift DCS is to record the following:
      a. T.F. 1, 2, 3, 4, and 5—Record the total frequency of 1, 2, 3, 4, and 5 scores that the resident obtained that week, in the appropriate column.
      b. % T.F. 1, 2, 3, 4, and 5
        1. % total frequency of 1 = $\dfrac{\text{frequency of 1 scores for the week}}{\text{TOTAL NUMBER OF ALL SCORES FOR WEEK}}$
        2. % total frequency of 2 = $\dfrac{\text{frequency of 2 scores for the week}}{\text{TOTAL NUMBER OF ALL SCORES FOR WEEK}}$
        3. % total frequency of 3 = $\dfrac{\text{frequency of 3 scores for the week}}{\text{TOTAL NUMBER OF ALL SCORES FOR WEEK}}$
        4. % total frequency of 4 = $\dfrac{\text{frequency of 4 scores for the week}}{\text{TOTAL NUMBER OF ALL SCORES FOR WEEK}}$
        5. % total frequency of 5 = $\dfrac{\text{frequency of 5 scores for the week}}{\text{TOTAL NUMBER OF ALL SCORES FOR WEEK}}$
      c. S. freq. of 1, 2, 3, 4, and 5—Record the frequency of 1, 2, 3, 4, and 5 scores for the week for each self-care skill.

d. DCS—Record the initials of the DCS making the weekly recordings on the Self-Care Skills Data Sheet
 B. Self-Care Skills Weekly Criterion Data Sheet (See Figure 2–11, p. 54.)
    1. There is to be one Self-Care Skills Weekly Criterion Data Sheet per resident.
    2. The Self-Care Skills Weekly Criterion Data Sheet is to be located in the resident's Individual Program Book.
    3. Each Monday evening the third shift DCS is to record the following:
       a. Date—Record the date from the last day of the week that the data were collected (this should always be the date for the Monday—the day this recording is to be done).
       b. For each self-care skill.
          (1) Criteria—Record whether the resident met the weekly criterion for each self-care skill.
             (a) If the resident met the weekly criterion for a self-care skill, place a check-mark (✓) in the appropriate column.
             (b) If the resident did *not* meet the weekly criterion for a self-care skill, place an *X* in the appropriate column.
          (2) Weekly criterion: Record whether the resident met the weekly criterion for every self-care skill:
             (a) If the resident met weekly criterion for every self-care skill, place a check mark (✓) in the appropriate space.
             (b) If the resident did *not* meet the weekly criterion for every self-care skill, place an *X* in the appropriate space.
          (3) Treatment Phase: The treatment phase the resident is currently in (B, $T1$, $T2$, $E1$, $E2$, $E3$, or $E4$):
             B: Record B if the resident is in the Self-Care Skills Baseline Period.
             T1: Record a $T1$ if the resident is in Phase I of the Self-Care Skills Program.
             T2: Record a $T2$ if the resident is in Phase II of the Self-Care Skills Program.
             E1: Record $E1$ if the resident is in Step 1 (five evaluations per week) of the Self-Care Skills elimination period.
             E2: Record $E2$ if the resident is in Step 2 (three evaluations per week) of the elimination period.
             E3: Record $E3$ if the resident is in Step 3 (one evaluation per week) of the elimination period.
             E4: Record $E4$ if the resident is in Step 4 (two evaluations per month) of the elimination period.
          (4) DCS—Record the initials of the DCS making the weekly recordings on the Self-Care Skills Weekly Criterion Data Sheet.
VI. Self-Care Skills Graphing Technique for Each Skill
    A. Each resident's data are to be plotted separately.
    B. There are to be three graph sheets per resident.
       The following skills are to be plotted on each of the three graph sheets:
       a. On one graph sheet:
          (1) Sleep data
          (2) Bedroom area preparation data
          (3) Locker data
       b. On the second graph sheet
          (1) Shower data
          (2) Medication data
          (3) Dental hygiene data
       c. On the third graph

                (1) Meal data
                (2) Dressing data
    D. Graphing is to be done by third shift on Monday evenings.
    E. Graph sheets are to be located in the resident's Individual Program Book.
VII. Total Self-Care Skill Graphing Technique
    A. The Self-Care Skills graph is to be done weekly.
    B. A week is to be from Tuesday through Monday.
    C. Plotting of data is to be done by third shift on Monday evening.
    D. The Self-Care Skills graph is to be located in the resident's Individual Program Book.
    E. Plot the percent total frequency of 1, 2, 3, 4, and 5 scores that the resident obtained each week from the Self-Care Skills Data Sheet row *% Total Frequency of 1, 2, and 3.*

LEVEL 3 DAILY EVALUATIONS SCHEDULE SHEET

NAME	BEGINNING DATE	TERMINATION DATE		

Figure 2-8

SELF-CARE SKILLS EVALUATION SCHEDULE SHEET

WEEKS OF MEETING CRITERION REQUIRED	ADMISSION TO PROGRAM	BASELINE	4	2	2	2	UNTIL DISCHARGE
			TREATMENT (7 TIMES/WEEK)	ELIMINATION STEP 1 (5 TIMES/WEEK)	ELIMINATION STEP 2 (3 TIMES/WEEK)	ELIMINATION STEP 3 (1 TIME/WEEK)	ELIMINATION STEP 4 (2 TIMES/MONTH)
NAME		B	T	E1	E2	E3	E4

Figure 2-9

SELF-CARE SKILLS DATA SHEET

DATE	SLEEPING		DENTAL HYGIENE	SHOWER	LOCKER	MEDIC.	MEALS	DRESSING	DAILY FREQ. OF 1	DAILY FREQ. OF 2	DAILY FREQ. OF 3	DAILY FREQ. OF 4	DAILY FREQ. OF 5	BONUS PYMT.	DCS
	SLEEP														
TUES															
WED.															
THURS.															
FRI.															
SAT.															
SUN.															
MON.															
T.F. 1, 2, 3, 4, 5															
%TF 1, 2, 3, 4, 5															
S. Freq. of 1															
S. Freq. of 2															
S. Freq. of 3															
S. Freq. of 4															
S. Freq. of 5															
DCS															

Figure 2-10

SELF-CARE SKILLS WEEKLY CRITERION DATA SHEET

DATE		SLEEPING AREA	WAKE-UP	DENTAL HYGIENE	SHOWER	LOCKER	MEDIC.	MEALS	DRESSING	WEEKLY CRITERION	TREAT-MENT PHASE	DCS
Mon.	Criteria											
Mon.	Criteria											
Mon.	Criteria											
Mon.	Criteria											
Mon.	Criteria											
Mon.	Criteria											
Mon.	Criteria											
Mon.	Criteria											
Mon.	Criteria											

Figure 2-11

LEVEL 1, LEVEL 2, AND LEVEL 3 BEDROOM AREA PREPARATION PROCEDURE

GENERAL STATEMENT

An individual living by him/herself or with roommates, typically does not have someone else to clean his/her living area. It is necessary for the individual to clean his/her own area. Many individuals living in a hospital do not have the skills, the motivation, or the need to take care of their own sleeping area. Taking care of one's sleeping area involves making one's bed regularly, periodically stripping all linen and replacing it with clean linen, and cleaning the general bedroom area.

PURPOSE

1. To help the resident develop good hygiene habits
2. To help increase the resident's pride in his/her living area
3. To help the resident maintain behavior that will allow him/her to remain out of the hospital
4. To help the resident develop a sense of independence
5. To help the resident increase his/her self-esteem
6. To help the resident develop habits of neatness

PROCEDURE

I. General Policies
   A. A resident's area is to be completely cared for by 8:00 A.M. without prompts.
   B. Cleanliness and neatness are the major criteria.
II. Bed-making
   A. Each resident is to make his/her own bed.
   B. The style of the bed-making is to be left to each resident's discretion.
   C. Regardless of the style of bed-making, the following will apply:
      1. The bed is to be made daily (i.e., cleaning and straightening under sheet and all top sheets and blankets).
      2. The cover sheet and blanket are to cover the mattress and bedframe on both sides of the bed and should not be touching the floor.
      3. Different layers of blankets and sheets are not to be visible from the side.
      4. Neatness is the major criterion for completeness (no folds or major wrinkles).
   D. Each Wednesday, residents are to
      1. Remove all bed linen from bed
      2. Wash mattress cover and wipe dry
      3. After mattress cover is dry, make bed with fresh linen
III. Clean Sleeping Area
   A. Each resident is to clean his/her own bedroom area.
   B. The resident is to keep his/her bedroom area free of dirt, dust, and trash.
   C. Once per week, the resident is to dust mop his/her bedroom floor.
   D. The resident is not to have his/her clothing lying around the bedroom.
IV. Evaluations
   A. The resident's room is to be evaluated each day.
   B. All evaluations are to be made by the Direct-Care Staff (DCS) member assigned to the resident or by his/her alternate.
   C. All evaluations are to be made in the presence of the resident whose room is being evaluated.
   D. Evaluations are to include the bed, the nightstand, and the floor (including under the bed).

E. Bedroom evaluations are to be made
   1. By 8:00 A.M.
   2. Before 8:00 A.M. if the resident says he/she has completed the task
   3. After the resident has taken a nap
F. Bedroom Evaluations
   1. All residents are to have a Bedroom Evaluation each day.
   2. Components to check:
      a. Bed
         (1) The bed is to be made with the cover sheet and blanket having approximately equal length sides. The cover sheet and blanket are to cover the bed frame and mattress on both sides of the bed and should not be touching the floor.
         (2) Different Layers of blankets and sheets are not to be visible from the sides.
         (3) There are to be no major folds or wrinkles.
         (4) Neatness is a major criterion for completeness.
      b. Sleeping Area
         (1) The sleeping area is to be free of trash.
         (2) Each Monday morning, the resident is to dust mop his/her bedroom floor.
         (3) The resident is not to have his/her clothing lying around the bedroom.
G. Stripped-Bed Evaluation
   1. Each Wednesday, all residents are to strip, wash, and remake their beds.
   2. Bed-stripping and washing are to be completed by 12:30 P.M.
      a. Evaluations of each resident's bed is to occur
         (1) By 12:30 P.M.
         (2) Before 12:30 P.M., if the resident states that he/she has completed the task
      b. Components to check
         (1) Dirty linens are to be placed in the laundry bag on each ward
         (2) The entire mattress cover is to be washed with soap and water, as provided, and dried.
         (c) At 12:30 P.M., if the resident has not appropriately stripped and washed his/her bed as defined above (G. 2.b.), begin prompting/correcting every 15 minutes until he/she appropriately completes the task, *or* until 1:30 P.M.
   3. Bed-making
      a. Residents' beds are to be left unmade for at least one hour after washing on Wednesdays for the purpose of drying.
      b. Residents may be granted free access to their bedrooms for bed-making purposes at anytime on Wednesday, as long as the bed is washed and dried.
      c. No nap time is permitted until the bed has been appropriately made.
      d. Evaluation of the resident's bed is to occur
         (1) By 5:30 P.M.
         (2) Before 5:30 P.M., if the resident states that he/she has completed the task.
      e. Components to check:
         (1) The bed is to be made with the cover sheet and blanket having approximately equal length sides. The cover sheet and blanket are to cover the bed frame and mattress on both sides of the bed, and should not be touching the floor.
         (2) Different layers of blankets and sheets are not be be visable from the sides.
         (3) There are to be no major wrinkles or folds.
         (4) Neatness is a major criterion for completeness.

f. At 5:30 P.M., if the resident has not appropriately made his/her bed as defined above (G. 3. E.), begin prompting/correcting every 15 minutes until he/she appropriately completes the task, *or* until 6:30 P.M.

V. Giving Prompts/Instructions
  A. The resident is to be given prompts/instructions on how the task can be completed properly.
  B. The resident is to be requested, not told, to complete the task.
  C. Repeat the prompts/instructions every 15 minutes until the task is completed properly or until five prompts have been given, whichever comes first.
  D. Always prompt and suggest that the resident comply.
  E. If the resident does not begin this skill by 8:00 A.M., he/she will be requested every 15 minutes to begin until the task is completed appropriately or until five prompts have been given.

VI. Reinforcement and Contingency Management
  A. Level 1 and Level 2 Reinforcement and Contingency Management
    1. Regular Bedroom Evaluation
      a. If the resident passes the bedroom evaluation with no prompts, give him/her
        (1) A 5¢ token payment
        (2) Verbal praise
        (3) A score of 1 on the data sheet
      b. If the resident does *not* pass the bedroom evaluation with no prompts
        (1) Always use a positive approach with the resident
        (2) Explain to the resident what needs to be done in order to pass the bedroom evaluation, and then ask him/her to make the necessary corrections
        (3) If the necessary corrections are made prior to 8:00 A.M., do *not* count as a prompt. Apply the same contingencies as in A. 1. a. above (i.e., 5¢ token payment, verbal praise, a score of 1)
        (4) Beginning at 8:00 A.M., prompt or correct the resident every 15 minutes until the task is completed appropriately, *or* until five prompts/corrections are given
      c. The following contingencies are to be applied when prompts/corrections are required as of 8:00 A.M.:
        (1) One prompt/correction
          (a) Give the resident a 3¢ token payment
          (b) Give the resident verbal praise
          (c) Give the resident a score of 2 on the data sheet
        (2) Two or three prompts corrections
          (a) Give the resident a 2¢ token payment
          (b) Give the resident verbal praise
          (c) Give the resident a score of 3 on the data sheet
        (3) Four or five prompts/corrections
          (a) Give the resident a 1¢ token payment
          (b) Give the resident verbal praise
          (c) Give the resident a score of 4 on the data sheet
        (4) If the task is *not* completed appropriately after five prompts
          (a) Do *not* give the resident token payment
          (b) Do *not* give the resident verbal praise
          (c) Give the resident a score of 5 on the data sheet
    2. Stripped-Bed Evaluations (Wednesdays)
      a. If the resident's bed is appropriately stripped and washed (as defined in IV. G. above) by 12:30 P.M., give him/her
        (1) A 5¢ token payment
        (2) Verbal praise
        (3) A score of 1 on the data sheet

b. If the resident does *not* pass the evaluation without prompts
   (1) Always use a positive approach
   (2) Explain to the resident what needs to be done in order to complete the task appropriately, and then ask him/her to make the necessary corrections
   (3) If the necessary corrections are made prior to 12:30 P.M., do *not* count as a prompt. Apply the same contingencies as in VI. A. 2. a. above (i.e., 5¢ token payment, verbal praise, a score of 1)
   (4) Beginning at 12:30 P.M., prompt or correct the resident every 15 minutes until the task is completed appropriately, or until five prompts/corrections are given
c. The following contingencies are to be applied when prompts/corrections are required as of 12:30 P.M.
   (1) One prompt/correction
      (a) Give the resident a 3¢ token payment
      (b) Give the resident verbal praise
      (c) Give the resident a score of 2 on the data sheet
   (2) Two or three prompts/corrections
      (a) Give the resident a 2¢ token payment
      (b) Give the resident verbal praise
      (c) Give the resident a score of 3 on the data sheet
   (3) Four or five prompts/corrections
      (a) Give the resident a 1¢ token payment
      (b) Give the resident verbal praise
      (c) Give the resident a score of 4 on the data sheet
   (4) If the task is *not* completed appropriately after five prompts
      (a) Do *not* give the resident token payment
      (b) Do not give the resident verbal praise
      (c) Give the resident a score of 5 on the data sheet
      (d) Assist the resident in completing the task
3. Regular evaluation of bed-making on Wednesday evenings (following Strippled bed Evaluation)
   —Implement reinforcement and contingency management procedure specified in Section VI. A. 1. above.
B. Level 3 Reinforcement and Contingency Management
   1. The following is applicable to both Stripped Bed Evaluations and Regular Bedroom Evaluations:
      a. Appropriate completion of task with no prompts
         (1) Give the resident a 2¢ token payment
         (2) Give the resident verbal praise
         (3) Give the resident a score of 1 on the data sheet
      b. Appropriate completion of task with no more than one prompt
         (1) Give the resident a 1¢ token payment
         (2) Give the resident verbal praise
         (3) Give the resident a score of 2 on the data sheet
      c. Appropriate completion of task with two or more prompts
         (1) Do not give the resident any token payment
         (2) Give the resident verbal praise
         (3) Give the resident a score of 3 on the data sheet
      d. When the resident refuses to do the task
         (1) Do *not* give him/her any token payment
         (2) Do not give him/her verbal praise unless the task is complete; then given verbal praise
         (3) Give him/her a score of 3 on the data sheet

e. When the resident completes the task, after two or more prompts
   (1) Do *not* give him/her any token payment
   (2) Give him/her verbal praise
   (3) Give him/her a score of 3 on the data sheet

VII. Bedroom Area Data Sheet (See Figure 2–12, p. 60)
   A. There is to be one data sheet per resident.
   B. The data sheet is to be located in the resident's Individual Program Book.
   C. Data to be recorded:
      1. Date—Always record the current date. Do not skip any dates.
      2. Bed-making—Record the score obtained by the resident.
      3. Stripped-bed evaluations (Wednesday morning)—Record the score obtained by the resident for stripped-bed evaluations. (See Section VI, p. 57.)
      4. Naps—Record the score obtained by the resident whenever he/she has lain down in bed (except for regular sleep) times: (Regular Evaluation) (Use the same square as often as necessary for that day) (See Section VI, p. 57.)
      5. Prompts—Record the number of times the resident had to be asked to complete the task. This includes the number of times the resident was asked to correct the task.
      6. Paid—Record the amount of money the resident was paid for the task
      7. DCS—Record the initials of the DCS who makes the evaluations and pays the resident.
      8. Highest Score—Each evening the second shift is to record the highest score the resident obtained that day for Bed-Making (mornings and Wednesday evening), Stripped-bed, and Nap evaluations.
      9. Each Monday, the second shift DCS is to record (from the Highest Score for the Day Column), in their respective spaces
         (1) Tot of Payment: Record the total amount of token payments made to the resident during the week
         (2) Frequency of 1, 2, 3, 4, or 5 HS: Record the total number of 1, 2, 3, 4, and 5 scores obtained that week (from the Highest Score for the Day Column) in their respective spaces

BEDROOM AREA PREPARATION DATA SHEET

DATE	BED-MAKING	STRIPPED BED	NAPS	PROMPT	PAID	DCS	DCS	DCS	DCS	DCS	DCS	HIGHEST SCORE
Tues.												
Wed.												
Thurs.												
Fri.												
Sat.												
Sun.												
Mon.												
Tot. Paym.	////	////	////	////		////	////	////	////	////		////
Freq. 1 HS	////	////	////	////	////	////	////	////	////	////		
Freq. 2 HS	////	////	////	////	////	////	////	////	////	////		
Freq. 3 HS	////	////	////	////	////	////	////	////	////	////		
Freq. 4 HS	////	////	////	////	////	////	////	////	////	////		
Freq. 5 HS	////	////	////	////	////	////	////	////	////	////		
Tues.												
Wed.												
Thurs.												
Fri.												
Sat.												
Sun.												
Mon.												
Tot. Paym.	////	////	////	////		////	////	////	////	////	////	////
Freq. 1 HS	////	////	////	////	////	////	////	////	////	////		
Freq. 2 HS	////	////	////	////	////	////	////	////	////	////		
Freq. 3 HS	////	////	////	////	////	////	////	////	////	////		
Freq. 4 HS	////	////	////	////	////	////	////	////	////	////		
Freq. 5 HS	////	////	////	////	////	////	////	////	////	////		

Figure 2-12

LEVEL 1, LEVEL 2, AND LEVEL 3 WAKE-UP PROCEDURE

GENERAL STATEMENT

One very essential determinant of one's physical and emotional health is the amount of sleep that he/she obtains. The actual amount of time an individual needs to sleep varies greatly. For an individual living independently, obtaining the proper amount of sleep is his/her responsibility. The amount of sleep one obtains while residing in the program is determined by the resident as long as he/she accepts the responsibility that must go along with that decision. Thus, should this independence be abused in such a way that it interferes with the resident's normal daily activities, efforts are made to teach the individual to properly judge the amount of sleep needed to meet the demands of daily living.

PURPOSE

1. To help in the development of self-control
2. To teach responsibility for one's actions
3. To help a resident develop time awareness
4. To help a resident develop good psychological and physiological habits
5. To help develop personal independence

PROCEDURE

I. General Policies
  A. Levels 1, 2, and 3
    1. The Wake-up procedure applies to both regular sleep and naps
       a. Wake-up from regular sleep is to be conducted at 6:00 A.M. (excluding Sunday and Saturday Special—see Section II below).
       b. Wake-up from naps is to be conducted at the end of the predetermined time unless the resident has already awakened.
    2. Being awake is defined as having both feet on the floor and being at least in a sitting position within five minutes of being prompted to awaken.
    3. A resident is to be allowed a maximum of two hours of nap time per day with one hour to occur in the morning and one hour to occur in afternoon, no later than 4:00 P.M. (exceptions may be made on an individual basis).
    4. A resident is not to be allowed to sleep anywhere other than his/her bedroom
       a. If a resident is observed sleeping anywhere other than in his/her bedroom, he/she is to be requested to wake-up and reminded that he/she is allowed time for sleep in his/her bedroom
       b. If a resident continues to sleep other than in his/her bedroom, after the first request, he/she is to be requested to wake-up every 15 minues until he/she remains awake
  B. Level 1
    1. The wake up procedure is divided into five categories (See Section II below).
    2. A resident may be allowed to stay up as late as 11:00 P.M. given that
       a. He/she did *not* require the fifth wake-up procedure from regular sleep and/or a nap(s) that day
       b. He/she is not disturbing other residents
    3. Bedroom doors are to be locked from 9:00 A.M. to 9:00 P.M. (except for shower period—4:00 to 5:00 P.M.)
  C. Level 2
    1. The wake-up procedure is divided into five procedures. (See Section II below.)
    2. A resident is to be in bed no later than 10:00 P.M. until he/she meets two consec-

utive weeks of weekly Self-Care Skills Criterion. (See Self-Care Skills Procedure, p. 41.)
   3. As soon as a resident meets two consecutive weeks of weekly Self-Care Skills Criterion, he/she is to be allowed to stay up until 12:00 P.M. (or later if prior permission is given, i.e., finishing watching a late show) provided that
      a. He/she did not receive a score of 4 or 5 in wake-up and/or in waking up from a nap that day (See Section II: Wake-up Procedure)
      b. He/she is not disturbing other residents.
   D. Level 3
   1. The wake up procedure is divided into three categories. (See Section II below.)
   2. A resident is to be allowed to stay up as late as he/she desires given that
      a. He/she did *not* require a strenuous prompt from regular sleep and/or a nap(s) that day (See Section II: Wake-up Procedures)
      b. He/she is not disturbing other residents
II. Wake-up Procedures
   A. Levels 1 and 2
   1. Initial Procedure
      a. The Direct-Care Staff (DCS) member is to announce wake-up time at approximately 6:00 A.M.
      b. When announcing wake-up time, the DCS is to
         (1) Knock on the resident's bedroom door
         (2) Pause for a few seconds
            (a) If the resident responds, the DCS is to ask for permission to enter, observe the resident, and reinforce him/her if appropriate
            (b) If there is no response, the DCS is to
               i. Open the door
               ii. Call the resident by name
               iii. Indicate that it is time to get up
   2. Second Procedure
   Five minutes after the first announcement (Initial Procedure), if any resident(s) is (are) not awake (as defined in I.A. above), the DCS is to repeat the Initial procedure.
   3. Third Procedure
   Five minutes after the completion of the Second Procedure, if any resident(s) is (are) not awake (as defined above), the DCS is to repeat the same procedure.
   4. Fourth Procedure
   If any resident(s) is (are) not awake (as defined in I.A. above) after completion of the Third Procedure, the DCS is to gently nudge the resident on the shoulder and tell him/her that it is time to wake up.
   5. Fifth Procedure
      a. If the resident does not awaken after the nudge
         (1) Take his/her blanket off
         (2) Gently but firmly take the resident's feet and move them off the bed
         (3) Place the resident in an erect sitting posture
         (4) Remain with the resident until he/she begins to verbally respond in a manner indicating that he/she is awake
         (5) Leave the resident's room and return within three to four minutes to ensure that he/she is awake. If awake when you return, give verbal praise
      b. Fifth Procedure Consequence
      Whenever a resident needs the fifth procedure to be awakened, initiate the following consequence:
         (1) The resident is to be required to be in bed for the evening between 8:45 P.M. and 9:15 P.M.
         (2) This requirement is to continue until the resident awakens with the First, Second, or Third Procedure for two consecutive days

B. Level 3
  1. Initial Procedure (Minimal Prompt)
     a. The DCS is to announce wake-up time at approximately 6:00 A.M.
     b. When announcing wake-up time the DCS is to
        (1) Knock on the resident's bedroom door
        (2) Pause for a few seconds
            (a) If the resident responds, the DCS is to ask for permission to enter, observe the resident, and reinforce him/her if appropriate
            (b) If there is no response, the DCS is to
                i. Open the door
                ii. Call the resident by name
                iii. Indicate that it is time to get up
        (c) The DCS is to then move on to the next resident
  2. Second Procedure (Medium Prompt)
     Five minutes after Minimal Prompt procedure, if any resident(s) is (are) not awake (as defined in I.A. above), the DCS is to repeat the Minimal Prompt procedure.
  3. Third Procedure (Strenuous Prompt)
     a. If any resident(s) is (are) not awake (as defined in I. A. above) after completion of the Medium prompt Procedure, the DCS is to
        (1) Gently nudge the resident on the shoulder
        (2) If the resident does not awaken after the nudge
            (a) Take his/her blanket off
            (b) Gently but firmly take the resident's feet and move them off the bed
            (c) Place the resident in an erect sitting posture
            (d) Remain with the resident until he/she begins to verbally respond in a manner indicating that he/she is awake
            (e) Leave the resident's room and return within three to five minutes to ensure that he/she is awake. (If the resident is awake when you return, give the resident verbal praise
     b. Strenuous Prompt Consequence
        Whenever a resident needs a strenuous prompt to be awakened, initiate the following consequences:
        1. The resident is to be required to be in bed for the evening between 8:45 P.M. and 9:15 P.M.
        2. This requirement is to continue until the resident awakens with either a minimal or average prompt for two consecutive days
III. Reinforcement and Contingency Management
  A. Level 1 and 2
    1. When a resident wakes up from regular sleep or a nap with the Initial Procedure, as soon as he/she is dressed and out of his/her room.
       a. Give the resident a 5¢ token payment
       b. Give the resident verbal praise
       c. Record a score of 1 on the data sheet
    2. When a resident wakes up from regular sleep or a nap with the Second Procedure, as soon as he/she is dressed and out of his/her room.
       a. Give the resident a 3¢ token payment
       b. Give the resident verbal praise
       c. Record a score of 2 on the data sheet
    3. When a resident wakes up from regular sleep or a nap with the Third Procedure, as soon as he/she is dressed and out of his/her room.
       a. Give the resident a 2¢ token payment
       b. Give the resident verbal praise
       c. Record a score of 3 on the data sheet

4. When a resident wakes up from regular sleep or a nap with the Fourth Procedure, as soon as he/she is dressed and out of his/her room.
   a. Give him/her a 1¢ token payment
   b. Give him/her verbal praise
   c. Record a score of 4 on the data sheet
5. When a resident wakes up from regular sleep or a nap with the Fifth Procedure, as soon as he/she is dressed and out of his/her room.
   a. Give him/her verbal praise
   b. Do *not* give him/her a token payment
   c. Record a score of 5 on the data sheet
   d. Always use a positive approach
   e. Inform the resident that he/she must go to bed between 8:45 P.M. and 9:15 P.M. each night until he/she receives a score of 1, 2, or 3 in wake-up for the day for two consecutive days

B. Level 3
1. When a resident wakes up from regular sleep or a nap with a minimal prompt
   a. Give him/her a 2¢ token payment
   b. Give him/her verbal praise
   c. Record a score of 1 on the data sheet
2. When a resident wakes up from regular sleep or a nap with an average prompt
   a. Give him/her a 1¢ token payment
   b. Give him/her verbal praise
   c. Record a score of 2 on the data sheet
3. When a resident wakes up from regular sleep or a nap with a strenuous prompt
   a. Do *not* give him/her any token payment
   b. Do *not* give him/her social praise
   c. Always use a positive approach with the resident
   d. Record a score of 3 on the data sheet

IV. Sunday and Saturday Special
A. Sunday Special
1. Sleeping late—residents are to be allowed to sleep as late as 10:00 A.M. on Sundays when
   a. The weekly self-care skills criterion is met for the week (See Self-Care Skills Procedure, p. 41.)
   b. All ward and individual criteria are met for the week
   c. All token debts are paid in full
   d. No restrictions are in effect as function of individual programs which would preclude this privilege and/or as a function of inappropriate behavior such as stealing, aggression, and/or sexual misconduct.
   e. The resident tells a second shift DCS before retiring on the preceding evening, when he/she would like to be awakened in the morning. (If the resident does *not* tell a second shift DCS on the preceding evening that he/she would like to sleep late the next morning, then the resident is to be awakened at the regular time, 6:00 A.M.) The second shift DCS is to make a recording in the Log Book indicating that the resident is engaging in the special and indicating the time that he/she would like to be awakened
2. Use of bedroom
Residents are to be allowed to use their bedrooms at their discretion on the day of the special with no token charge when
   a. The weekly self-care skills criterion is met for the week
   b. All ward and individual criteria are met for the week
   c. All token debts are paid in full
   d. No restrictions due to individual programs and/or inappropriate behavior such as stealing, aggression and/or sexual misconduct are in effect

B. Saturday Special
   1. Saturday specials are the same as Sunday specials (except for the additional criterion specified below).
   2. The resident needs to meet the self-care skills weekly criterion for the preceding two consecutive weeks and also the other criteria specified above for Sunday specials.
V. Financial Payment for Naps
   A. A resident is to pay 20¢ (tokens) for 30 minutes nap time, in advance, if in the token economy system.
   B. Free access to the bedroom is to be determined on an individual basis during Interdisciplinary Treatment Team Conferences.
   C. Payment for naps is to continue until the resident is no longer participating in the token economy.
   D. If a resident in the token economy system engages in nap time without paying (tokens) in advance
      1. Charge the resident twice the amount (40¢ tokens/30 minutes sleep) that is usually required (20¢ tokens/30 minutes sleep)
      2. Allow the resident to sleep for the remainder of the 30 minute period
      3. At the end of the 30 minute period, implement the Wake-Up Procedure
         a. If the resident continues to sleep following the completion of the Wake-Up Procedure, repeat Section D, Steps 1-3
         b. If the resident does *not* have sufficient tokens to pay for the sleep, the unpaid balance is to be recorded on his/her restitution sheet
   (NOTE: The procedure specified in Section D is to be implemented at the end of a 30 minute period until the resident discontinues sleeping.)
VI. Wake-up Data Sheet (See Figure 2-13, p. 66.)
   A. All data for naps and regular sleep are to be recorded on the Wake-Up Data Sheet.
   B. There is to be one Wake-Up Data Sheet per resident.
   C. The data sheet is to be located in the resident's Individual Program Book.
   D. Data to be recorded:
      1. Date—Always record the current date. Do not skip any dates.
      2. Wake-Up Procedure—Record how the individual responds when awakened in the morning.
         a. Record a 1 if Initial Procedure is required.
         b. Record a 2 if Second Procedure is required.
         c. Record a 3 if Third Procedure is required.
         d. Record a 4 if Fourth Procedure is required (Levels 1 and 2 only).
         e. Record a 5 if Fifth Procedure is required (Levels 1 and 2 only).
      3. Nap Wake-up Procedure—Record how the resident responds when awakened during any naps. Record a 1, 2, 3, 4, or 5. Use the same square as often as necessary per day.
      4. Paid—Record the amount of token money paid to the resident.
      5. DCS—Record the initials of the DCS waking the resident.
      6. Highest score—The highest score obtained that day, including naps, is to be recorded in this column, each evening, by the second shift DCS.
      7. Each Monday evening, the second shift assigned/alternate DCS is to record:
         a. Total of pay—Record the total amount of token payments that were given to the resident that week.
         b. Frequency of 1, 2, 3, 4, 5 highest score—Record the total number of 1, 2, 3, 4, and 5 scores obtained that week (from the highest score for the day row) in their respective spaces.
      8. DCS—Record the initials of the second shift DCS who recorded the weekly data on Monday evening.

WAKE-UP DATA SHEET

DATE	TUES.	WED.	THURS.	FRI.	SAT.	SUN.	MON.	TOTAL OF PAY	FREQ. OF 1 HIGH- EST SCORE	FREQ. OF 2 HIGH- EST SCORE	FREQ. OF 3 HIGH- EST SCORE	FREQ. OF 4 HIGH- EST SCORE	FREQ. OF 5 HIGH- EST SCORE	DCS
Wake up Procedure														
Nap Procedure														
Paid														
Highest Score														
DCS														
DATE	TUES.	WED.	THURS.	FRI.	SAT.	SUN.	MON.	TOTAL OF PAY	FREQ. OF 1 HIGH- EST SCORE	FREQ. OF 2 HIGH- EST SCORE	FREQ. OF 3 HIGH- EST SCORE	FREQ. OF 4 HIGH- EST SCORE	FREQ. OF 5 HIGH- EST SCORE	DCS
Wake up Procedure														
Nap Procedure														
Paid														
Highest Score														
DCS														
DATE	TUES.	WED.	THURS.	FRI.	SAT.	SUN.	MON.	TOTAL OF PAY	FREQ. OF 1 HIGH- EST SCORE	FREQ. OF 2 HIGH- EST SCORE	FREQ. OF 3 HIGH- EST SCORE	FREQ. OF 4 HIGH- EST SCORE	FREQ. OF 5 HIGH- EST SCORE	DCS
Wake up Procedure														
Nap Procedure														
Paid														
Highest Score														
DCS														

Figure 2-13

LEVEL 1, LEVEL 2, AND LEVEL 3 DENTAL HYGIENE PROCEDURE

GENERAL STATEMENT

Brushing one's teeth is a very important component of good personal hygiene. Brushing requires a deliberate attempt at thoroughly removing all dental plaque that may build up on and around an individual's teeth. By having well-brushed teeth, the individual will be more socially acceptable inasmuch as such personal care will help to maintain a good appearance and typically alleviates mouth odor. Moreover, properly caring for teeth reduces the chances of tooth decay and other physiological problems and the high medical expenses associated with dental care. Thus, it is extremely important that each individual learns to properly care for his/her teeth as efficiently as possible.

PURPOSE

1. To help develop appropriate self-control behavior suitable for good dental hygiene
2. To help develop and increase a resident's pride in his/her appearance
3. To help instill a feeling of confidence
4. To help the resident in decreasing dental difficulties and needless expense
5. To help increase self-esteem

PROCEDURE

I. General Policies
   A. To successfully meet the dental hygiene criteria the resident must
      1. Brush his/her teeth daily
      2. Have his/her teeth brushed by 8:00 A.M.
      3. Have the plaque removed from his/her teeth
   B. Exceptions to the rules are to be made on an individual basis, and are to be specified in the resident's Treatment Plan.
   C. Residents must meet dental hygiene criteria for seven days prior to being allowed to be a demonstrator.
II. General Procedure
   A. Each resident is to brush his/her teeth daily.
   B. Each resident is to have his/her teeth brushed by 8:00 A.M.
   C. Direct Care Staff (DCS) are to observe the occurrence of nonoccurrence of brushing teeth.
   D. If a resident has *not* brushed his/her teeth by 8:00 A.M., he/she is to be prompted every 15 minutes to brush until he/she does brush or until five prompts have been given.
III. Plaque Pill Procedure
   A. New residents
      1. Each new resident is to be given a complete set of verbal and nonverbal instructions by a DCS in the use of the plaque pill and proper brushing technique.
      2. Each new resident is to be given a demonstration, using another resident as a demonstrator.
   B. The Plaque Pill Procedure to be followed by both the DCS and the resident is as follows:
      1. Each day, Monday through Friday, five residents are to be chosen at random for the plaque pill procedure (each ward).
      2. The DCS is to give one plaque pill to each of the selected residents after they have brushed.
      3. The resident is to chew the pill after brushing.

4. The resident is to chew the pill for 30 seconds and then spit out the remains in the sink (DCS to insure chewing took place).
5. The resident is to be checked by the DCS for plaque (red indicates plaque).
6. If the resident failed to remove *all* plaque after the first brushing, he/she is to be prompted to brush again.
7. The brushing-evaluating process is to continue until all plaque is removed or until five prompts have been given.
8. If the resident refuses to continue the process of brushing-evaluating until all plaque is removed
    a. Prompt the resident every 15 minutes to finish his/her brushing until five prompts are given
    b. Always use a positive approach. *Never* force the resident to brush
    c. If the resident agrees to continue brushing after the passage of two or more hours since he/she last chewed a plaque pill, or if he/she has eaten since a plaque pill was chewed, ask him/her to chew another pill before brushing again

IV. Reinforcement and Contingency Management
   A. Level 1 and Level 2 Reinforcement and Contingency Management
      1. When teeth are brushed appropriately the first time with no prompts
         a. Give the resident a 5¢ token payment
         b. Give the resident verbal praise
         c. Give the resident a score of 1 on the data sheet
      2. When teeth are brushed appropriately after one prompt
         a. Give the resident a 3¢ token payment
         b. Give the resident verbal praise
         c. Give the resident a score of 2 on the data sheet
      3. When teeth are brushed appropriately after two or three prompts
         a. Give the resident a 2¢ token payment
         b. Give the resident verbal praise
         c. Give the resident a score of 3 on the data sheet
      4. When teeth are brushed appropriately after four or five prompts
         a. Give the resident a 1¢ token payment
         b. Give the resident verbal praise
         c. Give the resident a score of 4 on the data sheet
      5. When the resident refuses to properly brush his/her teeth after five prompts
         a. Do *not* give the resident any token payment
         b. Do *not* give the resident verbal praise
         c. Always use a positive approach
      6. When the demonstrator's behavior is appropriate as prescribed by instructions
         a. Give the resident a 5¢ token payment
         b. Give the resident verbal praise
   B. Level 3 Reinforcement and Contingency Management
      1. When teeth are brushed appropriately the first time with no prompts
         a. Give the resident a 2¢ token payment
         b. Give the resident verbal praise
         c. Give the resident a score of 1 on the dental hygiene data sheet
      2. When teeth are brushed appropriately after the second brushing (one prompt)
         a. Give the resident a 1¢ token payment
         b. Give the resident verbal praise
         c. Give the resident a score of 2 on the data sheet
      3. When teeth are brushed appropriately after two or more brushings (one prompt per brushing)
         a. Do *not* give the resident any token payment
         b. Give the resident verbal praise
         c. Give the resident a score of 3 on the data sheet

LEVEL 1, LEVEL 2, AND LEVEL 3 DENTAL HYGIENE PROCEDURE 69

    4. When the resident refuses to properly brush his/her teeth
       a. Do *not* give the resident any token payment
       b. Do *not* give the resident verbal praise
       c. Give the resident a score of 3 on the data sheet
       d. Always use a positive approach
    5. When the demonstrator's behavior is appropriate as prescribed by instructions
       a. Give the resident a 3¢ token payment
       b. Give the resident verbal praise
V. Dental Hygiene Data Sheet (See Figure 2-14, p. 70.)
   A. There is to be one Dental Hygiene Data Sheet per resident.
   B. The data sheet is to be located in the resident's Individual Program Book.
   C. Data to be recorded:
     1. Date—Always record the current date, even if brushing did not occur. Do not skip any dates.
     2. Score—Record the score the resident obtained for dental hygiene (See Section IV).
     3. Plaque Pill—Record a check (✓) if the resident was administered the plaque pill procedure, or an *X* if it was not administered.
     4. Prompt—Record the number of times the resident had to be asked to complete the skill appropriately. This includes the number of times the resident was asked to repeat the behavior.
     5. Paid—Record the amount of token money the resident was given for this skill.
     6. DCS—Record the initials of the DCS making the evaluation and paying the resident.
     7. Each Monday second shift DCS is to record:
       a. Total Paid—Record the total sum of token payments given to the resident that week.
       b. Frequency of 1, 2, 3, 4, and 5—Record the total number of 1, 2, 3, 4, and 5 scores for the week in their respective spaces.

DENTAL HYGIENE DATA SHEET

DATE	TUES.	WED.	THURS.	FRI.	SAT.	SUN.	MON.	TOTAL PAID	FREQ. 1	FREQ. 2	FREQ. 3	FREQ. 4	FREQ. 5
Score								/////					
Plaque Pill					/////	/////		/////	/////	/////	/////	/////	/////
Prompt								/////	/////	/////	/////	/////	/////
Paid									/////	/////	/////	/////	/////
DCS								/////	/////	/////	/////	/////	/////
Score								/////					
Plaque Pill					/////	/////		/////	/////	/////	/////	/////	/////
Prompt								/////	/////	/////	/////	/////	/////
Paid									/////	/////	/////	/////	/////
DCS								/////	/////	/////	/////	/////	/////
Score								/////					
Plaque Pill					/////	/////		/////	/////	/////	/////	/////	/////
Prompt								/////	/////	/////	/////	/////	/////
Paid									/////	/////	/////	/////	/////
DCS								/////	/////	/////	/////	/////	/////
Score								/////					
Plaque Pill					/////	/////		/////	/////	/////	/////	/////	/////
Prompt								/////	/////	/////	/////	/////	/////
Paid									/////	/////	/////	/////	/////
DCS								/////	/////	/////	/////	/////	/////

Figure 2-14

LEVEL 1, LEVEL 2, AND LEVEL 3 SHOWER PROCEDURE

GENERAL STATEMENT

Bathing or showering on a frequent basis is necessary for developing and maintaining good personal hygiene. In addition to washing one's body, most people in our society are expected to be clean-shaven (unless growing a beard), and to have their hair combed. By maintaining good personal hygiene, an individual can decrease the chances of disease, infections, odors, and various parasites. In addition, society will more readily accept a clean person than a dirty one.

PURPOSE

1. To help the resident develop socially adaptive behavior
2. To help increase the resident's pride in his/her appearance
3. To help the resident develop self-control techniques which are expected in today's society
4. To develop a skill that will greatly reduce body odors
5. To help the resident eliminate potential disease
6. To help the resident eliminate potential infections
7. To help the resident develop a better self-concept
8. To help the resident develop a concept of personal responsibility
9. To help the resident develop an independent attitude

PROCEDURE

I. Behavioral Requirements
   A. The shower procedure is to be observed daily.
   B. The resident is to wet his/her body completely (excluding the hair).
   C. The resident is to wash his/her hair at least once a week, unless otherwise specified in the resident's Treatment Plan.
   D. The resident is to lather his/her body completely with soap.
   E. The resident is to rinse all soap from his/her body.
   F. The resident is to towel dry his/her body completely.
   G. The resident is to put on clean undergarments after bathing or showering.
   H. The resident is to use a deodorant after bathing or showering.
   I. To meet the requirements for showering for the day, the resident must shower during one of the following times:
      1. 7:00 P.M.–9:00 P.M. (Shower time to be set according to ward activity schedule)
         a. The resident is to complete all requirements before 9:00 P.M.
         b. If the resident does not appropriately complete this skill before 9:00 P.M., he/she is to be prompted to do so every 15 minutes until the skill is completed appropriately or until five prompts have been given.
      2. 4:00 P.M.–5:00 P.M.—if the resident is engaging in an evening activity off the ward between 7:00 P.M. and 9:00 P.M.
         a. If the resident completes all requirements by 5:00 P.M., he/she is to be allowed to engage in the evening activity.
         b. If the resident *does not* complete all requirements by 5:00 P.M., or if he/she refuses to complete the task, he/she is not to be allowed to engage in the evening activity.
II. Evaluations
   A. Behavioral Component Evaluation
      1. Procedure
         a. During the two-week baseline period a Direct-Care Staff (DCS) member is to observe the resident engaging in a part of each behavioral component of

showering but does not need to observe on a continuous basis nor check for the total completion of each behavioral component.
    b. Evaluations are to be done as unobtrusively as possible.
    c. Every behavioral component of showering (i.e., wetting the body, soaping, rinsing, etc.) is to be engaged in.
    d. When a resident has *not* engaged in all the components of showering
       1. Always use a positive approach
       2. Explain to the resident how the skill can be completed appropriately (do not explain what was inappropriate)
  2. Assessment
    a. Following the two-week baseline period an assessment of the resident's showering performance is to be made.
    b. If the resident meets the shower procedure criterion for both weeks of the two-week baseline period, the General Evaluation procedure is to be followed (See II. B. below).
    c. If the resident does *not* meet the shower procedure criterion for both weeks of the two-week baseline period, the Behavioral Component Evaluation procedure is to continue until the criterion has been met for two consecutive weeks, or until otherwise decided in an Interdisciplinary Treatment Team staffing.
  B. General Evaluation
    1. General evaluations are *not* to include observation of the resident engaging in a part of each behavioral component of showering as in the Behavioral Component Evaluation.
    2. A DCS is to observe the occurrence or nonoccurrence of showering, shaving, and shampooing the hair.
    3. Evaluations are to be done as unobtrusively as possible.
III. Reinforcement and Contingency Management
  A. Levels 1 and 2
    1. Whenever the resident appropriately completes the skill with no prompts
       a. Give him/her a 5¢ token payment
       b. Give him/her verbal praise
       c. Give him/her a score of 1 on the data sheet
    2. Whenever the resident appropriately completes the skill with no more than one prompt
       a. Give him/her a 3¢ token payment
       b. Give him/her verbal praise
       c. Give him/her a score of 2 on the data sheet
    3. When the resident appropriately completes the skill with two or three prompts
       a. Give him/her a 2¢ token payment
       b. Give him/her verbal praise
       c. Give him/her a score of 3 on the data sheet
    4. When the resident appropriately completes the skill with four or five prompts
       a. Give him/her a 1¢ token payment
       b. Give him/her verbal praise
       c. Give him/her a score of 4 on the data sheet
    5. When the resident either does *not* appropriately complete the skill after a fifth prompt, or he/she refuses to complete the skill
       a. Do *not* give him/her any token payment
       b. Do *not* give him/her verbal praise
       c. Give him/her a score of 5 on the data sheet
       d. Always use a positive approach
  B. Level 3
    1. When the resident appropriately completes the skill

a. Give him/her a 2¢ token payment
b. Give him/her verbal praise
c. Give him/her a score of 1 on the data sheet
2. When the resident appropriately completes the skill with no more than one prompt
   a. Give him/her a 1¢ token payment
   b. Give him/her verbal praise
   c. Give him/her a score of 2 on the data sheet
3. When the resident either refuses to complete the skill appropriately, or requires more than one prompt
   a. Do not give the resident any payment
   b. Do not give the resident verbal praise unless he/she completes the skill appropriately; then give verbal praise
   c. Give the resident a score of 3 on the data sheet
   d. Always use a positive approach
IV. Shower Data Sheet (See Figure 2-15, p. 74.)
    A. There is to be one Shower Data Sheet per resident.
    B. The data sheet is to be located in the resident's Individual Program Book.
    C. Data to be recorded:
       1. Date: Record the current date, even if the behavior does not occur. Do *not* skip any dates.
       2. Eval. Type: Record the type of evaluation that was made.
          a. Record a *BC* if a Behavioral Component Evaluation was made.
          b. Record a *G* if a General Evaluation was made.
       3. Shower: Record the score obtained by the resident for showering. (See Section III, p. 72.)
       4. Hair: Record either a check mark (✓) or an *X*.
          a. Record a check mark (✓) if the resident washed his/her hair.
          b. Record an *X* if the resident did not wash his/her hair.
       5. Prompts: Record the total number of times the resident had to be asked to complete the skill appropriately.
       6. Paid: Record the total amount of token money the resident earned for the task.
       7. DCS: Record the initials of the staff member making the evaluation and reinforcing the resident.
       8. Each Monday, the second shift DCS is to record the following:
          a. Tot. Paid—Record the total sum of payments given to the resident that week.
          b. Freq. of score 1, 2, 3, 4, and 5—Record the total numbers of each score (i.e., 1, 2, 3, 4, and 5 scores on Levels 1 & 2; 1, 2, and 3 scores on Level 3) obtained that week in their respective spaces.

SHOWER DATA SHEET

DATE	TUES.	WED.	THURS.	FRI.	SAT.	SUN.	MON.	TOTAL PAID	FREQ. 1	FREQ. 2	FREQ. 3	FREQ. 4	FREQ. 5
Eval. Type (BC, or G)													
Shower													
Hair (√/X)													
Prompts													
Paid													
DCS													
Eval. Type (BC, or G)													
Shower													
Hair (√/X)													
Prompts													
Paid													
DCS													
Eval. Type (BC, or G)													
Shower													
Hair (√/X)													
Prompts													
Paid													
DCS													

Figure 2-15

LEVEL 1, LEVEL 2 AND LEVEL 3 LOCKER MAINTENANCE PROCEDURE

GENERAL STATEMENT

An individual living independently has the responsibility of caring for his/her own needs. Part of this responsibility involves the maintenance of his/her clothing and other personal items. This includes hanging up clothes, putting clothes away properly, putting personal items in appropriate locations, and ensuring that clean clothing is available. These responsibilities are an important component of the resocialization process.

PURPOSE

1. To help develop habits that are components of good hygiene
2. To help increase the resident's proper utilization of his/her property
3. To help decrease excessive wear and expense incurred by poor care of personal items
4. To develop habits which will be maintained after discharge from the facility
5. To help develop and increase the resident's positive self-esteem and self-worth
6. To help develop pride in one's appearance

PROCEDURE

I. General Policies
   A. Each resident is to be assigned his/her own locker.
   B. The locker is to be locked at the resident's discretion.
   C. Each resident is to have his/her own locker key.
   D. Each resident is to be responsible for his/her locker key.
   E. Each resident is to be responsible for his/her valuables.
   F. Each resident is to be responsible for the contents and total care of his/her locker.
   G. Any time a staff member opens a resident's locker, that resident must be present.
   H. Locker evaluations are to be conducted Monday through Friday.
II. Locker Requirements
   A. The following clothes are to be hung on either hangers or on hooks in the locker:
      1. Shirts
      2. Skirts
      3. Sweaters (may be folded)
      4. Slacks, pants, shorts, etc.
      5. Jackets
      6. Belts, ties
   B. The following personal items and undergarments are to be placed neatly on the locker shelves:
      1. Bras, girdles, underwear, undershorts, t-shirts, socks, etc.
      2. Toilet articles
      3. Cosmetics
      4. Jewelry
      5. Perfumes, deodorants, etc.
   C. All shoes, slippers, thongs, etc. are to be placed on the floor of the locker.
   D. All dirty or soiled clothing are to be placed in a laundry bag.
      1. There is to be one laundry bag per resident.
      2. Laundry bags are to be placed on the floor of the locker or in a convenient location as designated by staff.

III. Evaluations
   A. Residents are to be randomly selected for Locker Evaluations.
      1. Random Selection Procedure
         a. First shift Direct-Care Staff (DCS)
            (1) Write each resident's name on a separate name tag and place each name tag in a container.
            (2) Add an additional number of *blank* name tags to the container to produce a total number equal to the number of beds on the ward (i.e., resident's names + blank tags = total number of beds on ward).
            (3) Randomly select five name tags each day (Monday through Friday) from the container.
         b. Second shift DCSs, on a daily basis (Monday through Friday), are to
            (1) Evaluate the lockers of the residents whose names have been randomly selected from the container
            (2) Insofar as possible, randomize the time of day of the locker evaluations (NOTE: The resident *must* be present when his/her locker is evaluated. If not available during the evaluation time, the resident's locker is to be evaluated as soon as he/she is available.)
      2. When a resident receives a low score for Locker Evaluation (i.e., a score of 4 or 5 for Levels 1 & 2; a score of 3 for Level 3), he/she is to have a Locker Evaluation daily thereafter until a satisfactory score (i.e., a score of 1, 2, or 3 for Levels 1 and 2; a score of 1 for Level 3), is obtained (except during the baseline period).
   B. Locker Evaluation Procedure
      1. The DCS is to ask the resident to open his/her locker
      2. During the evaluation, check to determine whether
         a. The resident has his/her locker key
         b. The contents of the locker are appropriate
         c. The laundry bag is in the proper location and all dirty clothes are placed in the bag
IV. Master Key
   A. When a resident loses his/her locker key, the resident's locker is to be locked with the master key until his/her key is replaced.
   B. If the resident does not find his/her key within 48 hours, he/she is to be charged 75¢ (token money) and the actual replacement cost (real money) for the replacement of the key. If the resident is *not* in the token economy system he/she is to pay the actual replacement cost only.
V. Reinforcement and Contingency Management
   A. Levels 1 and 2
      1. When the resident passes the evaluation with no prompts
         a. Give him/her a 5¢ token payment
         b. Give him/her verbal praise
         c. Give him/her a score of 1 on the data sheet
      2. When the resident passes the evaluation with no more than one prompt
         a. Give him/her a 3¢ token payment
         b. Give him/her verbal praise
         c. Give him/her a score of 2 on the data sheet
      3. When the resident passes the evaluation with two or three prompts
         a. Give him/her a 2¢ token payment
         b. Give him/her verbal praise
         c. Give him/her a score of 3 on the data sheet
      4. When the resident passes the evaluation with four or five prompts
         a. Give him/her a 1¢ token payment
         b. Give him/her verbal praise
         c. Give him/her a score of 4 on the data sheet

5. When the resident does not pass the evaluation after five prompts or refuses to complete the task
   a. Do *not* give him/her any token payment
   b. Do *not* give him/her verbal praise
   c. Give him/her a score of 5 on the data sheet
6. Whenever the resident fails the evaluation
   a. The resident is to be given instructions on how the task can be completed appropriately
   b. The resident is to be requested (not told) to complete the task
   c. Repeat the instructions every 15 minutes until the task is completed properly or until five prompts have been given
   d. Always use a positive approach with the resident

B. Level 3
1. When the resident passes the evaluation with no prompts
   a. Give him/her a 2¢ token payment
   b. Give him/her verbal praise
   c. Give him/her a score of 1 on the data sheet
2. When the resident passes the evaluation with no more than one prompt
   a. Give him/her a 1¢ token payment
   b. Give him/her verbal praise
   c. Give him/her a score of 2 on the data sheet
3. When the resident either refuses to complete the task appropriately, and/or is given two or more prompts
   a. Do *not* give him/her any token payment
   b. Do *not* give the resident verbal praise (unless he/she completes the skill appropriately, regardless of the number of prompts)
   c. Give him/her a score of 3 on the data sheet
4. Whenever the resident fails the evaluation
   a. The resident is to be given instructions on how the task can be completed appropriately
   b. The resident is to be requested (not told) to complete the task
   c. Repeat the instructions every 15 minutes or until five prompts are given
   d. Always use a positive approach with the resident

VI. The Locker Evaluation Data Sheet (See Figure 2-16, p. 78)
A. There is to be one Locker Evaluation Data Sheet per resident
B. The data is to be located in the resident's Individual Program Book
C. Each time an evaluation is made, the data are to be recorded completely
D. Data to be recorded:
  1. Date—Always record the date of the evaluation.
  2. Eval.—Record the score obtained by the resident on the evaluation (See Section V above).
  3. Prompt—Record the number of times the resident is requested to complete the task.
  4. Paid—Record the amount of tokens paid to the resident for the task.
  5. Key Replacement Fee—Record the amount of money (token and/or real) paid by the resident to have his/her locker key replaced.
  6. DCS—Record the initials of the staff member reinforcing the resident and recording the data.
  7. Each Monday evening, second shift DCS is to record:
     a. Total Paid—Record the total sum of token payments given to the resident that week.
     b. Frequency of Scores—Record the total number of each score obtained that week in their respective places.

LOCKER DATA SHEET

DATE	TUES.	WED.	THURS.	FRI.	MON.	TOTAL PAID	FREQ. 1 SCORE	FREQ. 2 SCORE	FREQ. 3 SCORE	FREQ. 4 SCORE	FREQ. 5 SCORE
Eval.						/////					
Prompt						/////	/////	/////	/////	/////	/////
Paid							/////	/////	/////	/////	/////
Key Repl. Fee							/////	/////	/////	/////	/////
DCS											
Eval.						/////					
Prompt						/////	/////	/////	/////	/////	/////
Paid							/////	/////	/////	/////	/////
Key Repl. Fee							/////	/////	/////	/////	/////
DCS											
Eval.						/////					
Prompt						/////	/////	/////	/////	/////	/////
Paid							/////	/////	/////	/////	/////
Key Repl. Fee							/////	/////	/////	/////	/////
DCS											
Eval.						/////					
Prompt						/////	/////	/////	/////	/////	/////
Paid							/////	/////	/////	/////	/////
Key Repl. Fee							/////	/////	/////	/////	/////
DCS											

Figure 2–16

LEVEL 1, LEVEL 2, AND LEVEL 3 MEDICATION PROCEDURE

GENERAL STATEMENT

Medication is often necessary to alleviate, eliminate, or control a variety of physiological dysfunctions. Most medication must be taken at predetermined times and in prescribed amounts. Teaching a resident to willingly accept medication or to successfully self-medicate, is facilitative in the resocialization process and in the adjustment to the community, subsequent to discharge from the facility.

PURPOSE

1. To increase the probability that the resident will properly take his/her medication once discharged from the program
2. To help develop self-control techniques
3. To help develop within the resident, a time schedule awareness
4. To help develop an awareness of one's responsibilities
5. To teach self-medication techniques

I. General Policies
   A. Medication is always to be given or obtained during the following periods of time without variation unless medically necessary:
      1. 7:20–7:40 A.M.
      2. 11:20–11:40 A.M.
      3. 4:00–4:20 P.M.
      4. 8:20–8:40 P.M.
   B. The Medication procedure includes a four-step process (See Section IV: Four Step Process)
      1. Step I: Medication Given
      2. Step II: Medication Given but Asked For
      3. Step III: Medication Asked For and Obtained
      4. Step IV: Medication Prepared
   C. Step assignment and movement within the Medication Program is to be determined in an Interdisciplinary Treatment Team Conference. (See Interdisciplinary Treatment Team Conferences Procedure, p. 12)
      1. Level 1 residents are to be assigned to Step 1.
      2. Levels 2 & 3 residents are to be assigned to Steps 1, 2, 3 or 4 (See Section II: Baseline Period for Step Criteria).
   D. Possible Medication Scores
      1. Levels 1 and 2: 1, 2, and 5
      2. Level 3: 1, 2, and 3
   E. Never allow the resident to take the wrong medication.
   F. Always use a paper cup to dispense medication.
   G. Medication administered intramuscularly requires the completion of an appointment card by a Direct-Care Staff (DCS) member.
      1. The appointment card is to be given to the resident.
      2. Record on the card:
         a. Date to obtain the medication
         b. Time to obtain the medication
II. Baseline Period (two weeks)
   A. As soon as a resident enters the program he/she is to be given a thorough description of the Medication Program and instructions on how to participate in it.
   B. The baseline period is to begin as soon as the resident enters the program.

C. During the baseline period do *not* give the resident any token payment for appropriateness.
D. Step Placement during baseline period:
 1. Level 1
    Place resident in Step I: Medication Given
 2. Levels 2 and 3
    During the baseline period the resident is to be given the opportunity to engage in all four steps of the medication program.
    a. If the resident requests his/her medication (Step I—See Section IV: Four Step Process) within the scheduled medication time
       (1) Allow him/her to attempt the highest medication step he/she is capable of completing appropriately, starting with Step IV (See Section IV: Four Step Process)
       (2) If he/she attempts Step IV and fails, allow the resident to attempt Step III
       (3) If he/she attempts Step III and fails, implement Step II
       (4) (1), (2), and (3) above can occur during the same medication period, if necessary
       (5) Repeat this process (i.e., (1), (2), (3), and (4)) during each medication period
    b. If the resident needs to be prompted to take his/her medication (Step I) follow the procedure specified for Step I (See Section IV: Four Step Process).

III. Treatment Period (Post-baseline)
 A. The treatment period is to begin on the Monday following the Revised Rehabilitation Plan Review. (See Interdisciplinary Treatment Team Conferences Procedure, p. 12)
 B. Step placement at the beginning of the treatment period:
  1. Level 1
     Continue resident in Step 1: Medication Given
  2. Levels 2 and 3
     a. Step placement at the beginning of the treatment period is to be based on baseline period performance.
     b. Movement to higher medication steps during the treatment period is to occur when the resident meets the criterion for his/her current medication step for at least two consecutive weeks (to be determined in an Interdisciplinary Treatment Team Conference).

IV. Four Step Procedure
 A. Step I: Medication Given
    The resident is to be called by name to come to the medication room to receive his/her medication.
 B. Step II: Medication Given but Asked For (Levels 2 and 3 only)
    1. The resident is to request his/her medication within the 20 minute scheduled medication period.
    2. The medication is to be prepared by a nurse (to be placed in a paper cup).
    3. The medication is to be handed to the resident and he/she is to be observed taking the medication.
    4. When the resident does not ask for his/her medication(s) within the 20 minute scheduled medication period, follow the *Medication Given* step (Step I) procedure with the following change:
       Give him/her a score of 2 if he/she complies after one prompt
 C. Step III: Medication Asked For and Obtained (Levels 2 and 3 only)
    1. The resident is to request his/her medication within the 20 minute scheduled medication period.

2. The medication is to be prepared by a nurse (to be placed in a paper cup).
3. The resident is to observe the staff member preparing the medication.
4. The medication is to be placed on the medication tray by the staff member but in different locations at different times.
5. The resident is not to be allowed to observe where the staff member places the medication on the medication tray.
6. The staff member is to place all medications for residents in this category, on the tray, and place the medication cards on tops of medication cups before allowing the residents to obtain their medication.
7. The resident is to, under the supervision of the staff member, obtain his/her medication from the medication tray.
8. The staff member is to observe the resident taking his/her medication.
9. *Never* allow the resident to take the wrong medication.
10. When the resident obtains the wrong medication from the tray
    a. Ask the resident to check the accuracy of his choice
       If he/she again obtains the wrong medication, the staff member is to ask the resident which medication has his/her name on it and wait for a response. If the response is incorrect, or if there is no response within one minute, show the resident which card has his/her name on it.
11. When the resident does *not* ask for his/her medication within the scheduled 20 minute medication period, he/she is to be prompted to obtain his/her medication.
    a. If the resident refuses to comply, follow the *Medication Given* step (Step I) Procedure.
    b. If the resident agrees to take his/her medication after being prompted, follow the procedure specified in the medication step that he/she is currently in.

D. Step IV: Medication Prepared (Levels 2 and 3 only)
  1. The resident is to request his/her medication within the 20 minute scheduled medication period.
  2. The resident is to prepare his/her own medication (to be placed in a paper cup).
  3. The resident is to take his/her own medication.
  4. The resident is to be observed preparing and taking his/her own medication by a qualified staff member.
  5. *Never* allow the resident to prepare the wrong medication.
  6. If the resident attempts to prepare the wrong medication
     a. Ask him/her to check the accuracy of his/her choice and prepare the correct medication
     b. If the resident again attempts to prepare the wrong medication
        (1) The staff member is to ask the resident which medication has his/her name on it and wait for a response.
            i. If the response is incorrect, *or* if there is no response within one minute, show the resident which medication is his/hers.
            ii. If the response is correct, allow the resident to prepare to take his/her medication.
  7. When the resident does *not* ask for his/her medication within the 20 minute medication period
     a. He/she is to be prompted to obtain his/her medication
        (1) If the resident refuses, follow the *Medication Given* step (Step I) procedure.
        (2) If the resident agrees to take his/her medication after being prompted, follow the same procedures specified in the medication step currently in (Section D—Step IV).

V. Reinforcement and Contingency Management
   A. Levels 1, 2, and 3
      1. If the resident refuses to take his/her medication
         a. Always use a positive approach
         b. Do *not* give him/her a token payment
         c. Do *not* give him/her verbal praise
         d. Give him/her a score of 5 (if in Level 1 or 2) or 3 (if in Level 3)
         e. Notify the psychologist or nurse
         f. Write a progress note in the resident's chart
   B. Level 1
      1. Step I—Medication Given
         a. If the resident takes his/her medication after being called one time
            (1) Give him/her a 5¢ token payment
            (2) Give him/her a score of 1
            (3) Give him/her verbal praise
         b. If the resident requires a second call or prompt to take his/her medication
            (1) Give him/her a 3¢ token payment
            (2) Give him/her a score of 2
            (3) Give him/her verbal praise
         c. If the resident requires a third call or prompt to take his/her medication
            (1) Do *not* give him/her a token payment
            (2) Give him/her a score of 5
            (3) Do not give the resident verbal praise until he/she takes the medication
            (4) Always use a positive approach
   C. Levels 2 and 3
      1. Step I: Medication Given
         a. If the resident takes his/her medication after being called one time
            (1) Give him/her a 5¢ (if in Level 2) token payment
            (2) Give him/her a score of 1
            (3) Give him/her verbal praise
         b. If the resident requires a second call or prompt to take his/her medication
            (1) Give him/her a 3¢ (if in Level 2) token payment
            (2) Give him/her a score of 2
            (3) Give him/her verbal praise
         c. If the resident requires a third call or prompt to take his/her medication
            (1) Do *not* give him/her a token payment
            (2) Give him/her a score of 5 (Level 2) or 3 (Level 3)
            (3) Do *not* give the resident verbal praise until he/she takes the medication
            (4) Always use a positive approach
      2. Step II: Medication Given But Asked
         a. If the resident obtains medication appropriately
            (1) Give him/her a 5¢ (Level 2) or 1¢ (Level 3) token payment
            (2) Give him/her verbal praise
            (3) Give him/her a score of 1 on the data sheet
         b. If the resident obtains medication appropriately after one prompt
            (1) Give him/her a 3¢ (Level 2) token payment
            (2) Give him/her verbal praise
            (3) Give him/her a score of 2 on the data sheet
         c. If the resident requires more than one prompt to obtain medication
            (1) Do not give him/her any token payment
            (2) Do not give him/her verbal praise
            (3) Give him/her a score of 5 (Level 2) or 3 (Level 3) on the data sheet
      3. Step III: Medication Asked For and Obtained

a. If the resident meets all criteria
   (1) Give him/her a 5¢ (Level 2) or 2¢ (Level 3) token payment
   (2) Give him/her verbal praise
   (3) Give him/her a score of 1 on the data sheet
b. When the resident obtains the wrong medication on the first attempt or is prompted to take his/her medication
   (1) If he/she corrects himself/herself after requested to do so, or if he/she comes and appropriately obtains medication after one prompt
      (a) Give the resident a 3¢ (Level 2) or 1¢ (Level 3) token payment
      (b) Give the resident verbal praise
      (c) Give the resident a score of 2 on the data sheet
   (2) If the resident does *not* correct himself/herself after being requested to check his/her choice, *then* implement either (a) or (b) below
      (a) If when requested to check again he/she then corrects himself/herself
         i. Do *not* give the resident any token payment
         ii. Give the resident verbal praise
         iii. Give the resident a score of 5 (Level 2) or 3 (Level 3)
      (b) If when requested a second time to check again, he/she still doesn't correct himself/herself
         i. Always use a positive approach with the resident
         ii. Do *not* give the resident any payment
         iii. Do *not* give the resident verbal praise
         iv. Give the resident a score of 5 (Level 2) or 3 (Level 3) on the data sheet
c. When the resident does *not* ask for his/her medication within the scheduled 20 minute medication period
   (1) The resident is to be prompted to obtain his/her medication
      (a) If the resident refuses to comply follow the *Medication Given* step (Step I) procedure
      (b) If the resident agrees to take his/her medication after being prompted, follow the procedure specified in the medication step currently in (Step III)
   (2) Always use a positive approach with the resident
   (3) *Never* give him/her any token payment
   (4) Do not give him/her verbal praise
   (5) Always give him/her a score of 5 (Level 2) or 3 (Level 3)
4. Step IV: Medication Prepared Step
   a. If the resident meets all criteria
      (1) Give him/her a 5¢ (Level 2) or 3¢ (Level 3)
      (2) Give him/her verbal praise
      (3) Give him/her a score of 1 on the data sheet
   b. When the resident attempts to prepare the wrong medication on the first attempt
      (1) If he/she corrects himself/herself after requested to do so once
         (a) Give the resident a 3¢ (Level 2) or 1¢ (Level 3) token payment
         (b) Give the resident verbal praise
         (c) Give the resident a score of 2 on the data sheet
      (2) If he/she does not correct himself/herself after being requested to check his/her choice *then* implement either (a) or (b) below.
         (a) If when requested to check again, he/she then corrects himself/herself
            i. Do *not* give the resident any token payment

ii. Give the resident verbal praise
iii. Give the resident a score of 5 on (Level 2) or 3 (Level 3) on the data sheet
            (b) If when requested to check again, he/she still doesn't correct himself/herself
                i. Always use a positive approach with the resident
                ii. Do *not* give the resident any token payment
                iii. Do *not* give the resident verbal praise
                iv. Give the resident a score of 5 (Level 2) or 3 (Level 3) on the data sheet
        c. When the resident does not ask for his/her medication within the 20 minute scheduled medication period
            (1) The resident is to be prompted to obtain his/her medication
                (a) If the resident refuses, follow the *Medication Given* step (Step I) procedure
                (b) If the resident agrees to take his/her medication after being prompted, follow the procedures specified in the medication step currently in (Step IV)
            (2) Always use a positive approach with the resident
            (3) *Never* give the resident any token payment
            (4) Do *not* give him/her verbal praise
            (5) Always give him/her a score of 5 (Level 2) or 3 (Level 3) on the data sheet
VI. Medication Data Sheet (See Figure 2-17, p. 85.)
    A. There is to be one medication Data Sheet per resident.
    B. The data sheet is to be located in the resident's Individual Program Book.
    C. Data to be recorded:
        1. Date—Always record the current date. Do not skip any dates.
        2. Medication step—Record the medication step the resident is currently in. (During the baseline period record the medication step that the resident completed successfully.)
        3. Med.—Record the score the resident obtained for that medication period.
        4. Prompt—Record the number of times the resident was prompted.
        5. Paid—Record the amount of token money given to the resident.
        6. DCS—Record the initials of the Direct-Care Staff member responsible for observing medication and data recording during the medication period.
        7. Highest score—Record the highest score obtained that day across all medication periods—to be done by second shift DCSs each evening.
        8. Each Monday evening, second shift DCSs are to record the following:
            a. Total Paid—Record the total amount of token payments given that week.
            b. Freq. 1, 2, 3, and 5 highest score—Record the total number of 1, 2, 3, and 5 scores obtained that week (from the Highest Score for the Day column) in their respective spaces.

MEDICATION DATA SHEET

DATE	MED. STEP	MED.	MED.	MED.	MED.	PROMPT	PAID	DCS	DCS	DCS	DCS		HIGHEST SCORE
Tues.													
Wed.													
Thurs.													
Fri.													
Sat.													
Sun.													
Mon.													
Total Paid													
Freq. 1 Highest Score													
Freq. 2 Highest Score													
Freq. 3 Highest Score													
Freq. 5 Highest Score													
Tues.													
Wed.													
Thurs.													
Fri.													
Sat.													
Sun.													
Mon.													
Total Paid													
Freq. 1 Highest Score													
Freq. 2 Highest Score													
Freq. 3 Highest Score													
Freq. 5 Highest Score													

Figure 2-17

LEVEL 1, LEVEL 2, AND LEVEL 3 MEAL PROCEDURE

GENERAL STATEMENT

Most people enjoy having, and need, three nutritious meals a day. Meal time is a time to relax, socialize, make friends, and simply enjoy oneself. An important aspect of meal enjoyment is the atmosphere in which the meal is eaten. Having to eat a meal next to a loud, sloppy, inconsiderate person decreases the pleasure obtained from that meal. Some institutionalized people have developed very poor eating habits. They sometimes tend to be sloppy with food, steal food from other plates, grab food, and in general, have little regard for others.

PURPOSE

1. To increase appropriate social interactions
2. To create a normal meal atmosphere
3. To increase one's self-awareness
4. To increase pride in oneself
5. To develop appropriate eating skills
6. To help develop pleasant peer relationships
7. To help the resident become an acceptable member of society

PROCEDURE

I. Meal Arrangements
   A. Residents are to pick up their own trays and carry them to the designated program eating area in the dining room.
   B. There are to be small tables with no more than four residents per table.
   C. Generally, residents have the option to select their own table and seat. Residents may be assigned tables within the designated program eating area. Table assignment, if used, must be approved by the program psychologist. This table assignment is to be made for the purpose of improving meal behavior.
   D. Males and females may sit together at their own discretion, as long as there is no established seating arrangement.
II. Behavioral Requirements
   A. *All* residents are to attend each meal. Meals are to be brought to the ward only when necessary for medical or behavioral reasons (e.g., resident is on bed rest or in seclusion).
   B. Residents are allowed to eat or not eat their meals—it is their choice.
   C. Residents are to eat only their own food.
   D. If a meal is *not* eaten, this is to be recorded on the Meals Data Sheet, and a Progress Note is to be written regarding the incident in the resident's chart.
   E. Residents are expected to use a napkin properly.
   F. Residents are to clean their own meal area.
   G. Residents are to be appropriately dressed, and hands are to be clean for each meal (including fingernails).
   H. Residents are required to attend breakfast even when sleeping late during a Saturday or Sunday special. (See Wake-up Procedure, Section IV, p. 61.)
   I. Residents may return to bed after breakfast when engaging in a Saturday or Sunday special.
III. Evaluations
   A. Each resident is to be unobtrusively observed and evaluated on the ward prior to each meal for
      1. Clean hands
      2. Appropriate dress (See Level 1 Dressing Procedure, p. 91.)

B. Each resident is to be observed during meals. The frequencies of the following behaviors are to be recorded:
   1. Stealing—defined as taking food that belongs to another resident without that resident's consent
   2. Gorging—defined as putting too much food in the mouth such that food falls out of the mouth or hangs out while chewing
   3. Sloppiness—defined as
      a. Spilling of food caused by gross carelessness
      b. Eating with the hands (unless the particular food is customarily eaten with the hands)
   4. Failure to clean up area—defined as
      a. Not wiping up food accidentally spilled on the table or on oneself
      b. Not carrying one's own tray, silverware, and containers to the disposal after the meal
      c. Not properly disposing of one's own tray (e.g., not scraping left-over food from the tray into the garbage and not placing silverware and tray in the proper area)

IV. Evaluation Outcome
   A. Appropriate appearance and clean hands evaluation (to be conducted unobtrusively on the ward)
      1. If the resident is not dressed appropriately and/or has dirty hands
         a. Ask resident to correct problem(s) prior to going to dining room
         b. Always use a positive approach
      2. If the resident complies with the instructions and appropriately corrects the problem(s)
         a. Give him/her verbal praise
         b. Allow him/her to go to the dining room
         c. Record a check mark (on the Meal Data Sheet) (See Figure 2-18, p. 90 under "Appearance and Hands.")
      3. If the resident does *not* comply with the instructions, *or* if the resident returns and the problem(s) has (have) not been corrected
         a. Do *not* give him/her any token money payment for the meal
         b. Do *not* give him/her verbal praise
         c. Record an *X* on the Meals Data Sheet under "Appearance and Hands"
         d. Inform him/her of what is inappropriate
         e. Allow him/her to go to the dining room
         f. Always use a positive approach
   B. If the resident engages in stealing during the meal
      1. Taken *stolen* food away
      2. Explain to him/her why food was taken away
      3. Always use a positive approach
      4. Ask him/her to apologize to the person from whom the food was stolen
      5. Do *not* give the resident any token money payment for the meal
      6. Do *not* give him/her verbal praise
      7. Give him/her a score of 5 (Levels 1 and 2) or a score of 3 (Level 3) on the Meal Data Sheet
      8. If the resident engages in stealing a second time during one meal
         a. Have the resident sit alone at a separate table to finish his/her meal
         b. He/she is to complete the meal within the regular time limit
         c. Do *not* allow resident to leave the table until other residents are ready to leave dining room area
         d. If there is not enough time to finish the meal, have him/her bring the food back to the ward and eat in the hallway
      9. Record a slash mark (i.e., 1 = 1, 2 = 11, 3 = 111, etc.) for each occurrence of stealing during a meal on the Meal Data Sheet under "Stealing"

C. When gorging *or* sloppiness with food occurs
  1. Ask the resident to apologize to the other residents sitting at the table for his/her poor manners
  2. Record 1 prompt on the Meal Data Sheet under the behavior that occurred
  3. If the resident apologizes, give him/her verbal praise
  4. If the resident receives a second prompt for gorging or a second prompt for sloppiness (during the same meal), or if the resident refuses to apologize
    a. Do *not* give him/her token money payment for the meal
    b. Do *not* give him/her verbal praise
    c. Give him/her a score of 5 (Levels 1 and 2) or a score of 3 (Level 3) for the meal
D. When the resident does not clean his/her area after eating
  1. Prompt him/her to clean the area
  2. Record a 1 prompt on the Meal Data Sheet under "Not Clean Area"
  3. If he/she complies and appropriately cleans area give him/her verbal praise
  4. If the resident does *not* comply or complies but does not appropriately clean up area
    a. Do *not* give him/her any token money payment for the meal
    b. Do *not* give him/her verbal praise
    c. Give him/her a score of 5 (Levels 1 and 2) or a score of 3 (Level 3) on the Meal Data Sheet for that Meal
    d. Continue prompting him/her (once every 5 minutes until time for residents to leave the dining room)
    e. Always use a positive approach
V. Reinforcement and Contingency Management
  A. Whenever the resident engages in stealing
    1. Do not give him/her any token payment
    2. Do not give him/her verbal praise
    3. Give him/her a score of 5 (Levels 1 and 2) or 3 (Level 3) for the meal
    4. Always use a positive approach
  B. *Whenever* a resident is prompted for inappropriate dress and clean hands and does *not* comply
    1. Do not give him/her any token payment
    2. Do not give him/her verbal praise
    3. Always use a positive approach
  C. Whenever a second prompt is required during one meal for the same inappropriate meal behavior (i.e., gorging, sloppy with food, or failure to clean area)
    1. Do not give him/her any token payment
    2. Do not give him/her verbal praise
    3. Give him/her a score of 5 (Levels 1 and 2) or 3 (Level 3) for that meal
  D. Following the meal, if the resident has *not* received a score of 5 (Levels 1 and 2) or 3 (Level 3) for his/her meal behavior (see paragraphs A and C, above), add the total number of prompts for gorging, sloppy with food, and not clean area.
    1. If the resident received no prompts
      a. Give him/her a score of 1 for the meal
      b. Give him/her a token payment (5¢ cor Levels 1 and 2; 2¢ for Level 3)
      c. Give him/her verbal praise
    2. If the resident received one prompt
      a. Give him/her a score of 2 for the meal
      b. Give him/her a token payment (3¢ for Levels 1 and 2; 1¢ for Level 3)
      c. Give him/her verbal praise
    3. If the resident received two or three prompts, with each prompt for a different inappropriate meal behavior
      a. Give him/her a score of 3 for the meal

LEVEL 1, LEVEL 2, AND LEVEL 3 MEAL PROCEDURE

  b. Give him/her a 2¢ token payment (Levels 1 and 2 only)
  c. Give him/her verbal praise (Levels 1 and 2 only)
VI. Meals During Seclusion
  A. Meals are to be brought to the ward when a resident is in seclusion and may be withheld *only* while he/she is dangerous to himself/herself or others.
  B. Meals for residents in seclusion are to be served on plastic plates with plastic cups (no knives, forks or spoons).
  C. Meals for residents in seclusion are to be hand-eaten meals (e.g., sandwiches).
VII. Meal Data Sheet (See Figure 2-18, p. 90.)
  A. There is to be one Meal Data Sheet per resident.
  B. The Meal Data Sheet is to be located in the resident's Individual Program Book.
  C. Data to be recorded daily:
    1. Date—Always record the current date. Do not skip any dates.
    2. Inappropriate Appearance and Hands:
      a. Record a check mark (✓) if the resident is prompted for inappropriate appearance or dirty hands.
      b. If the resident fails to correct the deficiency, record an *X*.
      c. If no prompts are required, record a 0.
    3. Stealing:
      a. Record a slash (i.e., 1 = 1, 2 = 11, 3 = 111) each time the resident engages in stealing
      b. If no stealing occurs, record a 0
    4. Gorging, sloppy with food, not clean mess:
      a. Record a slash each time the resident is prompted for engaging in the behavior.
      b. Record a 0 if the behavior does not occur.
    5. Paid—Record the amount of token money the resident was paid.
    6. DCS—Record the initials of the Direct-Care Staff (DCS) member who is observing and paying the resident, and recording the data.
    7. Score—Record a score of 1, 2, 3, or 5, according to the criteria established in section V: Reinforcement and Contingency Management.
    8. Highest score—Record the highest score the resident obtained that day for all three meals.
    9. Meals eaten at mealtime:
      a. Record a check mark (✓) if the resident ate his/her meal
      b. Record an *S* if the resident did not eat because he/she was physically sick.
      c. Record an *X* if the resident refused to eat his/her meal.
      d. Record an *NA* if the resident was not available for his/her meal.
      e. Record an *MO* if the resident was not able to eat his/her meal due to medical orders.
    10. Each Monday evening second shift DCSs are to record:
      a. Total of *P-P*—Record the total sum of prompts, and payments given to the resident that week.
      b. Frequency of 1, 2, 3, and 5 highest score—Record the total number of 1, 2, 3, and 5 scores obtained that week (from the Highest Score for the day column), in their respective spaces.
      c. Total meals eaten—Record the total number of meals the resident ate that week.
      d. Total meals not eaten—Record the total number of meals the resident did not eat that week.
      e. DCS—Record the initials of the DCS doing the weekly recording.

MEAL DATA SHEET

DATE	APPEAR & HANDS	STEAL-ING	GORG-ING	SLOPPY WITH FOOD	NOT CLEAN AREA	PAID	DCS	SCORE	HIGH SCORE FOR DAY	MEALS EATEN			
B													
L													
S													
B													
L													
S													
B													
L													
S													
B													
L													
S													
B													
L													
S													
B													
L													
S													
B													
L													
S													
Total of p-p													
Freq. of 1 Hi Sc													
Freq. of 2 Hi Sc													
Freq. of 3 Hi Sc													
Freq. of 4 Hi Sc													
Freq. of 5 Hi Sc													
Total Meals Eaten													
Total Meals Not Eaten													
DCS													

Figure 2–18

LEVEL 1
DRESSING PROCEDURE

GENERAL STATEMENT

Proper dress is essential to satisfactory adjustment in the community. Some individuals living in institutional settings have difficulty maintaining the basic requirements of dress and grooming. The components of proper dressing behavior include: (1) selecting clothes appropriate for the weather and the day's activities; (2) keeping these clothes clean and neat; (3) ensuring that all buttons and zippers are fastened to preserve modesty; and (4) wearing proper shoes. Each resident in the Level 1 program is responsible for maintaining standards of proper dress as part of his/her preparation for community placement.

PURPOSE

1. To help the resident to properly select and wear his/her clothes
2. To help the resident develop pride in his/her personal appearance
3. To increase self-esteem
4. To increase the resident's potential for successful living in a community setting

PROCEDURE

I. General Policies
   A. Residents are to maintain proper dress (as defined in II. below) during the entire day.
   B. The major criteria are that the resident's appearance is clean, neat, and appropriate.
   C. Dressing evaluations are to be completed for each resident on Monday through Friday.
   D. If a staff member feels that the attire of any resident is inappropriate (i.e., too tight, too revealing, or in poor taste), the following steps are to be taken:
      1. Two other staff members are to assess the resident's attire.
      2. If two or more of the staff members concur that the resident's attire is inappropriate, then the consequences outlined in III. C. or III. D., below, are to be implemented.
II. Dressing Criteria
   A. Clean Clothing:
      1. Clothes are to be clean from odor, major food stains, and major wrinkles.
      2. All clothing worn must meet criterion of clean before wearing.
   B. Appropriate Dress (Females)
      1. A top is to be worn at all times—tee shirts, tank tops, blouses, etc.
      2. A dress, skirt, pants, or shorts is/are to be worn at all times, except as noted below.
      3. Style of clothing is to be determined by the resident.
      4. Bathing suits may be worn from June through September if the temperature is above 70°F.
         a. Bathing suits are to be worn at supervised activities only, whether swimming or sunbathing.
         b. Bathing suits are not permitted in the sunbathing area around Harper Building. Residents are to wear shorts and appropriate top while sunbathing around Harper Building.
         c. A cover is to be worn over bathing suits when going to and from any supervised activity.
      5. Tears in clothing must be repaired before wearing (patched, sewn together).

6. Bedroom dress is at resident's own discretion, but when in state of undress, door is to be closed.
7. When leaving bedroom, resident must wear robe or street clothes. When wearing bathrobes, residents may not leave the ward.
8. If resident is to attend an activity where dress codes are required, he/she must follow code or decline going.

C. Appropriate Dress (Males)
1. Shirts are to be worn at all times, except as noted below (e.g., athletic function, swimming)
2. Style of shirts and pants is to be determined by the resident.
3. Bathing suits may be worn from June through September if the temperature is above 70°F.
    a. Bathing suits are to be worn at supervised activities only, whether swimming or sunbathing.
    b. Bathing suits are not permitted in the sunbathing area around Harper Building. Residents are to wear shorts while sunbathing around Harper Building.
    c. A cover is to be worn over bathing suits when going to and from any supervised activity.
4. Tears must be repaired before wearing any clothing.
5. If an activity has a specified dress code, resident must meet code before attending or may not attend.
6. Bedroom dress is totally at resident's discretion, but when in state of undress, door is to be closed.
7. When leaving bedroom, resident must wear robe or street clothes; when wearing bathrobe, resident may not leave ward area.

D. Socks
1. Socks must be worn with leather shoes.
2. Hose are considered the same as socks.
3. Socks are to be worn at resident's own discretion in resident's own bedroom.

E. Shoes
1. Shoes or slippers must be worn in all enclosed areas.
2. Slippers may be worn outside or to meals.
3. Type of shoes worn is left up to resident's discretion.
4. Shoes and boots with eyelets above ankles are to be laced and tied, at least up to ankle level.
5. Shoes may be removed at outside activity or sunbathing area, but must be worn going to and returning from activity or area.
6. Shoes are to be worn when participating in physical activity (bowling, tennis, baseball, basketball), unless permission is given by staff member.
7. Shoes are to be worn in resident's bedroom at resident's own discretion.

F. Combed Hair
1. Hair should be brushed or combed in the morning before breakfast.
2. Resident's hair is to be neat, clean, and free from tangles.
3. Teased hair must be thoroughly brushed or combed once a week as described above.

G. Shaving
1. All male residents are to shave each morning except Saturday and Sunday unless growing or maintaining a beard.
2. A resident with an extremely sparse or light-colored beard may skip shaving if, in the judgement of staff, it does not detract from his appearance.
3. Prompting for shaving should be recorded on the Dressing Data Sheet in the "Neat and Clean" category.

III. Dressing Evaluation Procedure
   A. 1st shift Direct-Care Staff (DCS) members are to evaluate each resident in the morning following the bedroom area evaluation Monday through Friday.
   B. This evaluation is to include the following criteria:
      1. Clothes are to be clean and generally neat (as described in Section II, A., above).
      2. Clothes are to be appropriate (including proper socks and shoes, as described in Section II., B., C., D., and E. above).
      3. Hair must be combed (as described in paragraph II., F., above)
      4. Shaving is to be completed appropriately (males).
   C. If deficiencies are noted, DCSs are to
      1. Prompt/correct resident every 15 minutes until deficiencies are corrected or until five prompts/corrections are given
      2. Record a slash in the proper column on the Dressing Data Sheet (i.e., Neat and Clean, Appropriate, Hair Combed) for each prompt/correction
      3. Record the total number of prompts on the Dressing Data Sheet under "Total Prompts"
   D. In addition to the daily Dressing Evaluation, each resident is to be briefly evaluated before leaving the ward (Monday through Sunday).
      1. Before the resident leaves the ward for normal individual or group outside privileges
         a. Dress is to be appropriate for the weather
         b. Dress is to be clean and appropriately modest
      2. Before the resident leaves the ward to attend any hospital-wide social function (e.g., the Wednesday night dance) or any off-campus activity
         a. All dressing criteria, as described above in paragraph II. A. through G., are to be met
         b. Any special dress requirements for the planned activity are to be met
      3. No data are to be recorded for the dressing checks prior to leaving the ward.
      4. If the resident does not meet the relevant dressing criteria, he/she is not to be permitted to leave the ward.
IV. Reinforcement and Contingency Management Procedure
   A. When the resident passes the evaluation with no prompts
      1. Give him/her a 5¢ token payment
      2. Give him/her verbal praise
      3. Give him/her a score of 1 on the Dressing Data Sheet (See Figure 2-19, p. 95.)
   B. When the resident passes the evaluation with no more than one prompt
      1. Give him/her a 3¢ token payment
      2. Give him/her verbal praise
      3. Give him/her a score of 2 on the Dressing Data Sheet
   C. When the resident passes the evaluation with two or three prompts
      1. Give him/her 2¢ token payment
      2. Give the resident verbal praise
      3. Give him/her a score of 3 on the Dressing Data Sheet
   D. When the resident passes the evaluation with four or five prompts
      1. Give him/her a 1¢ token payment
      2. Give him/her verbal praise for completing the task appropriately
      3. Give him/her a score of 4 on the Dressing Data Sheet
   E. When the resident does not pass the evaluation after five prompts, or refuses to complete the task
      1. Do *not* give him/her any token payment
      2. Give him/her a score of 5 on the Dressing Data Sheet
      3. Do *not* give him/her any verbal praise

94 PSYCHIATRIC UNIT PROCEDURES

    F. Whenever the resident fails the evaluation
        1. The resident is to be given instructions on how the tasks can be completed appropriately
        2. The resident is to be requested to complete the task, not told
        3. Repeat the instructions every 15 minutes until the task is completed properly, or until five prompts have been given
        4. Always use a positive approach with the resident

VI. Dressing Data Sheet (See Figure 2-19, p. 95.)
    A. There is to be one Dressing Data Sheet per resident.
    B. The data sheet is to be filed alphabetically in the Dressing Data Chart.
    C. Each time an evaluation is made, the data are to be recorded completely.
    D. Data to be recorded
        1. Date—Always record the date of the evaluation.
        2. Neat and Clean, Appropriate, Hair Combed—Record a slash in the appropriate column each time the resident is prompted/corrected for each particular deficiency.
        3. Total Prompts—Record the total number of times the resident is prompted to complete/correct the task.
        4. Score—Record the score (1, 2, 3, 4, or 5) obtained by the resident on the morning evaluation.
            a. Record a score of 1 when the task is completed appropriately with no prompts.
            b. Record a score of 2 when the task is completed appropriately with one prompt.
            c. Record a score of 3 when the task is completed appropriately with two or three prompts.
            d. Record a score of 4 when the task is completed appropriately with four or five prompts.
            e. Record a score of 5 when the task is *not* completed appropriately after five prompts.
        5. Tokens Paid—Record the amount of token money paid to the resident for the task.
        6. DCS—Record the initials of the DCS reinforcing the resident and/or recording the data.
        7. Each Monday evening, second shift DCS is to record:
            a. Frequency of 1, 2, 3, 4, and 5 scores—Record the total number of 1, 2, 3, 4, and 5 scores obtained that week in their respective place.
            b. Total paid—Record the total sum of token payments given to the resident that week.

DRESSING DATA SHEET

DATE	TUES.	WED.	THURS.	FRI.	MON.	FREQ. 1 SCORE	FREQ. 2 SCORE	FREQ. 3 SCORE	FREQ. 4 SCORE	FREQ. 5 SCORE	TOTAL PAID
Neat & Clean											
Appropriate											
Hair Combed											
Total Prompts											
Score											
Tokens Paid											
DCS											
Neat & Clean											
Appropriate											
Hair Combed											
Total Prompts											
Score											
Tokens Paid											
DCS											
Neat & Clean											
Appropriate											
Hair Combed											
Total Prompts											
Score											
Tokens Paid											
DCS											

Figure 2-19

LEVEL 3
COMMUNICATION SKILLS PROGRAM

General Statement

Ordinarily, people are socially oriented. Part of sociability is engaging in interpersonal activities that require a variety of social behaviors and skills. This includes any activity or appointment shared by two or more people. The people involved may be of the same or opposite sex, and the activity may be totally social in nature, or totally business in nature, or a combination of the two. A large percentage of one's time is spent engaging in interpersonal activities of one type or another. As such, it is important for the institutionalized individual to develop or redevelop skills that will enable him/her to engage in interpersonal activities with as many appropriate responses as possible for each situation. Thus, an intensive communication skills program is used to teach appropriate skills in this area.

Terminal Objective

The terminal objective is to have the resident successfully complete both Unit 1 and Unit 2 by meeting the criteria specified for each unit.

Purpose

1. To help increase self-esteem
2. To increase appropriate social relationships
3. To increase the probability of engaging in a satisfactory dating relationship
4. To help encourage involvement in various social activities
5. To help increase appropriate social behaviors
6. To explore various types of social relationships (i.e., love, platonic, business, male-female, female-female, male-male)
7. To help encourage proper money management

Procedure

I. General Policies
   A. Communication Skills training is to be conducted for one hour every other day, Monday through Friday.
      1. Classes are to be held from 1:30 to 2:30 P.M. or from 3:30 to 4:30 P.M.
      2. Classes are to consist of
         a. Verbal instruction, group discussion, and classroom assignments and/or
         b. Video-taping and feedback
   B. At the completion of each class period the instructor is to post the date and the time of the next class.
   C. When a Communication Skills Unit is not completed by the end of a class period, continue that unit during the following class period scheduled for Communication Skills.
   D. The Communication Skills Program is divided into two units.
   E. A resident may begin instruction with either Unit 1 or Unit 2. (Note: A resident may only begin a unit at the beginning of the unit.)
   F. Individual programs based on the specific needs of the resident may be developed, which supersede the Communication Skills Program.
II. Outline of Communication Skills Program
   A. Unit 1: Meeting People
      1. Unit 1 Sections
         a. Section 1: High probability places for meeting people
         b. Section 2: Interactions

(1) Introducing oneself and beginning conversations
(2) Possible conflicts while trying to meet someone
(3) Developing and maintaining conversations
(4) Closing conversations
2. Unit 1 Training procedure
3. Unit 1 Review
4. Unit 1 Test
5. Unit 1 Criteria
6. Unit 1 Reinforcement
7. Unit 1 Data Collection
B. Unit 2: Dates
1. Unit 2 Sections:
a. Section 1: Date Making
(1) Selecting an individual to ask for a date
(2) Asking for a date
(3) Being asked for a date
b. Section 2: Deciding on an activity and time
c. Section 3: During the date
(1) Appropriate attire
(2) Appropriate behavior
2. Unit 2 Training Procedure
3. Unit 2 Review
4. Unit 2 Test
5. Unit 2 Criteria
6. Unit 2 Reinforcement
7. Unit 2 Data Collection
III. Instructional Procedure
A. Unit 1: Meeting People
1. Unit Sections:
a. Section 1: High probability places for meeting people
b. Section 2: Interactions
2. Training
a. Section 1: High probability placed for meeting people
(1) Possible places
(a) Work
(b) Church
(c) Social Activities (dance, athletic activities, etc.)
(d) Other
(2) Teaching Technique
(a) Discussion of the places listed above by instructor and class
(b) Classroom Assignment 1-1 (CS CA1-U1S1)
i. Each resident is to list (in writing) at least five places where he/she could meet people
ii. Each resident is to be asked to discuss his/her list with the class
b. Section 2: Interactions
(1) Introducing oneself and beginning conversation
(a) Necessary Components
i. Pleasant voice
ii. Courteousness and friendliness
iii. Smile
iv. Positive attitude
(b) Teaching Technique
i. The instructor and class are to discuss the appropriate way to approach someone, introduce oneself, and begin a conversation.

ii. The instructor is to model an inappropriate way to meet someone (with another staff member). This interaction should last approximately three minutes and is to be video-taped.
iii. The video-taped interaction is to be reviewed and discussed by the class.
iv. The instructor is to model the appropriate way to meet someone (using another staff member). This interaction should last approximately three minutes and is to be video-taped.
v. The video-taped interaction is to be reviewed and discussed by the class.
vi. Each resident is to be asked to role play meeting another person (with the instructor). This interaction should last approximately three minutes and is to be video-taped.
vii. The video-tape is to be reviewed and discussed by the class.
viii. Repeat steps vi and vii (role playing by residents).

(2) Possible conflicts while trying to meet someone
(a) Examples of conflicts
Refer to Table 2-1 Possible Difficulties When Trying to Meet People (p. 110)
(b) Teaching Technique
i. The instructor is to present five situations from Table 2-1.
ii. The instructor and the class are to discuss these situations.
iii. The instructor is to model an inappropriate way of handling one of the situations discussed (Using another staff member). To be video-taped.
iv. The video-tape is to be reviewed and discussed by the class.
v. The instructor is to model an appropriate way of handling the same conflict situation (using another staff member). To last approximately three minutes. To be video-taped.
vi. The video-tape is to be reviewed and discussed by the class.
vii. Each resident is to be asked to role play a proper way of handling a conflict situation (with the instructor). This interaction should last approximately three minutes and is to be video-taped.
viii. The video-tape is to be reviewed and discussed by the class.
ix. Repeat steps vii and viii (role playing by residents).

(3) Developing and Maintaining Conversations
(a) Verbal behavior
i. Important verbal behavior
(i) Small talk
(ii) Asking questions, open ended questions (questions requiring more than a yes or no response)
(iii) Positive statements (statements expressing understanding, interest, or rapport)
(iv) Attentiveness
(v) Pursuing topics the other person seems interested in
(vi) Not making negative statements
(vii) Not interrupting
(viii) Sincerity
(ix) Appropriate level of assertiveness
(x) Positive attitude
ii. Teaching Techniques
(i) The instructor and class are to discuss the important verbal behaviors.

(ii) The instructor is to model an inappropriate attempt at developing and maintaining a conversation (Using another staff member). To last approximately five minutes. To be video-taped.
(iii) The video-tape is to be reviewed and discussed by the class.
(iv) The instructor is to model an appropriate way to develop and maintain a conversation (with another staff member). To last approximately five minutes. To be video-taped.
(v) The video-tape is to be reviewed and discussed by the class.
(vi) Each resident is to be asked to role play the development and maintenance of a conversation (with the instructor). This interaction should last approximately five minutes and is to be video-taped.
(vii) The video-tape is to be reviewed and discussed by the class.
(viii) Repeat steps (vi) and (vii) (role playing by the students).
(b) Nonverbal Behavior
i. Important nonverbal behaviors
(i) Eye contact
(ii) Gestures (affect)
(iii) Posture
(iv) General body position
ii. Teaching Technique
(i) The instructor and class are to discuss the important verbal behaviors.
(ii) The instructor is to model inappropriate nonverbal behavior in an interaction with one of the residents. To last approximately five minutes. To be video-taped.
(iii) The video-tape is to be reviewed and discussed by the class.
(iv) The instructor is to model appropriate nonverbal behavior in an interaction with one of the residents. To last approximately five minutes. To be video-taped.
(v) The video-tape is to be reviewed and discussed by the class.
(vi) Each resident is to be asked to role play appropriate nonverbal behavior in an interaction with the instructor. Each interaction should last approximately five minutes. To be video-taped.
(vii) The video-tape is to be reviewed and discussed by the class.
(viii) Repeat steps (vi) and (vii) (role playing by residents).
(4) Closing Conversations
(a) Necessary Components
i. Ensuring that the other individual is also ready to close the conversation
ii. Smooth transition from the topic discussed to the closing statement
iii. Indicating the pleasure resulting from the interaction, i.e., "It was pleasant talking to you." (if appropriate)
iv. Closings (i.e., Good-bye, etc.)

(b) Teaching Technique
   i. The instructor and the class are to discuss the necessary components of closing conversations.
   ii. The instructor is to model an inappropriate way to close a conversation (with a resident). To last approximately three minutes. To be video-taped.
   (iii) The video-tape is to be discussed and reviewed by the class.
   (iv) The instructor is to model an appropriate way to close a conversation (with the instructor). Each interaction should last approximately three minutes. To be video-taped.
   (v) Each resident is to be asked to role play the proper way to close a conversation (with the instructor). Each interaction should last approximately three minutes. To be video-taped.
   (vi) The video-tape is to be reviewed and discussed by the class.
   (vii) Repeat steps v. and vi. (role playing by students).
3. Unit Review
   a. Sections to be reviewed
      (1) Section 1: High probability places for meeting individuals
      (2) Section 2: Interactions
         (a) Introducing oneself and beginning conversation
         (b) Possible conflicts while trying to meet someone
         (c) Developing and maintaining conversations
         (d) Closing conversations
   b. Teaching Technique
      The instructor and class are to review and discuss the sections of the unit.
4. Unit 1 Test (CS–T1)
   a. Method
      (1) The unit test is to be administered during class time.
      (2) The unit test is to involve the resident role playing (with the instructor) the behaviors covered in Section 2 of this unit (i.e., introducing oneself, developing and maintaining a conversation, and closing a conversation).
      (3) The role playing is to last approximately five to ten minutes. To be video-taped.
   b. Evaluation
      (1) The instructor is to evaluate the video-tape recording of the interaction using the Unit 1 Role Playing Evaluation Form. (Form DS-RPEF1; See Figure 2-20, p. 111.)
      (2) The resident is to be present during the evaluation.
      (3) The resident is to be given feedback during the evaluation.
      (4) The completed evaluation form is to be retained by the staff and a copy given to the student.
   c. Unit 1 Test Criterion
      Achievement of *at least* an 80% level of accuracy
5. Unit 1 Criteria
   a. Completion of the classroom assignment with *at least* an 80% level of accuracy
   b. Achievement of *at least* an 80% level of accuracy on the Unit 1 Test.
   c. Attendance at a minimum of 90% of the classes conducted on this unit (unless excused from class)
   d. All assignments are to be handed in on time

6. Unit 1 Reinforcement
   a. When a resident attends a class
      (1) Give him/her verbal praise
      (2) Gove him/her a 10¢ token money payment
      (3) Record the appropriate data on his/her Communication Skills Data Sheet
   b. When a resident appropriately completes a classroom assignment (*at least 80% level of accuracy*)
      (1) Give him/her verbal praise
      (2) Give him/her a 10¢ token money payment
      (3) Record the appropriate data on his/her Communication Skills Data Sheet
   c. When a resident appropriately engages in role-playing during a class
      (1) Give him/her verbal praise
      (2) Give him/her a 5¢ token money payment
      (3) Record the appropriate data on his/her Communication Skills Data Sheet
   d. Token money payment for classroom participation is to be determined on an individual basis in Interdisciplinary Treatment Team Conference. (See Interdisciplinary Treatment Team Conference Procedure, p. 12.)
   e. When a resident meets the unit criteria
      (1) Give him/her verbal praise
      (2) Give him/her a 50¢ token money payment
      (3) Record the appropriate data on his/her Communication Skills Data Sheet
7. Unit 1 Data Collection
   a. There is to be one Unit 1 Data Sheet per resident. (See Figure 2-21, p. 112.)
   b. If a resident needs to repeat Unit 1 of the Dating Skills Program, a new data sheet is to be used.
   c. The data sheet is to be kept in the resident's Individual Program Book.
   d. The class instructor and/or the staff member who evaluates an assignment is to record the data.
   e. Data to be recorded:
      (1) Name: Record the name of the resident.
      (2) Course: Record whether the resident is enrolled in this unit of the Communication Skills Program for the first, second, third, etc., time.
      (3) Date: Record the date on which the resident attended a class, engaged in role playing, completed an assignment and/or completed the unit test.
      (4) Class attend.: Record either a check mark (✔) or an *X*.
         (a) ✔: Record a check mark (✔) each time the resident attends a Communication Skills Class. (Also, record the date in the "Date" column and a slash (i.e., 1 = 1; 2 = 11; 3 = 111; 4 = 1111; 5 = 1̶1̶1̶1̶1̶, etc.) in the "Total Number" row for each occurrence.)
         (b) *X*: Record an *X* each time a Communication Skills Class is conducted on Unit 1 and the resident did *not* attend. (Also, record the date in the "Date" column.)
         (c) *E*: Record an *E* when a Communication Skills class is conducted on Unit 1 and the resident is excused from attending.
      (5) Role P1: Record a check mark (✔) each time the resident engages in role playing. (Note: Record the check mark (s) in the same row as the recordings for class attendance.)
      (6) Class.Assign. 1-1: Record the percent level of accuracy achieved by the resident on the Unit 1 Section 1 Classroom assignment (High probability places for meeting people).

(7) Unit 1 Test: Record the percent level of accuracy achieved by the resident on the Unit 1 Test.
(8) Staff: Record the initials of the staff members recording the data.
(9) Comments: Record any comment(s) relevant to the recorded data.
(10) Total # ✓s: Record a slash mark (i.e., 1 = 1; 2 = 11; 3 = 111; 4 = 1111; 5 = ~~1111~~, etc.) in the appropriate column each time the resident attends class, attempts an assignment, engages in role playing, and/or takes the unit test. (Attempts are to be recorded whether the resident is successful *or* not successful.)
(11) Crit.: Record either a check mark (✓), an *X*, or an *L*.
  (a) ✓: Record a check mark (✓) in the appropriate column if the individual met the criterion for the classroom assignment (crit. = 80%), class attendance (crit. = 90%), or the Unit Test (Crit. = 80%).
  (b) *X*: Record an *X* in the appropriate column if the resident did not meet the specified criterion for the classroom assignment, class attendance, and/or the unit test.
  (c) *L*: Record an *L* in the appropriate column if the resident met the specified criterion for the classroom assignment but turned it in late.
(12) Unit 1 Crit.: Record either a check mark (✓) or an *X*.
  (a) ✓: Record a check mark if the resident
    i. Completed the classroom assignment with *at least* an 80% level of accuracy
    ii. Achieved *at least* an 80% level of accuracy on the Unit 1 test
    iii. Attended *at least* 90% of the classes conducted on Unit 1 (excluding times when the resident was excused from class)
  (b) *X*: Record an *X* if the resident did not
    i. Complete the classroom assignment with *at least* an 80% level of accuracy
    ii. Achieve *at least* an 80% level of accuracy on the Unit 1 test
    iii. Attend *at least* 90% of the classes conducted on Unit 1 (excluding times with the resident was excused from class)

B. Unit 2: Dates
  1. Unit Sections:
    a. Section 1: Date Making
    b. Section 2: Deciding on an activity and a time
    c. Section 3: During the date
  2. Training
    a. Section 1: Date Making
      (1) Selecting an individual to ask for a date
        (a) Factors to consider:
          i. Probability of a common interest(s)
          ii. Positive feedback from individual prior to asking
          iii. Encouragement from individual
          iv. Other nonspecific cues (friendliness, dropping hints, etc.)
          v. Compatable time schedules
        (b) Teaching technique
          i. The instructor and class are to discuss the factors listed above.
          ii. Class is to be divided into groups of two.
            (i) The pairs of residents are to discuss the factors listed above and the idiosyncratic (to each individual) factors.
          ii. The instructor is to oversee and guide discussions.
      (2) Asking for a date
        (a) The invitation

i. Factors to consider
   (i) Appropriate context (i.e., in a social situation, by telephone, etc.)
   (ii) Positive attitude
   (iii) Possible statements (ways to ask)
ii. Teaching Technique
   (i) The instructor and class are to discuss the factors listed above.
   (ii) The instructor is to model an inappropriate way to ask for a date (with a staff member). To last approximately two minutes. To be video-taped.
   (iii) The video-tape is to be reviewed and discussed by the class.
   (iv) The instructor is to model an appropriate way to ask for a date (with a staff member). To last approximately two minutes. To be video-taped.
   (v) The video-tape is to be reviewed and discussed by the class.
   (vi) Each resident is to be asked to role play asking for a date (with the instructor). To last approximately two minutes. To be video-taped.
   (vii) The video-tape is to be reviewed and discussed by the class.
   (viii) Repeat steps (vi) and (vii) (role playing by residents).
(b) Negative response from person asked (being turned down)
   i. Components
      (i) Acceptance of negative response
      (ii) Appropriate reaction
      (iii) Evaluation of situation
         ((i)) Was the invitation appropriate?
         ((ii)) Dissimilar interests?
         ((iii)) Prior negative interactions?
         ((iv)) Other
      (iv) Maintain positive self-concept
      (v) Possible constructive criticisms
   ii. Teaching Technique
      (i) The instructor and the class are to discuss the components listed above.
      (ii) The instructor is to model an inappropriate way to react to being turned down (with another staff member). To last approximately two minutes. To be video-taped.
      (iii) The video-tape is to be reviewed and discussed by the class.
      (iv) The instructor is to model an appropriate way to react to being turned down (with another staff member). To last approximately two minutes. To be video-taped.
      (v) The video-tape is to be reviewed and discussed by the class.
      (vi) Class is to be divided into groups of two for the purpose of discussing
         ((i)) The components listed above
         ((ii)) How they would react in such a situation
         ((iii)) An appropriate way of reacting that would be comfortable for them

(vii) Each resident is to be asked to role play an appropriate way to react in such a situation (with another resident). To last approximately two minutes. To be video-taped.
(viii) The video-tape is to be reviewed and discussed by the class.
(ix) Repeat steps (vii) and (viii) (role playing by resident).
(3) Being asked for a date
   (a) Possible responses
      i. Positive
      ii. Negative
   (b) Teaching Technique
      i. The instructor and class are to discuss the two responses listed above and how they can be accomplished.
      ii. The instructor is to model an inappropriate way to respond affirmatively and then negatively to a request for a date (with a resident). Each interaction is to last approximately two minutes. To be video-taped.
      iii. The video-tape is to be reviewed and discussed by the class.
      iv. The instructor is to model an appropriate way to respond affirmatively and then negatively to a request for a date (with a resident). To last approximately two minutes. To be video-taped.
      v. The video-tape is to be reviewed and discussed by the class.
      vi. Each resident is to be asked to role play an appropriate way to respond affirmatively and then negatively to a request for a date (with another resident). Each interaction is to last approximately two minutes and is to be video-taped.
      vii. The video-tape is to be reviewed and discussed by the class.
      viii. Repeat steps vi and vii (role playing by residents).
b. Section 2: Deciding on an activity and a time
   (1) Factors to consider:
      (a) Possible activities
         i. Movie
         ii. Dance
         iii. Restaurant
         iv. Party
         v. Picnic
         vi. Sports activities
         vii. Walk
         viii. Other
      (b) Expenditures
         i. Who is to pay for the activity?
         ii. Available money
         iii. Cost of activity
      (c) Transportation
         i. Location of activity (distance from the participants)
         ii. Distance participants are from one another
         iii. Vehicle
            (i) Privately owned
            (ii) Bus
            (iii) Cab
            (iv) Friend's vehicle
            (v) Other
      (d) Amount of time necessary for activity

(e) Time schedules of participants
(f) Mutually agreeable activity
(2) Teaching Technique
 (a) The instructor and class are to discuss the factors listed above.
 (b) The instructor is to describe a dating situation and develop the structure of date by incorporating the factors listed above. This is to be done with the class involved in the process.
 (c) Section 2 Classroom Assignment 2-2 (CS CA2-U2S2)
  i. The class is to be divided into groups of two.
  ii. Each group is to be given a dating assignment.
  iii. The assignment is to include:
   a. Number of participants involved in the date.
   b. Amount of money available for the date.
   c. Type of transportation available (if any).
  iv. Each pair of residents is to be given a Section 2 Activity and Time Answer Sheet (Form CS-ATAS). (See Figure 2-22, p. 113.)
  v. Each pair of residents is to make the decisions specified on the form.
  vi. Each pair of residents is to write the answers on the form.
  vii. The completed CS-ATAS forms are to be reviewed and discussed in class by the class and instructor.
 (d) Section 2 Homework Assignment 2-1 (CS HA1-U2S2)
  i. Each resident is to be given another dating assignment of the same type as the one given for the classroom assignment (the specifics of the dating situation are to differ).
  ii. Each resident is to be given another Section 2 Activity and Time Answer Sheet (Form CS-ATAS).
  iii. Each resident is to complete the form.
  iv. The completed form is due the next day.
  v. The completed forms are to be reviewed and evaluated in the next Communication Skills Class.
c. Section 3: During the date
 (1) Appropriate Attire
  (a) Factors to consider
   i. Weather
   ii. Type of activity
   iii. Time of day
   iv. Partner's Attire
   v. Neatness
  (b) Teaching Technique
   i. The instructor and the class are to discuss the factors listed above.
   ii. Section 3 Classroom Assignment 2-3 (CS CA2-U2S3)
    (i) The class is to be divided into groups of two.
    (ii) Each pair of residents is to be given three contrived dating activities.
    (iii) Each pair of residents is to discuss the type of attire that would be appropriate for each of the three contrived dating activities.
    (iv) Each pair of residents is to then describe to the class, the type of attire they decided would be appropriate for each of the three contrived activities.

(2) Appropriate behavior
　(a) Components
　　i. Initial greeting
　　ii. Courteousness
　　iii. Appropriate affect
　　iv. Attentiveness
　　v. Positive attitude
　　vi. Development and maintenance of a conversation
　(b) Teaching Technique
　　i. The instructor and the class are to discuss the components listed above. The instructor is to integrate the information from Unit 1 on conversations.
　　ii. The instructor is to model an inappropriate way to greet a date (with a resident). This interaction is to include approximately three minutes of conversation subsequent to the greeting. To be video-taped.
　　iii. The video-tape is to be reviewed and discussed by the class.
　　iv. The instructor is to model an appropriate way to greet and converse with a date (with a resident). To last approximately three minutes. To be video-taped.
　　v. Each resident is to be asked to role play greeting his/her date and conversing for approximately three minutes (with another resident). To be video-taped.
　　vi. The video-tape is to be reviewed and discussed by the class.
　　vii. Repeat steps v. and vi. (role playing by residents).
3. Unit 2 Review
　a. Sections to be reviewed
　　(1) Section 1: Date Making
　　　(a) Selecting an individual to ask for a date
　　　(b) Asking for a date
　　　(c) Being asked for a date
　　(2) Section 2: Deciding on an activity and time
　　(3) Section 3: During the date
　　　(a) Appropriate attire
　　　(b) Appropriate behavior
　b. Teaching Technique
　　The instructor and the class are to review and discuss the sections of the unit.
4. Unit 2 Test (CS-T2)
　a. Method
　　(1) The unit test is to be administered during class time.
　　(2) The unit test is to consist of a written exam (Form CS-T2a; See Figure 2-23, p. 114) and role playing (with the instructor) asking for a date.
　　(3) There is a time limit of approximately thirty minutes for the written portion of the test.
　　(4) The role playing is to last approximately two minutes.
　　(5) The role playing is to be video-taped.
　b. Evaluation
　　(1) The instructor is to evaluate and return a copy of the written portion of the test to the resident within two days.
　　(2) The original written portion of the test is to be retained by the staff.
　　(3) The instructor is to evaluate the video-tape recording of the request for a date using the Unit 2 Role Playing Evaluation Form. (Form CS-RPEF2; See Figure 2-24, p. 116.)

(4) The resident is to be present during the evaluation.
(5) The resident is to be given feedback during the evaluation.
(6) The completed evaluation form is to be retained by the staff and a copy given to the student.
  c. Unit 2 Test Criteria
    (1) Achievement of *at least* an 80% level of accuracy on the written portion of the test
    (2) Achievement of *at least* an 80% level of accuracy on the video-tape recording.
5. Unit 2 Criteria
  a. Completion of each classroom assignment with *at least* an 80% level of accuracy
  b. Completion of each homework assignment with *at least* an 80% level of accuracy
  c. Achievement of *at least* an 80% level of accuracy on the Unit 2 test (both the written portion and the video-taped portion)
  d. Attendance at a minimum of 90% of the classes conducted on this unit (excluding times when the resident was excused from class)
  e. All assignments are to be handed in on time
6. Reinforcement
  a. When a resident attends a class
    (1) Give him/her verbal praise
    (2) Give him/her a 10¢ token money payment
    (3) Record the appropriate data on his/her Communication Skills Data Sheet
  b. When a resident appropriately completes a classroom assignment (at least an 80% level of accuracy)
    (1) Give him/her verbal praise
    (2) Give him/her a 10¢ token money payment
    (3) Record the appropriate data on his/her Communication Skills Data Sheet
  c. When a resident appropriately completes a homework assignment (*at least* an 80% level of accuracy)
    (1) Give him/her verbal praise
    (2) Give him/her a 25¢ token money payment
    (3) Record the appropriate data on his/her Communication Skills Data Sheet
  d. When a resident appropriately engages in role-playing during class
    (1) Give him/her verbal praise
    (2) Give him/her a 5¢ token money payment
    (3) Record the appropriate data on his/her Communication Skills Data Sheet
  e. Token money payment for classroom participation is to be determined on an individual basis in Interdisciplinary Treatment Team Conferences
  f. When a resident meets the Unit 2 criteria
    (1) Give him/her verbal praise
    (2) Give him/her a 50¢ token money payment
    (3) Record the appropriate data on his/her Communication Skills Data Sheet
7. Unit 2 Data Collection
  a. There is to be one Unit 2 Data Sheet per resident. (See Figure 2-25, p. 117.)
  b. If a resident needs to repeat Unit 2 of the Communication Skills Program, a new data sheet is to be used.

c. The data sheet is to be kept in the resident's Individual Program Book.
d. The class instructor and/or staff member who evaluates an assignment is to record the data.
e. Data to be recorded:
   (1) Name: Record the name of the resident.
   (2) Course: Record whether the resident is enrolled in this unit of the Communication Skills Program for the first, second, third, etc., time.
   (3) Date: Record the date on which the resident attended a class, engaged in role playing, completed a class assignment, and/or completed a Unit test.
   (4) Class attend.: Record either a check mark (✓) or an *X*, or an *E*.
      (a) ✓: Record a check mark (✓) each time the resident attends a Communication Skills class. (Also, record the date in the "Date" column and a slash (i.e., 1 = 1; 2 = 11; 3 = 111; 4 = 1111; 5 = ⊬⊬⊤, etc.) in the "Total Number" row for each occurrence.)
      (b) *X*: Record an *X* each time a Communication Skills Class is conducted on Unit 2 and the resident did *not* attend and he/she did not have a valid excuse. (Also record the date.)
      (c) *E*: Record an *E* when a Communication Skills Class is conducted on Unit 2 and the resident is excused from attending.
   (5) Role Pl: Record a check mark (✓) each time the resident engages in role playing. (NOTE: Record the check mark(s) in the same row as the recordings for class attendance.)
   (6) Class. Assign. 2-2: Record the % level of accuracy achieved by the resident on the Unit 2 Section 2 Classroom assignment.
   (7) Homew. Assign. 2-1: Record the % level of accuracy achieved by the individual on the Unit 2 Section 2 homework assignment.
   (8) Class. Assign. 2-3: Record the % level of accuracy achieved by the resident on the Unit 2 Section 3 Classroom assignment.
   (9) Unit Test - T2a: Record the % level of accuracy achieved by the resident on the written portion of the Unit 2 Test.
   (10) Unit Test-RPEF2): Record the % level of accuracy achieved by the resident on the video-taped portion of the Unit 2 test.
   (11) Staff: Record the initials of the staff members recording the data.
   (12) Comments: Record any comments relevant to the recorded data.
   (13) Total # ✓s: Record a slash mark (i.e., 1 = 1; 2 = 11; 3 = 111; 4 = 1111; 5 = ⊬⊬⊤, etc.) in the appropriate column each time the resident attends class, attempts an assignment, engages in role playing, and/or completes the unit test. (Attempts are to be recorded whether the resident is successful *or* not successful.)
   (14) Crit.: Record either a check mark (✓), an *X*, or an *L*.
      (a) ✓: Record a check mark (✓) in the appropriate column if the individual met the criterion for Classroom Assignment 2-2 (crit. = 80%), Homework Assignment 2-1 (Crit. = 80%), Classroom Assignment 2-3 (Crit. = 80%), Class Attendance (Crit. = 90%), Unit Test T2a (Crit. = 80%) or Unit Test RPEF2 (crit. = 80%).
      (b) *X*: Record an *X* in the appropriate column if the resident did *not* meet the specified criterion for Classroom Assignment 2-2, Homework Assignment 2-1, Classroom Assignment 2-3, Class Attendance, Unit Test T2a, or Unit Test RPEF2.
      (c) *L*: Record an *L* in the appropriate column if the resident met the specified criterion for the Classroom Assignment 2-2, Homework Assignment 2-1, or Classroom Assignment 2-3, but turned the assignment in late.

(15) Unit 2 Crit.: Record either a check mark (✓) or an *X*.
   (a) ✓: Record a check mark (✓) if the resident
      i. Completed the Classroom Assignment 2-2 with *at least* an 80% level of accuracy
      ii. Completed Homework Assignment 2-1 with *at least* an 80% level of accuracy.
      iii. Completed Classroom Assignment 2-3 with *at least* an 80% level of accuracy
      iv. Attended *at least* 90% of the classes conducted on Unit 2 (excluding times with the resident was excused from class)
      v. Achieved *at least* an 80% level of accuracy on Unit Test T2a
      vi. Achieved *at least* an 80% level of accuracy on Unit Test RPEF2
   (b) *X*: Record an *X* if the resident did *not*
      i. Complete the Classroom Assignment 2-2 with *at least* an 80% level of accuracy
      ii. Complete Homework Assignment 2-1 with *at least* an 80% level of accuracy
      iii. Complete Classroom Assignment 2-3 with *at least* an 80% level of accuracy
      iv. Attend *at least* 90% of the classes conducted on the Unit 2 (excluding times when the resident was excused from class)
      v. Achieve *at least* an 80% level of accuracy on Unit Test T2a
      vi. Achieve *at least* an 80% level of accuracy on Unit Test RPEF2

Table 2-1 Communication Skills Program
Unit 1
Possible Difficulties When Trying to Meet People
(Form CS-DMP)

1. You approach someone to introduce yourself and the individual tells you to leave him/her alone.

2. You introduce yourself and the individual appears to be shy.

3. You approach an individual to begin a conversation and he/she starts putting you down.

4. You approach an individual who may not like you.

5. You're at a party and don't know anyone but the host/hostess and he/she is busy.

6. You've just moved into a new neighborhood and you go over to meet your neighbor who appears to be friendly.

7. You've just moved into a new neighborhood and you go over to meet your next door neighbor who does not appear to be friendly.

8. You introduce yourself to an individual and the individual appears to be friendly but does not tell you his/her name.

9. You're eating lunch alone and you approach and individual to ask if you may join him/her at his/her table. The individual invites you to sit down.

10. You're eating lunch alone and you approach an individual to ask if you may join him/her at his/her table. The individual responds by saying he/she would prefer eating alone.

11. You invite a new co-worker to your house for a game of cards and he/she responds by saying he/she does not know how to play cards.

12. You're a new employee and your co-workers invite you to go to lunch with them but you don't have enough money to go to the restaurant they have chosen.

13. A new employee is looking up the number of a taxi cab company and you offer him/her a ride home and he/she accepts.

14. A new employee is looking up the number of a taxi cab company and you offer him/her a ride home and he/she states that he/she never accepts rides from strangers.

15. You invite a new employee to go to a party and he/she responds by stating that he/she never forms personal relationships with people he/she works with.

COMMUNICATION SKILLS PROGRAM
UNIT 1
ROLE PLAYING EVALUATION FORM
(FORM CS-RPEF1)

Resident's Name: _____

Date: _____

Instructor: _____

	APPROPRIATE	INAPPROPRIATE	COMMENTS
Introducing Oneself	/////	/////	/////
Pleasant Greeting			
Positive Attitude			
Clear Introduction			
Conversation	/////	/////	
Open Ended Questions			
Positive Statements			
Absence of Negative Statements			
Absence of Interrupting			
Sincerity			
Assertiveness			
Positive Attitude			
Closing	/////	/////	
Transition			
Statement regarding pleasure talking to individual			
General	/////	/////	
Speech Level			
Affect			
Posture			
Eye Contact			
Total Appropriate		/////	
Total Inappropriate	/////		
% Appropriate		/////	

Figure 2-20

COMMUNICATION SKILLS PROGRAM DATA SHEET
UNIT 1
MEETING PEOPLE

DATE	CLASS ATTEND (√, X OR E)	ROLE P1. (√)	CLASS ASSIGN 1-1(%)	UNIT 1 TEST (%)	STAFF	COMMENTS
Total # √s						
Crit. (√, X, or L)						
Unit 1 Crit. (√ or X)						

Figure 2-21

COMMUNICATION SKILLS PROGRAM
UNIT 2
SECTION 2 ACTIVITY AND TIME ANSWER SHEET
(FORM CS-ATAS)

1. Where are you going for the date? _____
   _____

2. Is the date going to be in the evening, afternoon, or morning? _____
   _____

3. What time does the activity begin? _____
   _____

4. What time has been scheduled for the date? _____
   _____

5. How much time is needed for the activity? _____
   _____

6. Where are you going to meet your date(s)? _____
   _____

7. What type of transportation is going to be used? _____
   _____

8. Approximately how much money is the activity going to cost? _____
   _____

9. Who is going to pay for the date? _____
   _____

10. What is the approximate time that the date is to end? _____
    _____

Number Correct: _____

Number Incorrect: _____

% Correct: _____

Figure 2-22

**COMMUNICATION SKILLS PROGRAM
UNIT 2
WRITTEN EXAM
(FORM CS-T2a)**

Resident's Name _____ Date _____

Instructor _____

1. Name four possible activities that could be scheduled for a date (four different dates).

   a. _____

   b. _____

   c. _____

   d. _____

2. Name two things that should be considered when deciding on what you will wear when going out on a date.

   a. _____

   b. _____

3. Name two activities that you could participate in if you wanted to get together with a friend or new acquaintance but neither of you have any money that you can spend on a recreational activity.

   a. _____

   b. _____

4. Do you think it is appropriate to turn down a date when you're asked for a date by someone you don't particularly care for? (yes or no)
   _____

5. If you were talking to someone you recently met, what sorts of things could that person do or say in order to let you know that he/she wants to stop talking to you without actually telling you?

   a. _____

   b. _____

   c. _____

6. If you asked someone for a date and he/she said no how would you react and/or what would you say? _____

   _____

Figure 2-23

COMMUNICATION SKILLS PROGRAM (CONT.)
UNIT 2
WRITTEN EXAM
(FORM CS-T2a)

7. An important component of appropriate behavior during a date is "attentiveness". Name two other important behaviors.
   a. _____
   b. _____

8. Name two places where you could go or two activities you could plan with a friend on a Sunday afternoon.
   a. _____
   b. _____

9. If someone asks you for a date and you want to go but you cannot go because you already have other plans what would you say to him/her? _____
   _____
   _____

10. Name two factors you should think about when selecting an individual to ask for a date (example: encouragement from individual).
    a. _____
    b. _____

11. Name three things that should be considered when deciding on something to do when going out on a date.
    a. _____
    b. _____
    c. _____

12. If someone asks you for a date and you don't want to go with that person what would you say to him/her? _____
    _____

13. If you met someone whom you like and want to encourage that person to ask you for a date what could you do to appropriately express your feelings without actually telling him/her or asking for a date yourself? _____
    _____
    _____

Number Correct: _____

Number Incorrect: _____

% Correct: _____

COMMUNICATION SKILLS PROGRAM
UNIT 2
ROLE PLAYING EVALUATION FORM
(FORM DS-RPEF2)

Resident's Name: _____

Date: _____

Instructor: _____

	APPROPRIATE	INAPPROPRIATE	COMMENTS
Pleasant Greeting			
Positive Attitude			
Clarity			
Sincerity			
Assertiveness			
Speech Level			
Affect			
Posture			
Eye Contact			
Closing			
Total Appropriate		/////	
Total Inappropriate	/////		
% Appropriate		/////	

Figure 2-24

COMMUNICATION SKILLS PROGRAM DATA SHEET
UNIT 2
DATES

DATE	CLASS ATTEND (√, X OR E)	ROLE PL. (√)	CLASS ASSIGN 2-2 (%)	HOMEW. ASSIGN 2-1 (%)	CLASS ASSIGN 2-3 (%)	UNIT TEST T2A (%)	UNIT TEST RPEF2 (%)	STAFF	COMMENTS
NAME: COURSE:									
Total #√s									
Crit. (√, X or L)		▨							
Unit 2 Crit. (√ or X)	▨	▨	▨	▨	▨	▨	▨		

Figure 2-25

LEVEL 3
PROBLEM SOLVING SKILLS PROGRAM
(DAILY DIARY)

GENERAL STATEMENT

Everyone encounters problems. Thus, it is important for an individual to be able to detect, specify, and deal with problems as they arise. The types of problems, the degree of emotion aroused, and the coping strategies and solutions used, vary greatly between individuals and within the same individual at differing times.

When not dealt with effectively, common every day problems can have very debilitating effects. Typically, unresolved problems cause a decrease in happiness and, depending upon the severity of the unresolved problems, a decrease in effectiveness and successful living. Fortunately, most environmental, interpersonal and intrapersonal problems can be dealth with and solved.

The Problem Solving Skills Program is designed to teach the requisite skills for solving problems appropriately. The procedure takes into consideration four components necessary for successful problem solving: motiviation, responses, environmental stimuli, and environmental consequences. Motivation includes the extent to which an individual desires change and believes a change can be accomplished. An individual's degree of motivation is a function of his/her learning history, intellectual level of functioning, competing responses, perceived reinforcements, and physiology. Responses are the actual behaviors that the individual is emitting. In order for the individual to implement behavioral change, it is extremely important for him/her to be aware of the responses he/she is currently emitting. Environmental stimuli, or antecedents, are the situations, the people, the behavior, the objects, the conditions, etc., that may be influential in the emission of responses. Awareness of antecedents facilitates an accurate analysis and understanding of the problem or situation, thus increasing the probability of the individual solving the problem appropriately. Environmental consequences are the events that follow a response. A consequence can be either positive or negative, with the former increasing the probability of a response and the latter decreasing the probability of a response. Awareness of the consequences that are maintaining, increasing, or decreasing the probability of responses or behaviors, increases the likelihood of successful problem solving and behavioral change.

PURPOSE

1. To help increase motivation to produce desired changes
2. To help develop self-confidence
3. To help improve understanding of the environment
4. To help develop the ability to generate alternative responses for given situations
5. To help develop a means to express moods, emotions, and feelings
6. To help develop new and more appropriate modes of behavior
7. To help develop problem solving skills

I. General Policies
   A. This procedure is to be followed by both residents in the token economy system and residents not in the token economy system. Residents not in the token economy system are not to be given the specified token payments.
   B. Each resident in the Level 3 program is to participate in the Problem Solving Skills Program.
   C. Participation begins upon arrival into the Level 3 program (see Section II: Baseline Period).
   D. Each resident is to complete the Problem Solving Skills Program (i.e., Daily Diary)

daily (except when engaging in a Sunday Special or Saturday Special). (See Section III. G. 6: Saturday and Sunday Specials, p. 125.)
   E. The Daily Diary is to be appropriately completed by 6:30 P.M. (during the Baseline Period and the Treatment Period).
   F. Those residents not able to write are to tape record their Daily Diaries using the Daily Diary format.
   G. After the resident completes his/her Daily Diary, he/she is to give it to his/her assigned or alternate Direct-Care Staff (DCS) member. All diaries are to be retained by the staff, whether completed properly or not.
   H. Individual programs, based on the specific needs of the resident, may be developed which supersede the Problem Solving Skills Program.
II. Baseline Period
   A. Baseline data are to be collected on each resident until the Sunday following his/her Revised Treatment Plan Conference. (See Section V: Data Collection, p. 126 and the Interdisciplinary Treatment Team Conferences Procedure, p. 12.)
   B. During the Baseline Period there are no contingencies or token reinforcement for participation in the Problem Solving Skills Program.
   C. The resident is to be prompted, but not required to participate.
   D. The resident is to be given the option of completing any number of the four steps of the Simple Daily Diary form.
   E. Staff may give the resident assistance and instruction when he/she attempts to complete the Simple Daily Diary. Instruction is to consist of
      1. The resident's assigned or alternate DCS is to assist the resident
      2. The DCS is to describe each component of the Simple Daily Diary
      3. The DCS is to ask the resident to describe each component of the Simple Daily Diary
      4. The DCS is to demonstrate how to complete the Simple Daily Diary
III. Treatment Period
   A. The Treatment Period begins on the Monday following the resident's Revised Treatment Plan Conference. (See the Interdisciplinary Treatment Team Conferences Procedure, p. 12.)
   B. During the Treatment Period, completion of the Simple Daily Diary is *required*.
   C. When incidents occur during the day which seem to be appropriate for the resident to record in his/her diary, encourage him/her to remember the incident (s) for later use when completing the diary.
   D. The resident is to complete and give his/her completed diary to his/her assigned or alternate DCS by 6:30 P.M. This is to occur daily unless the resident is engaging in a Sunday Special or Saturday Special. (See Section III. G. 6: Saturday and Sunday Specials, p. 125.)
   E. Daily Diary Shaping Program
      1. The Daily Diary procedure involves a shaping program consisting of four diary steps:
         a. Step I: General Diary
         b. Step II: Positive-Negative Behavior
         c. Step III: Antecedents and Consequences
         d. Step IV: Positive Alternatives
      2. Step placement at the beginning of the Treatment Period is to be based on the resident's baseline period performance (to be determined in the resident's Revised Treatment Plan Conference).
      3. Movement to higher diary steps during the Treatment Period is to occur when the resident meets the Daily Diary Weekly Criterion (95%) for his/her current diary step for at least two consecutive weeks (to be determined by the resident's assigned or alternate DCS and the program psychologist).

F. The treatment period includes two different diary forms (Simple Daily Diary and Complex Daily Diary).
 1. Simple Daily Diary (See Table 2-26, p. 129.)
    a. The resident is to begin using the Simple Daily Diary form on the first day of the Treatment Period.
    b. Simple Daily Diary steps
       (1) Step I: General Diary
           (a) To consist of
               i. A statement consisting of 30 or more words concerning his/her emotions that day. The statement should
                  (i) Be specific
                  (ii) Include the type(s) of feeling(s) experienced
                  (iii) Include what caused the feeling(s)
               ii. Today's Goal Met: The resident is to record a yes if his/her goal for the day was met or a no if his/her goal for the day was *not* met.
               iii. How met or why *not* met?: The resident is to write a statement describing how the goal was met, if it was met, or a statement describing why it was not met, if it was *not*.
               iv. Tomorrow's goal: The resident is to specify at least one measurable (objective) goal which he/she plans on accomplishing the next day. This must be a goal other than the one specified for the current day.
           (b) The requirements for the General Diary step
               i. At least 30 words long
               ii. Description of his/her emotions
               iii. Description of the cause of his/her emotions
               iv. Completion of the goal related statements below
                   (i) Today's goal met (yes or no)
                   (ii) How met or why *not* met?
                   (iii) Tomorrow's goal
           (c) When the resident appropriately completes at least 95% (or six) of the six requirements for the General Diary step
               i. Give him/her verbal praise
               ii. Give him/her a 4¢ token money payment
               iii. Record the appropriate data on his/her Daily Diary Data Sheet (See Section V. A.: Daily Diary Data Sheet, p. 126.)
       (2) Step II: Positive-Negative Behavior
           (a) To consist of
               i. Completion of the General Diary step (Step I)
               ii. Two statements describing two specific events (one positive and one negative) that occurred during the day
                   (i) A positive behavior the resident engaged in during the day or a positive thought the resident had during the day as a function of some event that occurred during the day.
                   (ii) A negative behavior the resident engaged in during the day or a negative thought the resident had during the day as a function of some event that occurred during the day.
           (b) The requirements for the Positive-Negative Behavior step are
               i. Appropriate completion of the six General Diary step (Step I) components
               ii. Appropriate completion of Section 2.a. ii. above (i.e., two statements describing two specific events (one positive and one negative) that occurred during the day) (Step II).

LEVEL 3 PROBLEM SOLVING SKILLS PROGRAM (DAILY DIARY)   121

  (c) When the resident appropriately completes at least 95% (or eight) of the eight requirements for the Positive-Negative Behavior step
     i. Give him/her verbal praise
     ii. Give him/her a 8¢ token money payment
     iii. Record the appropriate data on his/her Daily Diary Data Sheet (See Section V.A: Daily Diary Data Sheet, p. 126.)
  (3) Step III: Antecedents and Consequences
    (a) To consist of
      i. Completion of the General Diary Step (Step I)
      ii. Completion of the Positive-Negative Behavior Step (Step II)
      iii. Specification of the antecedent for each Positive-Negative behavior entry
      iv. Specification of the consequence for each Positive-Negative Behavior entry
    (b) The requirements for the Antecedents and Consequences Step are
      i. Appropriate completion of the six General Diary Step (Step I) components
      ii. Appropriate completion of the two Positive-Negative Behavior Step (Step II) components
      iii. Specification of the antecedent and consequence for each Positive-Negative Behavior entry (Step III)
    (c) When the resident appropriately completes at least 95% (or 12) of the 12 requirements for the Antecedents and Consequences Step
      i. Give him/her verbal praise
      ii. Give him/her a 12¢ token money payment
      iii. Record the appropriate data on his/her Daily Diary Data Sheet (See Section V.A: Daily Diary Data Sheet, p. 126.)
  (4) Step IV: Positive Alternatives
    (a) To consist of
      i. Completion of the General Diary Step (Step I)
      ii. Completion of the Positive-Negative Behavior Step (Step II)
      iii. Completion of the Antecedents and Consequences Step (Step III)
      iv. Specification of two positive alternatives for each negative behavior entry (Step IV)
    (b) The requirements for the Positive-Alternatives Step are
      i. Appropraite completion of the six General Diary Step (Step I) components
      ii. Appropriate completion of the two Positive-Negative behaviors Step (Step II) components
      iii. Appropriate completion of the four Antecedents and Consequences Step (Step III) components
      iv. Specification of at least two positive alternatives for the *Negative* behavior entry (Step IV)
    (c) When the resident appropriately completes at least 95% (or 14) of the 14 requirements for the Positive Alternative Step
      i. Give him/her verbal praise
      ii. Give him/her a 16¢ token money payment
      iii. Record the appropriate data on his/her Daily Diary Data Sheet (See Section V.A: Daily Diary Data Sheet, p. 126.)
2. Complex Daily Diary (See Table 2-27, p. 130.)
  a. Movement to the Complex Daily Diary Form is to be determined in an Interdisciplinary Treatment Team Conference
  b. The resident is to begin using the Complex Daily Diary form when

(1) He/she has met the Simple Daily Diary Weekly Criterion (through Step IV) for at least eight consecutive weeks
(2) He/she has met all individual and ward criteria specified in his/her Treatment Plan
c. The resident is to complete all four steps of the Complex Daily Diary.
d. When necessary, the four step shaping program (see Section III. E. Daily Diary Shaping Program, p. 119 is to be used (to be determined in an Interdisciplinary Treatment Team Conference).
e. Complex Daily Diary Steps
  (1) Step I: General Diary
    (a) To consist of
      i. A statement consisting of 30 or more words concerning his/her emotions that day. The statement should
        (i) Be specific
        (ii) Include the type(s) of feeling(s) experienced
        (iii) Include what caused the feeling(s)
      ii. Today's Goal Met: The resident is to record a yes if his/her goal for the day was met, or a no if his/her goal for the day was *not* met
      iii. How met or why *not* met?: The resident is to write a statement describing how the goal was met, if it was met, or a statement describing why it was not met, if it was *not*
      iv. Tomorrow's goal: The resident is to specify at least one measurable (objective) goal which he/she plans on accomplishing the next day. This must be a goal other than the one specified for the current day
    (b) The requirements for the General Diary Step
      i. At least 30 words long
      ii. Description of his/her emotions
      iii. Description of the cause of his/her emotions
      iv. Completion of the goal related statements below:
        (i) Today's goal met (Yes or No)
        (ii) How met or why *not* met?
        (iii) Tomorrow's goal
    (c) When the resident appropriately completes at least 95% (or six) of the six requirements for the General Diary Step
      i. Give him/her verbal praise
      ii. Give him/her a 4¢ token money payment
      iii. Record the appropriate data on his/her Daily Diary Data Sheet (See Section V.A: Daily Diary Data Sheet, p. 126.)
  (2) Step II: Positive-Negative Behavior
    (a) To consist of
      i. Completion of the General Diary Step (Step I)
      ii. Four statements describing four specific events that occurred during the day (no more than one thought):
        (i) A positive behavior the resident engaged in during the day or a positive thought the resident had during the day as a function of some event that occurred during the day.
        (ii) A negative behavior the resident engaged in during the day or a negative thought the resident had during the day as a function of some event that occurred during the day.
        (iii) A positive behavior engaged in during the day by another person that was directed toward or affected the resident.

(iv) A negative behavior engaged in during the day by another person that was directed toward or affected the resident.
- (b) The requirements for the Positive-Negative Behavior Step are
  - i. Appropriate completion of the six General Diary Step (Step I) components
  - ii. Appropriate completion of Section 2. a. ii. above (i.e., four statements describing four specific events (one positive self; one negative self; one positive other; one negative other) that occurred during the day (Step II)
- (c) When the resident appropriately completes at least 95% (or ten) of the ten requirements for the Positive-Negative Behavior Step
  - i. Give him/her verbal praise
  - ii. Give him/her a 8¢ token money payment
  - iii. Record the appropriate data on his/her Daily Diary Data Sheet (See Section V.A: Daily Diary Data Sheet, p. 126.)

(3) Step III: Antecedents and Consequences
- (a) To consist of
  - i. Completion of the General Diary Step (Step I)
  - ii. Completion of the Positive-Negative Behavior Step (Step II)
  - iii. Specification of the antecedent for each Positive-Negative Behavior entry
  - iv. Specification of the consequence for each Positive-Negative Behavior entry
- (b) The requirements for the Antecedents and Consequences Step are
  - i. Appropriate completion of the six General Diary Step (Step I) components
  - ii. Appropriate completion of the four Positive-Negative Behavior Step (Step II) components
  - iii. Specification of the antecedent and consequence for each Positive-Negative Behavior entry (Step III)
- (c) When the resident appropriately completes at least 95% (or 18) of the 18 requirements for the Antecedents and Consequences Step
  - i. Give him/her verbal praise
  - ii. Give him/her a 12¢ token money payment
  - iii. Record the appropriate data on his/her Daily Diary Data Sheet (See Section V. A: Daily Diary Data Sheet, p. 126.)

(4) Step IV: Positive Alternatives
- (a) To consist of
  - i. Completion of the General Diary Step (Step I)
  - ii. Completion of the Positive-Negative Behavior Step (Step II)
  - iii. Completion of the Antecedents and Consequences Step (Step III)
  - iv. Specification of two positive alternatives for each *Negative* behavior entry (Step IV)
- (b) The requirements for the Positive-Alternatives Step are
  - i. Appropriate completion of the six General Diary Step (Step I) components
  - ii. Appropriate completion of the four Positive-Negative Behavior Step (Step IV) components
  - iii. Appropriate completion of the eight Antecedents and Consequences Step (Step III) components
  - iv. Specification of at least two positive alternatives for each of the two negative behavior entries (Step IV)

(c) When the resident appropriately completes at least 95% (or at least 21) of the 22 requirements for the Positive Alternatives Step
  i. Give him/her verbal praise
  ii. Give him/her a 16¢ token money payment
  iii. Record the appropriate data on his/her Daily Diary Data Sheet (See Section V.A: Daily Diary Data Sheet, p. 126.)

G. Reinforcement and Contingency Management (For both Simple *and* Complex Daily Diary Forms)
  1. When the resident is in Step I and he/she appropriately completes at least 95% of the requirements for this step (by 6:30 P.M.) on the first attempt
     a. Give him/her verbal praise
     b. Give him/her a 4¢ token money payment
     c. Record the appropriate data on his/her Daily Diary Data Sheet (See Section V.A: Daily Diary Data Sheet, p. 126.)
  2. When the resident is in Step II and he/she appropriately completes at least 95% of the requirements for this step (by 6:30 P.M.) on the first attempt
     a. Give him/her verbal praise
     b. Give him/her a 8¢ token money payment
     c. Record the appropriate data on his/her Daily Diary Data Sheet (See Section V.A: Daily Diary Data Sheet)
  3. When the resident is in Step III and he/she appropriately completes at least 95% of the requirements for this step (by 6:30 P.M.) on the first attempt
     a. Give him/her verbal praise
     b. Give him/her a 12¢ token money payment
     c. Record the appropriate data on his/her Daily Diary Data Sheet (See Section V.A: Daily Diary Data Sheet)
  4. When the resident is in Step IV and he/she appropriately completes at least 95% of the requirements for this step (by 6:30 P.M.) on the first attempt:
     a. Give him/her verbal praise
     b. Give him/her a 16¢ token money payment
     c. Record the appropriate data on his/her Daily Diary Data Sheet (See Section V.A: Daily Diary Data Sheet)
  5. When the resident does not appropriately complete the diary on the first attempt (as defined by the step he/she is currently in) by 6:30 P.M.
     a. Do *not* give him/her verbal praise (unless he/she appropriately completes the diary later in the evening; then give him/her verbal praise
     b. Do *not* give him/her any token money payment
     c. Record the appropriate data on his/her Daily Diary Data Sheet (See Section V.A: Daily Diary Data Sheet, p. 126.)
     d. Restrict him/her to a chair at a table located in the bedroom hall area until the diary is completed appropriately or until 9:00 P.M.
     e. While on diary restriction do *not* allow the following privileges:
        (1) Any activities requiring the individual to leave the hall area except for the use of the telephone
        (2) Canteen
        (3) On ward activities
        (4) Token earning power
        (5) Smoking
        (6) Bedroom Area
        (7) Ward Jobs
     f. Record the appropriate data on the resident's Individual Restriction Sheet
     g. If the resident completes the diary appropriately at least 95% of the step requirements) before or by 9:00 P.M. (but after 6:30 P.M.)
        (1) Give him/her verbal praise

(2) Do *not* give him/her any token money payment
(3) Record the appropriate data on his/her Daily Diary Data Sheet (See Section V.A: Daily Diary Data Sheet)
(4) Record the appropriate data on his/her Individual Restriction Sheet (i.e., time Daily Diary restriction ended)

6. Saturday and Sunday Specials
   a. Sunday Special
      The resident is *not* required to complete the Daily Diary on Sundays when
      (1) He/she has met the weekly Self-Care Skills criterion for the week (See Self-Care Skills Procedure, p. 41.)
      (2) He/she has met the Daily Diary Daily criterion every day of the week (Monday through Saturday)
      (3) There are no restrictions in effect as a function of individual and/or ward programs and/or inappropriate behavior such as stealing, aggression, or sexual inappropriateness
   b. Saturday Special
      The resident is *not* required to complete the Daily Diary on Saturday when
      (1) He/she has met the weekly Self-Care Skills criterion for the preceding four consecutive weeks
      (2) He/she has met the Daily Diary Weekly criterion for the preceding four consecutive weeks
      (3) There are no restrictions in effect as a function of individual and/or ward programs and/or inappropriate behavior such as stealing, aggression, or sexual inappropriateness
   c. When the resident is engaging in a Saturday and/or Sunday Special, specify this on the Daily Diary Data Sheet.

IV. Daily Diary Evaluations
   A. Daily Diary evaluations are to occur during the Baseline Period and Treatment Period.
   B. The resident's assigned or alternate DCS is to evaluate his/her diary.
   C. There are two types of evaluation methods:
      1. Mechanics evaluation
         a. Those residents *not* randomly selected for a close evaluation (See Section IV.C.2: Close Evaluation) are to be given a mechanics evaluation.
         b. The mechanics evaluation consists of checking for
            (1) Completion of all requirements of the diary step the resident is currently in (e.g., general diary, goal for the day, turned in on time, etc.)
            (2) Appropriate length
      2. Close evaluation
         a. Each DCS on duty is to randomly choose one resident from the group of residents assigned to him/her, for a close evaluation.
         b. Evaluation method
            (1) Carefully read the contents of the diary.
            (2) Check for completion of all requirements of the diary step the resident is currently in.
            (3) Give feedback to the resident concerning
               (a) Appropriateness (use actual examples)
               (b) Inappropriateness (use actual examples)
               (c) Suggestions for improving entries (when needed)
            (4) If changes (additions, corrections, etc.) are needed, return the diary to the resident.
            (5) The corrected diary is to be returned to the DCS by 9:00 P.M.
            (6) Repeat evaluation steps 1-5 above as often as necessary for appropriate completion of the diary.

c. If the diary was not completed appropriately, continue close evaluations on subsequent days until the diary is completed appropriately on the first attempt.
   D. Token payments are to be given to the resident *only* when he/she appropriately completes the diary on the first attempt.
V. Data Collection
   A. Daily Diary Data Sheet (See Figure 2-28, p. 132.)
      1. There is to be one Daily Diary Data Sheet per resident.
      2. The data sheet is to be located in the resident's Individual Program Book.
      3. Data to record:
         a. Date: Always record the current date.
            (1) The current date is the date on which the diary was completed and turned in.
            (2) The date is to be recorded above the day of the week.
            (3) Do *not* skip any dates.
            (4) Color code
               (a) Record the date in *red* when a close evaluation was given.
               (b) Record the date in *black* when a mechanics evaluation was given.
         b. Diary/Step #: Record the diary form (Simple or Complex) the individual used, and the diary step he/she is currently in (Diary Form/Step #).
            (1) Diary Form
               (a) Record an *S* if the resident used the Simple Diary Form.
               (b) Record a *C* if the resident used the Complex Diary Form.
            (2) Diary Step
               (a) Record a 1 if the resident is currently in Step I.
               (b) Record a 2 if the resident is currently in Step II.
               (c) Record a 3 if the resident is currently in Step III.
               (d) Record a 4 if the resident is currently in Step IV.
         c. # Appr. Comp./# Requir: Record the number of requirements that were appropriately completed on the first attempt *and* the number of requirements for the step the resident is currently in (# requir. appropriately completed/# requirements for the step). (See Section III. F., p. 120.)
            (1) Step I: General Diary (Simple *and* Complex Diaries) - six requirements
            (2) Step II: Positive-Negative Behavior
               (a) Simple Diary - eight requirements
               (b) Complex Diary - ten requirements
            (3) Step III: Antecedents and Consequences
               (a) Simple Diary - twelve requirements
               (b) Complex Diary - eighteen requirements
            (4) Step IV: Positive Alternatives
               (a) Simple Diary - fourteen requirements
               (b) Complex Diary - twenty-two requirements
         d. # Not Appr. Comp: Record the number of requirements that were not appropriately completed on the first attempt (# Not appr. comp. = # of requirements for the step the resident is currently in *minus* # of requirements the resident appropriately completed).
         e. % Appr. Comp: Record the percent of requirements that were appropriately completed on the first attempt (% appr. comp. = # appr. comp. *divided by* # requirements) (round to the nearest hundreth, e.g., .954 = .95; .955 = .96).
         f. D. Crit.: Record whether the resident met the Daily Diary Criterion (Daily Diary Daily Criterion = 95% appropriately completed or greater).
            (1) If the resident met the Daily Diary Daily Criterion record a check mark (✓).
            (2) If the resident did *not* meet the Daily Diary Daily Criterion record an *X*.

g. # Feel. Stmt.: Record the number of different "feeling" statements that the resident included in his/her general diary statement.
h. # NonFeel. Stmt.: Record the number of different "nonfeeling" statements that the resident included in his/her general diary statement.
i. Amt. paid: Record the amount of token money given to the resident.
j. Goals 1-2-3: Record either a 1, 2, or 3:
   (1) Record a 1 when the goal was met and a statement was written concerning how the goal was met.
   (2) Record a 2 when the goal was not met.
   (3) Record a 3 when the goal was not attempted.
k. # Attempts: Record the number of attempts necessary before the resident completed the diary appropriately.
l. DCS: Record the initials of the DCS recording the data.
m. Each Sunday evening second shift DCSs are to record
   (1) Tot. Paid: Record the total amount of token money payments given to the resident that week.
   (2) T. # Ap. Comp/T. # Requir.: Record the total number of requirements that were appropriately completed that week *and* the total number of requirements for the week (total number of requirements that were appropriately completed that week/total number of requirements for the week).
   (3) T. # N. Ap. Comp.: Record the total number of requirements that were *not* appropriately completed that week (T. # N. Ap. Comp. = total number of requirements for the week *minus* total number of requirements that were appropriately completed that week).
   (4) T. Feel: Record the total number of "feeling" and "nonfeeling" statements for the week in the appropriate squares.
   (5) Goal 1: Record the total number of "Goal 1s" the resident obtained that week.
   (6) Goal 2: Record the total number of "Goal 2s" the resident obtained that week.
   (7) Goal 3: Record the total number of "Goal 3s" the resident obtained that week.
   (8) Tot. attempts: Record the total number of attempts for the week.
   (9) DCS: Record the initials of the DCS recording the weekly data.
B. Daily Diary Summary Sheet (Weekly) (See Figure 2-29, p. 133.)
   1. There is to be one Daily Diary Summary Table per resident.
   2. The Summary Table is to be located in the resident's Individual Program Book.
   3. The data recorded on the resident's Daily Diary Data Sheet are to be used to complete the resident's Daily Diary Summary Table.
   4. Data are to be recorded once each week.
   5. Data are to be recorded on Sunday evenings by third shift DCSs.
   6. Data to record:
      a. Date: Record the date of the last day of the week for which the data are being recorded.
      b. Diary/Step #: Record the diary form (Simple or Complex) the resident used and the diary step he/she is currently in (Diary Form/Step #).
         (1) Diary Form
            (a) Record an *S* if the resident used the Simple Diary Form.
            (b) Record a *C* if the resident used the Complex Diary Form.
         (2) Diary Step
            (a) Record a 1 if the resident is currently in Step I.
            (b) Record a 2 if the resident is currently in Step II.
            (c) Record a 3 if the resident is currently in Step III.
            (d) Record a 4 if the resident is currently in Step IV.

c. T. #. Ap. Comp./T. # Requir.: Record the total number of requirements that were appropriately completed by the resident that week on the first attempt each day, *and* record the total number of requirements for the week for the step the resident is currently in (tot. number of requirements that were appropriately completed that week/total number of requirements for the week for the step).
d. % T. Ap. Comp: Record the percent of requirements appropriately completed for the week (% T. AP. Comp. = T. # ap. comp. *divided by* T. # requir) (round to the nearest hundreth, e.g., .954 = .95; .955 = .96)
e. W. Crit.: Record whether the resident met the Daily Diary Weekly Criterion (Daily Diary Weekly Criterion = 95% T. Ap. Comp. or greater).
f. T. D. Crit.: Record the total number of days that the resident met the Daily Diary Daily Criterion that week.
g. T. Feel: Record the total number of "feeling" statements that the resident recorded that week.
h. T. Nonfeel: Record the total number of "nonfeeling" statements that the resident recorded that week.
i. % T. Feel: Record the percent of "feeling" statements that the resident recorded that week (% T. Feel. = T. Feel. *divided by* T. Feel + T. Non-feel.).
j. T. Goal 1: Record the total number of "Goal 1s" the resident obtained that week.
k. T. Goal 2: Record the total number of "Goal 2s" the resident obtained that week
l. T. Goal 3: Record the total number of "Goal 3s" obtained by the resident that week
m. % T. Goal 1: Record the percent of "Goal 1s" obtained by the resident that week (% T. Goal 1 = T. Goal 1 *divided by* T. Goal 1 *plus* Goal 2 *plus* T. Goal 3).
n. T. Attem: Record the total number of attempts that week.
o. $\bar{x}$: Record the monthly means (divide the total of each column by the number of weeks that weekly data were recorded).
p. DCS: Record the initials of the DCS recording the data.

VI. Daily Diary Graphing Technique
A. There is to be one Daily Diary Graph per resident.
B. The graph is to be located in the resident's Individual Program Book.
C. The data recorded on the resident's Daily Diary Summary Sheet are to be used for graphing.
D. Data are to be graphed once each week.
E. Data are to be graphed on Sunday evenings by third shift DCSs.
F. The following data are to be graphed:
1. T.D. Criterion: Total number of days that the resident met the Daily Diary Daily Criterion that week (use open circles: ○———○).
2. % T. Ap. Comp: Percent of requirements appropriately completed that week (use closed triangles: ▲———▲).
3. % T. Goal 1: Percent of "Goal 1s" obtained by the resident that week (use open triangles: △———△).
4. T. Attem.: Total number of attempts that week (use closed circles: ●———●).
5. When the resident advances to the Complex Daily Diary, place a vertical dotted line on the graph to indicate the date on which this advancement took place.

SIMPLE DAILY DIARY

NAME _____ DATE _____

I. <u>GENERAL DIARY:</u> (Write a paragraph concerning the events of the day, feelings you experienced today, and the cause(s) for these feelings) _____
_____
_____
_____
_____

Was today's goal met?   Yes _____ No _____
If it was met, explain how _____
_____

If it was not met, explain why it wasn't _____
_____

What is your goal for tomorrow? _____

II. <u>POSITIVE (GOOD) AND NEGATIVE (BAD) BEHAVIOR:</u> (Describe one of your positive (good) and one of your negative (bad) behaviors or thoughts that occurred today:

1. Positive thought or behavior: _____
_____

2. Negative thought or behavior: _____
_____

III. <u>ANTECEDENTS AND CONSEQUENCES:</u>
Antecedents: (What happened to cause each of your positive (good) and negative (bad) behaviors or feelings to occur?)

1. _____
_____

2. _____
_____

Consequences: (What happened or how did you feel after each of your positive (good) and negative (bad) behaviors and/or thoughts?)

1. _____
_____

2. _____
_____

IV. <u>ALTERNATIVE BEHAVIORS:</u> (Describe at least two better ways of dealing with the situation that produced your negative (bad) thought or behavior. What could you have done or thought that would have been better than what actually occurred?)

1. _____
_____

2. _____
_____

Figure 2-26

COMPLEX DAILY DIARY

NAME _____ DATE _____

I. GENERAL DIARY: (Write a paragraph concerning the events of the day, feelings you experienced today, and the cause(s) for these feelings)
_____
_____
_____
_____

Was today's goal met? Yes_____ No_____
If it was met, explain how_____
_____
If it was not met, explain why it wasn't _____
_____
What is your goal for tomorrow?_____

II. POSITIVE (GOOD) AND NEGATIVE (BAD) BEHAVIOR: (Describe one of your positive (good) and one of your negative (bad) behaviors or thoughts that occurred today)

1. Positive-self thought or behavior: _____
_____

2. Negative-self thought or behavior: _____
_____

(Describe one of someone else's positive (good) and one of someone else's negative (bad) behaviors that occurred and affected you today)

3. Positive-other behavior: _____
_____

4. Negative-other behavior: _____
_____

III. ANTECEDENTS AND CONSEQUENCES: Antecedents: (What happened to cause each of the positive (good) and each of the negative (bad) behaviors or feelings that you listed in Section II above?)

1. _____
_____
2. _____
_____
3. _____
_____
4. _____
_____

Figure 2-27

COMPLEX DAILY DIARY (CONT.)

    Consequence: (What happened or how did you feel after each of the positive (good) and each of the negative (bad) behaviors or thoughts occurred that you listed in Section II above?)

    1. _____

    2. _____

    3. _____

    4. _____

IV.   **ALTERNATIVE BEHAVIORS:** (Describe at least two better behaviors or thoughts that could have occurred instead of each of the <u>negative</u> behaviors or thoughts that you listed in Section II above. Describe two for each behavior or thought.

    2. _____

    2. _____

    4. _____

    4. _____

DAILY DIARY DATA SHEET

	Step	Token Payment	Requirements Simple	Complex
1 = Goal Met	I	4¢	6	6
2 = Goal not met but attempted	II	8¢	8	10
3 = Goal not attempted	III	12¢	12	18
	IV	16¢	14	22

DATE	DIARY /STEP #	#APPR. COMP./# REQUIR.	#NOT APPR. COMP.	# APPR. COMP.	D.CRIT. (√ OR X)	# FEEL STMT.	#NON FEEL STMT.	# PROMPTS	AMT. PAID	GOALS 1-2-3	# ATTEMPTS	DCS
Mon.												
Tues.												
Wed.												
Thurs.												
Fri.												
Sat.												
Sun.												
Tot. Paid												
T. # Ap. Comp./T. # Requir.												
T. # N P. Comp.												
T. Feel												
Goal 1												
Goal 2												
Goal 3												
Tot. Attempts												
DCS												

Figure 2-28

DAILY DIARY SUMMARY SHEET (WEEKLY)

DATE	DIARY FORM STEP #	T. #AP. COMP./ T. # REQUIR.	% T. AP. COMP.	W. CRIT.	T.D. CRIT.	T. FEEL.	T. NON-FEEL.	% T. FEEL.	T. GOAL 1	T. GOAL 2	T. GOAL 3	% T. GOAL	T. ATTEM.	DCS
$\overline{X}$	▨			▨										
$\overline{X}$	▨			▨										
$\overline{X}$	▨			▨										
$\overline{X}$	▨			▨										

Figure 2-29

LEVEL 3
GOAL ORIENTATION PROCEDURE
(DAILY LIVING SCHEDULE)

GENERAL STATEMENT

Inactivity can be a major contributing factor to the development of inappropriate feelings and behaviors. An individual who is constantly inactive may easily become bored, probably has few sources of reinforcement or gratification, and could eventually become depressed, angry and/or lose his/her motivation to continue. This is especially true of the chronically institutionalized individual. The institutionalized individual typically engages in few activities unless prompted to do so, seldom schedules appointments, and usually when an appointment is scheduled there is a high probability that the appointment will not be met by the individual unless he/she is reminded to do so. The Goal Orientation Procedure has been developed to serve as a means for individuals in the Level 3 program to structure their days, schedule appointments and activities, and help alleviate or prevent depression and boredom.

PURPOSE

1. To help goal development
2. To teach dependability
3. To teach organizational skills
4. To develop self-reliance
5. To increase self-esteem
6. To help develop an active daily schedule
7. To reduce inactivity and boredom
8. To increase gratification and reinforcement
9. To teach adherance to schedules
10. To help teach the individual that he/she can control his/her own life

PROCEDURE

I. General Policies
A. This procedure is to be followed by residents in the token economy system and residents not in the token economy system, with the exception that individuals *not* in the token economy system are not given the specified token money payments.
B. Each resident in the Level 3 program is to participate in the Goal Orientation Procedure unless otherwise specified in his/her treatment plan.
C. Participation begins upon arrival into the Level 3 program (See Section: IV: Baseline Period).
D. Each resident is to complete a Daily Living Schedule (D.L.S.) daily.
E. The D.L.S. is to be completed by 8:00 A.M.
F. The resident is to make a carbon copy of each D.L.S.
G. The original D. L. S. is to be turned in to the resident's assigned or alternate Direct-Care Staff (DCS) member.
H. The D.L.S. is to be divided into half-hour periods.
I. At least one behavior is to be scheduled for each half-hour period. The behavior(s) scheduled is(are) to be different from the behavior(s) scheduled for the preceding half-hour period unless the behavior(s) requires more than the amount of time allocated during the preceding half-hour period; unless the resident elects to allocate additional time for the behavior(s) using proper judgement concerning time; and/or unless the resident is given permission by a staff member to repeat/continue the behavior(s). Behavior(s) scheduled for a half-hour period must require a total of at *least* 15 minutes for completion.

LEVEL 3 GOAL ORIENTATION PROCEDURE DAILY LIVING SCHEDULE

J. The D.L.S. is to cover the time period from 8:30 A.M. to 9:00 P.M.
K. Each schedule is to include at least
 1. Four ward jobs (See Level 1, 2, & 3 Job Assignment Procedure, p. 182.)
    a. The resident is to record his/her job choice on the Job Assignment Sheet.
    b. Two residents cannot sign-up for the same job at the same time.
    c. Jobs can be repeated *only* after all jobs have been completed once.
    d. Token economy participants are to be paid for the four required ward jobs prior to meeting the Self-Care Skills weekly criterion for two consecutive weeks, if they indicate on their schedules the four jobs they wish to be paid for (must place a check mark (✓) besides each of these jobs). After meeting the Self-Care Skills weekly criterion for two consecutive weeks, token economy participants are to be paid for ward jobs as specified in the Level 3 Job Assignment Program
 2. Four different cooperative and/or competitive recreational or leisure activities (See Level 1, 2, and 3 Recreation - Leisure Activities Program, p. 179.)
    a. Each activity is to involve *at least* one other resident.
    b. The resident is to list the name(s) of the individual(s) participating in the activity.
    c. For each of the four required cooperative and/or competitive recreational or leisure activities a resident schedules on his/her Daily Living Schedule, the resident is to have each listed participant (on DLS) sign his/her first name and first letter of last name beside the agreed upon activity listed on his/her D.L.S.
    d. If a resident schedules an activity with a potential participant and this participant has not signed the individual's D.L.S., as described in c above, then the activity is not to be counted as one of the four required cooperative and/or competitive recreational or leisure activities.
    e. Passive activities (e.g., TV, etc.) are *not* to be accepted as one of the four required activities.
    f. Listening to records may be accepted as one of the four activities if active participation such as dancing is included in the activity. Socializing may be accepted as one of the four activities if a specific resident is included.
    g. Token economy participants are *not* to be charged for engagement in the four required activities.
    h. Token economy participants are to indicate which activities on their D.L.S.s they are selecting as their required activities, by placing a check mark beside each of these activities. If an activity requires more than a half-hour to complete, the token economy participant is to pay for the additional time required, in half-hour increments of time.
L. Unscheduled behavior/activity/sleep
 1. When a token economy resident is observed engaging in a behavior/activity that he/she has not scheduled on his/her D.L.S. *and* the behavior/activity requires a token payment, the assigned/alternate DCS is to
    a. Charge the resident twice the amount (in tokens) that is usually required
    b. Give the resident a "Not Met" for the D.L.S.
    c. *Prompt* the resident to follow his/her D.L.S.
 2. If the resident decides to continue engaging in the behavior/activity
    a. Allow the resident to engage in the behavior/activity for the remainder of the current D.L.S. half-hour period
    b. At the end of the D.L.S. half-hour period, *prompt* the resident to follow his/her D.L.S.
 3. If the resident continues to engage in the behavior/activity after he/she is given the prompt specified above in 2.b., implement the procedure specified above in Sections 1 and 2. The procedure specified in Sections 1 and 2 is to be im-

plemented at the conclusion of each D.L.S half-hour period until the resident discontinues engaging in the behavior/activity, which has not been scheduled, and follows his/her schedule.
- M. D.L.S.s are not to be accepted as being appropriate, if scheduled events are not consistent among residents as to time and activity. When an error is made in judging the amount of time allowed for a scheduled event, the assigned/alternate DCS is to discuss the error with the resident (e.g., scheduling half-hour segments of time for medication). The schedule is not to be considered appropriate if the resident does not make the necessary change in the schedule following discussion(s) with the DCS. For residents who repeatedly schedule several hours of "rest," assigned/alternate DCSs are to write a progress note in the resident's chart concerning this problem.
- N. Scheduled activities are to be recorded by the resident as specifically as possible (e.g., when the resident plans on going outside he/she should specify the activity to be engaged in while outside and also whether he/she will be alone or with others).
- O. The resident is responsible for meeting the schedule.
- P. Schedule Changes
    1. The resident is excused from a scheduled activity, ward job, etc., only after being given approval by his/her assigned or alternate DCS prior to the scheduled time for the activity. Examples of situations warranting approval of a request to be excused from a scheduled activity are as follows:
        a. Appointments made by staff without the resident's awareness (e.g., medical, testing, etc.)
        b. Activities beyond the resident's control (e.g., unexpected visits by family members)
        c. Medical reasons (e.g., sickness)
        d. Spontaneous activities (e.g., no advance notice)
        e. When a scheduled activity requires more time than anticipated and this activity continues into the next 1/2-hour period
    2. Approved schedule changes or approved excuses are to be initialed by the individual's assigned or alternate DCS.
- Q. Individual programs, based on the specific needs of the resident, may be developed which supersede the Goal Orientation Procedure

II. Daily Living Schedule Observational System
- A. The Daily Living Schedule Observational System is to be observed during Baseline and Treatment Periods with the exception that the Reinforcement and Contingency Management procedure is *not* to be followed during the Baseline Period.
- B. Second and Third Shift DCS responsibilities
    1. Third shift is to randomly select a Daily Living Schedule Observation Schedule (variable-interval 30-minute schedule (VI 30)) Data Sheet (from the sixteen possible schedules for First and Second shifts) for each DCS on both First and Second shifts. (See Figures 2-30 and 2-31, pp. 146-147—Examples selected from the sixteen possible VI 30 schedules.)
    2. DCS Daily Living Schedule Variable-Interval Schedules Sheet
        a. There is to be one D.L.S. Daily Living Schedule Variable-Interval Schedules Sheet on each ward.
        b. Data to record:
            (1) Date: Record the date for which the Daily Living Schedule Observation Schedule Data Sheets were randomly selected.
            (2) Names: Record the names of all DCSs on 1st and 2d shifts.
            (3) VI Schedule: Record the number of the variable-interval schedule that was randomly selected for each DCS.
        c. The completed DCS Daily Living Schedule Variable-Interval Schedules Sheet is to be posted on the bulletin board in each DCS Office.

C. First Shift DCS Responsibilities
1. At the beginning of the shift, each DCS is to refer to the DCS Daily Living Schedule Variable-Interval Schedules Sheet to find out which observational schedule has been randomly selected for him/her for the day.
2. The randomly selected schedule is to be used with all the residents assigned to the DCS on that day (including both regular and alternate assignments).
3. The DCS is to observe the resident(s) assigned to him/her on that day as unobtrusively as possible when prescribed on the observational schedule randomly selected for him/her for that day. If a resident is not on the ward but DCS can assume resident is following his/her schedule (e.g., resident at work), the DCS is to indicate that the resident is following his/her schedule and record *O* for activity task (See Section VII: Data Collection).
4. Daily Living Schedule Observation Schedule Data Sheet (See Figure 2-30, p. 00)
   a. There is to be one Daily Living Schedule Observation Schedule Data Sheet per resident per shift.
   b. Data to record:
      (1) Date: Record the current date.
      (2) Name: Record the name of the resident.
      (3) Met: Record either a check mark ✓, and *X*, or an *E* for each variable-interval observation.
         (a) "✓": Record a check mark (✓) if the resident was following his/her schedule at the time of the observation.
         (b) *X*: Record an *X* if the resident was not following his/her schedule at the time of the observation.
         (c) *E*: Record an *E* if the resident was not following his/her schedule during a variable-interval observation *but* was given prior approval for a schedule change (See Section I. P.: Schedule Changes).
      (4) Behav.: Record either an *A*, *J*, *AI*, *I*, or an *O* for each variable-interval observation.
         (a) *A*: Record an *A* if the resident was engaging in a cooperative and/or competitive recreational or leisure activity involving at least one other resident.
         (b) *J*: Record a *J* if the resident was engaging in a ward job.
         (c) *AI*: Record an *AI* if the resident was engaging in a recreational or leisure activity by him/herself (e.g. reading a book, watching television, etc.).
         (d) *I*: Record an *I* if the resident was isolated from other people and not engaging in an activity.
         (e) *O*: Record an *O* if the resident was engaging in something other than isolation (*I*), activity isolation (*AI*), a ward job (*J*), or a recreational/leisure activity involving at least one other individual (*A*).
      (5) Observ. Pymnt: Record the amount of token money given to the resident for appropriately engaging in his/her schedule during each variable-interval observation.
      (6) DCS: Record the initials of the DCS that made each variable-interval observation.
      (7) After the last variable-interval observation for the shift record
         (a) Tot. Met: Record the total number of check marks (✓) that were recorded in each "Met" column.
         (b) Tot. Not Met: Record the total number of *X*s that were recorded in each "Met" column.
         (c) Tot. Exc.: Record the total number of *E*s that were recorded in each "Met" column.
         (d) Tot. Observ.: Record the total number of variable-interval observations of the resident.

(e) Tot. *A*: Record the total number of *A*s that were recorded in each "Behavior" column.
(f) Tot. *J*: Record the total number of *J*s that were recorded in each "Behavior" column.
(g) Tot. *AI*: Record the total number of *AI*s that were recorded in each "Behavior" column.
(h) Tot. *I*: Record the total number of *I*s that were recorded in each "Behavior" column.
(i) Tot. *O*: Record the total number of *O*s that were recorded in each "Behavior" column.
(j) Tot. Observ. Pymnt: Record the total amount of token money payments that were recorded in each "Observ. Pymnt" column.
(k) Shift Totals: Sum across the appropriate rows to determine the totals for the shift. Record the resulting sums for each row.
(l) DCS: Record the initials of the DCS who calculated and recorded the Shift Totals.

III. Goal Orientation Program Criteria
  A. Daily Criterion: To meet the daily criterion the resident needs to
    1. Appropriately complete his/her schedule by 8:00 A.M.
    2. Specify a behavior for every half-hour period on his/her schedule (8:30 A.M. to 9:00 P.M.) (as specified in Section I: General Policies)
    3. Specify at least four different cooperative and/or competitive recreational or leisure activities on his/her schedule involving at least one other individual (as specified in Section I. General Policies)
    4. Specify four ward jobs on his/her schedule (as specified in Section I: General Policies)
    5. Meet at least 90% of his/her schedule as determined by variable-interval observations
  B. Weekly Criterion: To meet the weekly criterion the resident needs to meet the Daily Criterion every day of the week (exceptions: days on which the resident is engaging in a Saturday and/or Sunday Special see Section V.D., and days on which the resident is excused from writing a schedule).

IV. Baseline Period
  A. Baseline data are to be collected on each resident until the Sunday following his/her Revised Rehabilitation Plan Staffing (See Section VII: Data Collection; and the Interdisciplinary Treatment Team Procedure, p. 12.)
  B. During the baseline period there are no contingencies or token reinforcement for participation in the Goal Orientation Procedure.
  C. The resident is to be prompted to participate in the program but *not* required.
  D. Staff may give the resident assistance and instruction when he/she attempts to complete the schedule.
    1. The resident's assigned or alternate DCS is to assist the resident
    2. The DCS is to describe each component of the D.L.S.
    3. The DCS is to ask the resident to describe each component of the D.L.S.
    4. The DCS is to demonstrate how to complete the schedule
    5. Do *not* require or coerce the resident to complete and/or follow the D.L.S.

V. Treatment Period
  A. The treatment period begins on the Monday following the individual's Revised Rehabilitation Plan Staffing.
  B. During the Treatment Period completion of the Daily Living Schedule is required.
  C. Reinforcement and Contingency Management
    1. Writing schedule
      a. When the schedule is completed appropriately on the first attempt and turned in by 8:00 A.M. and there are at least four different jobs listed, at least

four competitive and/or cooperative recreational or leisure activities listed *and* all half-hour periods are filled in (See Section I: General Policies for specific requirements)
    (1) Give the resident verbal praise
    (2) Give the resident a 10¢ token payment
    (3) Record the appropriate data on the resident's Daily Living Schedule Data Sheet (See Section VII: Daily Living Schedule Data Sheet
  b. When the schedule is *not* completed appropriately (i.e., less than four different ward jobs listed, and/or less than four competitive and/or recreational or leisure activites listed, and/or all half-hour periods are *not* filled in by 8:00 A.M.
    (1) Do not give the resident verbal praise
    (2) Do not give the resident token money payment
    (3) Record the appropriate data on the resident's Daily Living Schedule Data Sheet (See Section VII: Daily Living Schedule Data Sheet
    (4) Restrict the resident to a chair at a table located in the bedroom hall area until he/she completes the schedule appropriately or until 12:00 noon (assistance may be given to him/her if required by the resident)
    (5) While on Daily Living Schedule restriction do *not* allow the following privileges:
        (a) Any activities requiring the resident to leave the hall area (except for the use of the telephone)
        (b) Canteen
        (c) On-ward activities
        (d) Token earning power
        (e) Smoking
        (f) Bedroom area
        (g) Ward jobs
    (6) If the resident completes the schedule appropriately (as defined above) before or by 12:00 noon (but after 8:00 A.M.)
        (a) Give him/her verbal praise
        (b) Do *not* give him/her any token money payment
        (c) Record the appropriate data on his/her Daily Living Schedule Data Sheet (See Section VII: Daily Living Schedule Data Sheet)
2. Engaging in Scheduled Activities
  a. When the resident is observed appropriately engaging in his/her schedule during a variable-interval (VI) observation (See Section: II: Daily Living Schedule Observational System for a description of the VI observation schedule)
    (1) Give the resident verbal praise
    (2) Give the resident a 1¢ token payment
    (3) Record the appropriate data on his/her Observation Schedule Data Sheet
  b. When the resident is observed *not* engaging in his/her scheduled behavior during a variable-interval observation *and* he/she has *not* been excused from engaging in the behavior he/she scheduled
    (1) Do *not* give the resident verbal praise
    (2) Do *not* give the resident any token money payment
    (3) Prompt him/her to engage in the behavior he/she scheduled
    (4) Record the appropriate data on his/her Observation Schedule Data Sheet
    (5) Always use a positive approach
  c. When the resident completes a scheduled behavior prior to the end of a half-hour period for which the behavior was scheduled and prior to a variable-

interval (VI) observation that is to occur during that same half-hour period *and*
   (1) He/she informs his/her assigned/alternate DCS immediately following completion of the behavior
      (a) Give the resident verbal praise
      (b) Give the resident a 1¢ token money payment
      (c) Record the behavior as being met on his/her Observation Schedule Data Sheet for that VI observation (at the time of VI observation)
   NOTE: Resident is to specify how he/she is going to utilize the remaining time in the half-hour period for (a), (b), and (c) above to occur.)
   (2) He/she does *not* inform his/her assigned/alternate DCS immediately following completion of the behavior
      (a) Do *not* give the resident verbal praise
      (b) Do *not* give the resident any token payment
      (c) Remind him/her to report completion of scheduled behaviors if a behavior is completed prior to the end of a half-hour period for which it was scheduled.
      (d) Record the behavior as *not* met on his/her Observation Schedule Data Sheet (at the time of VI observation)
      (e) Always use a positive approach
   d. When the resident states that he/she has completed a scheduled behavior prior to the end of the half-hour period for which the behavior was scheduled and prior to a VI observation that is to occur during that same half-hour *and,* in actuality, he/she did *not* complete the behavior
      (1) Do *not* give the resident verbal praise
      (2) Do not give the resident any token money payment
      (3) Prompt him/her to engage in the behavior he/she scheduled
      (4) Record the behavior as *not* met on his/her Observation Schedule Data Sheet for that VI observation
      (5) Write a progress note in the resident's chart describing the incident
   e. When a token economy participant is observed engaging in an on-ward cooperative and/or competitive recreational or leisure activity (other than those activities indicated on his/her DLS as free), which he/she has not paid (tokens) to participate in, the assigned or alternate DCS is to charge the resident double the standard token charge for that activity. If the resident does not have a sufficient number of tokens to pay the fine (on the first occurrence) the unpaid balance is to be recorded on the residents restitution sheet and he/she is not to be permitted to participate in subsequent recreational and leisure activities (other than the four free activities required by the D.L.S. program) until the balance is paid in full.
D. Saturday and Sunday Specials
   1. Sunday Special - The resident is *not* required to complete the Daily Living Schedule when
      a. He/she has met the weekly Self-Care Skills criterion for the week (Monday through Saturday) (See Self-Care Skills Procedure, p. 41.)
      b. He/she has met the Goal Orientation Procedure criterion every day of the week (Monday through Saturday)
      c. There are no restrictions in effect as a function of individual and/or ward programs and/or inappropriate behavior such as stealing, aggression, or sexual inappropriateness
   2. Saturday Special - The resident is *not* required to complete the Daily Living Schedule on Saturday when
      a. He/she has met the weekly Self-Care Skills criterion for the preceding four consecutive weeks (See Self-Care Skills Procedure, p. 41.)

b. He/she has met the Goal Orientation Procedure Weekly criterion for the preceding four consecutive weeks
c. There are no restrictions in effect as a function of individual and/or ward programs and/or inappropriate behavior such as stealing, agression, or sexual inappropriateness
3. If the resident meets the criteria to engage in a Saturday Special (i.e., Self-Care Skills, Daily Living Schedule, *and* absence of restrictions in effect) and then subsequent to the day of the Saturday Special, he/she fails to meet the Self-Care Skills and/or Daily Living Schedule criteria/criterion to engage in a Saturday Special, he/she may engage in a Saturday Special after meeting the Self-Care Skills *and* Daily Living Schedule criteria for *two* consecutive weeks.
4. When the resident is engaging in a Saturday and/or Sunday Special specify this on the Daily Living Schedule Data Sheet.

VI. Daily Living Schedule Elimination Procedure
   A. Procedure
      1. After the resident has met the Goal Orientation Procedure weekly criterion for eight consecutive weeks
         a. He/she is only required to complete the Daily Living Schedule three days per week (Monday, Wednesday, and Friday)
         b. His/her assigned 3rd shift DCS is to indicate on the resident's Daily Living Schedule Data Sheet that he/she is to complete the Daily Living Schedule on Monday, Wednesday, and Friday by placing a check mark beside each of these days
         c. Continue this procedure until the resident has met the Goal Orientation Procedure weekly criterion for four consecutive weeks.
      2. After the resident has meet the Goal Orientation Procedure weekly criterion for four consecutive weeks of three days per week
         a. He/she is only required to complete the daily Living Schedule two days per week (Tuesday and Friday)
         b. His/her assigned 3rd shift DCS is to indicate on the individual's Daily Living Schedule Data Sheet, that he/she is to complete the Daily Living Schedule on Tuesday and Friday, by placing a check mark beside each of these days.
         c. Continue the above procedure until the individual has met the Goal Orientation Procedure weekly criterion for four consecutive weeks.
      3. After the resident has met the Goal Orientation Procedure weekly criterion for four consecutive weeks of two days per week
         a. He/she is only required to complete the Daily Living Schedule one day per week (Wednesday)
         b. His/her assigned 3rd shift DCS is to indicate on the individual's Daily Living Schedule Data Sheet, that he/she is to complete the Daily Living Schedule on Wednesday, by placing a check mark beside this day
         c. Continue the above procedure until the resident leaves the Level 3 Program
   B. Whenever a resident does *not* meet the Goal Orientation Procedure weekly criterion during the elimination procedure, he/she is to be placed in the elimination step preceding the step he/she is currently in. If he/she is in the first elimination step (i.e., three Daily Living Schedules per week) he/she is to be required to complete the Daily Living Schedule daily until he/she meets the weekly criterion for *two* consecutive weeks before returning to the first elimination step.
   C. Changes in a resident's elimination step (regressions and progressions) are to occur on Wednesday.
   D. Throughout the elimination procedure variable-interval observations of the resident are to continue on a daily basis (Monday through Friday). The observation, data collection, and reinforcement procedures prescribed in Section II: Daily Living Schedule Observational System are to be observed.

1. On days that the resident is required to complete the Daily Living Schedule he/she is to be observed (VI observations) for
   a. Following his/her schedule (✓)
   b. Not following his/her schedule (*X*)
   c. Excused from his/her schedule (*E*)
   d. Engagement in cooperative and/or competitive recreational or leisure activities involving at least one other resident (*A*)
   e. Engagement in ward jobs (*J*)
   f. Engagement in activity isolation (*AI*)
   g. Engagement in isolation (*I*)
   h. Engagement in other (*O*)
2. On days that the resident is *not* required to complete the Daily Living Schedule he/she is to be observed (VI observations) for
   a. Engagement in cooperative and/or competitive recreational or leisure activities involving at least one other individual (A)
   b. Engagement in ward jobs (J)
   c. Engagement in activity isolation (AI)
   d. Engagement in isolation (I)
   e. Engagement in other (O)
E. Daily Living Schedule Elimination Schedule Sheet (See Figure 2-32, p. 148.)
   1. There is to be one Daily Living Schedule Elimination Schedule Sheet displayed in each of the two DCS offices.
   2. On each Daily Living Schedule Elimination Schedule Sheet, the assigned third shift DCS is to record the following:
      a. Name: Record the resident's name (on Tuesday evening).
      b. Step: Record the date on which the resident entered the Level 3 Program and the date on which he/she was placed into a given step.
      c. When the resident moves from one step to another (regression or progression) draw a single line through the date in the previously indicated step. (Changes in the resident's step are to be noted in the ward log book.)
VII. Data Collection
   A. Daily Living Schedule Data Sheet (See Figure 2-33, p. 149.)
      1. There is to be one Daily Living Schedule Data Sheet per resident.
      2. The Daily Living Schedule Data Sheet is to be kept in the resident's Individual Program Book.
      3. Data to be recorded:
         a. The resident's first shift assigned DCS (or alternate, if assigned DCS is not on duty) is to record the following data daily:
            (1) Date: Always record the current date.
               (a) The current date is the date on which the schedule was completed and turned in.
               (b) The date is to be recorded above the day of the week.
               (c) Do *not* skip any dates.
            (2) Ap. Time: Record either a check mark (✓) or an *X*:
               (a) "✓": Record a check mark if the schedule was completed by 8:00 A.M.
               (b) *X*: Record an *X* if the schedule was *not* completed by 8:00 A.M.
            (3) Periods: Record either a check mark (✓) or an *X*:
               (a) "✓": Record a check mark if the resident specified a behavior for every half-hour period on his/her schedule (8:30 A.M. to 9:00 P.M.).
               (b) *X*: Record an *X* if the individual did *not* specify a behavior for every half-hour period on his/her schedule (8:30 A.M. to 9:00 P.M.).
            (4) *A*: Record the number of cooperative and/or competitive recreational or leisure activities the resident recorded on his/her schedule involving *at least* one other resident.

(5) *J*: Record the number of different ward jobs the resident has specified on his/her schedule.

(6) Ap. Comp.: Record either a check mark (✓) or an *X*:
  (a) "✓": Record a check mark if the resident (on the first attempt)
    (i) Completed his/her schedule appropriately by 8:00 A.M.
    (ii) Specified a behavior for every half-hour period (8:30 A.M. to 9:00 P.M.),
    (iii) Specified at least four cooperative and/or competitive recreational and/or leisure activities involving at least one other resident
    (iv) Specified four different ward jobs
  (b) *X*: Record an *X* if the resident did *not* complete (i), (ii), (iii), and (iv) above on the first attempt (exceptions: when he/she is engaging in Saturday and/or Sunday Special and when he/she is excused from writing a schedule).

(7) Ap. Comp. Paid: Record the amount of token money given to the resident for appropriately completing his/her schedule.

b. Third shift DCSs are to record the following data daily (data are to be taken from first and second shift *Observation Schedule Data Sheets*):

  (1) D.T. Met: Record the Daily Total Met (D.T. Met = 1st Shift T. Met *plus* 2d Shift Tot. Met).
  (2) D.T.N. Met: Record the Daily Total Not Met (D.T.N. Met = 1st Shift T. Not Met *plus* 2d Shift T. Not Met).
  (3) D.T. Exc.: Record the Daily Total Excused (D.T. Exc. = 1st Shift T. Exc. *plus* 2d Shift T. Exc.).
  (4) D.T. Observ.: Record the Daily Total number of observations of the resident (D.T. Observ. = 1st Shift Tot. Observ. *plus* 2d Shift Tot. Observ.).
  (5) D. % Met: Record the percent met for the day (D. % Met = D. T. Met *plus* D.T. Excused *divided by* D. T. Observ.).
  (6) D. % N. Met: Record the percent *not* met for the day (D. % N. Met = D.T.N. Met *divided by* D. T. Observ.).
  (7) D. % Exc.: Record the percent excused for the day (D. % Excused = D.T. Exc. *divided by* D. T. Observ.).
  (8) D.T. *A*: Record the Daily Total *A* (D.T. *A* = 1st Shift Tot. *A plus* 2d Shift Tot. *A*).
  (9) D.T. *J*: Record the Daily Total *J* (D.T. *J* = 1st Shift Tot. *J plus* 2d shift Tot. *J*).
  (10) D.T. *AI*: Record the Daily Total *AI* (D.T. *AI* = 1st Shift Tot. *AI plus* 2d Shift Tot. *AI*).
  (11) D.T. *I*: Record the Daily Total *I* (D.T. *I* = 1st Shift Tot. *I plus* 2d Shift Tot. *I*).
  (12) D.T. *O*: Record the Daily Total *O* (D.T. *O* = 1st Shift Tot. *O plus* 2d Shift Tot. *O*).
  (13) D.T. Paid: Record the Daily Total Paid (D.T. Paid = 1st Shift Tot. Observ. Pymnt *plus* 2d Shift Tot. Observ. Pymnt. *plus* Ap. Comp. Paid (on Daily Living Schedule Data Sheet)).
  (14) D. Crit.: Record either a check mark (✓) or an *X*
    (a) "✓": Record a check mark (✓) if the resident
      (i) Appropriately completed his/her schedule for the day on the first attempt (See "Ap. Comp." on Daily Living Schedule Data Sheet)
      (ii) Met at least 90% of his/her schedule (See "Daily % Met" on Daily Living Schedule Data Sheet)
    (b) *X*: Record an *X* if the resident

144 PSYCHIATRIC UNIT PROCEDURES

          (i) Did *not* appropriately complete his/her schedule for the day on the first attempt (See "Ap. Comp." on Daily Living Schedule Data Sheet) unless he/she was excused from completing a schedule or he/she is engaging in a Saturday and/or Sunday Special)

          (ii) Did *not* meet at least 90% of his/her schedule (See "*D. %* Met" on Daily Living Schedule Data Sheet)

    (15) DCS: Record the initials of the third shift DCS recording the data.

B. Daily Living Schedule Weekly Summary Data Sheet (See Figure 2-34, p. 150.)
   1. There is to be one Daily Living Schedule Weekly Summary Table per resident.
   2. The Summary Table is to be located in the resident's Individual Program Book.
   3. The data recorded on the resident's Daily Living Schedule Data Sheet are to be used to complete the resident's Daily Living Schedule Weekly Summary Table.
   4. Data are to be recorded on the Summary Table once each week.
   5. Data are to be recorded by third Shift DCSs on Tuesday evenings.
   6. Data to record:
     (a) Date: Record the date of the last day of the week for which data are being recorded.
     (b) Step: Indicate the step (e.g., Baseline, Treatment, Elimination 1, etc.) the resident was in that week by recording either a *B*, *T*, *E*1, *E*2, or *E*3.
        (1) *B*: Record *B* if the resident was in the baseline period.
        (2) *T*: Record *T* if the resident was in the standard treatment period.
        (3) *31*: Record *E*1 if the resident was in the first step of the elimination procedure.
        (4) *E*2: Record *E*2 if the resident was in the second step of the elimination procedure.
        (5) *E*3: Record *E*3 if the resident was in the third step of the elimination procedure.
     (c) W. Ap. Comp.: Record the total number of times the resident completed his/her schedule appropriately that week.
     (d) W. % Ap. Comp.: Record the percent of schedules that were appropriately completed that week (W. % Ap. Comp. = W. Ap. Comp. *divided by* number of days the schedule should have been written that week).
     (e) W. T. Met: Record the total number of times the resident met his/her schedule that week.
     (f) W.T.N. Met: Record the total number of times the resident did *not* meet his/her schedule that week.
     (g) W.T. Exc.: Record the total number of times the resident was excused from engaging in his/her schedule that week.
     (h) W.T. Observ.: Record the total number of observations of the resident that week.
     (i) W. %. Met: Record the percent met that week (W. % Met = W. T. Met *plus* W.T. Exc. *divided by* W.T. Observ.).
     (j) W. % N. Met: Record the percent *not* met that week (W. % N. Met = W.T.N. Met *divided by* W. T. Observ.).
     (k) W. % Exc.: Record the percent excused that week (%Exc. = W.T. Exc. *divided by* W.T.Observ.).
     (l) W.T. *A*: Record the total number of *A*s recorded for the week.
     (m) W.T. *J*: Record the total number of *J*s recorded for the week.
     (n) W.T. *AI*: Record the total number of *AI*s recorded for the week.
     (o) W.T. *I*: Record the total number of *I*s recorded for the week.
     (p) W.T. *O*: Record the total number of *O*s recorded for the week.
     (q) W.T. Paid: Record the total amount of token money given to the resident that week as a function of the Daily Living Schedule Procedure.

(r) T.D. Crit.: Record the total number of times the daily criterion was met that week.
(s) W. Crit.: Record a check mark (✓) or an *X*:
(1) "✓": Record a check mark (✓) if the resident met the Goal Orientation Procedure Criterion (D. Crit.) every day of the week (exceptions: days on which the resident is engaging in a Saturday and/or Sunday Special and days on which the resident was excused from writing a schedule. See Section V: Saturday and Sunday Specials).
(2) *X*: Record an *X* when the resident did *not* meet the Goal Orientation Procedure Daily Criterion every day of the week that it was required.
(t) DCS: Record the initials of the DCS recording the data.
C. Observation Schedule Data Sheet (See Section II: Daily Living Schedule Observational System)
VIII. Graphing Technique
A. There is to be one Daily Living Schedule graph per resident.
B. The graph is to be located in the resident's Individual Program Book.
C. The data recorded on the resident's Daily Living Schedule Weekly Summary Table are to be used for graphing.
D. Data are to be graphed once each week.
E. Data are to be graphed on Tuesday evenings by third shift DCSs.
F. The following data are to be graphed:
1. W. % Ap. Comp.: Percent of Schedules that were appropriately completed that week (use open circles: ○———○)
2. W. % Met: Percent met that week (use closed circles: ●———●)
3. W.% N. Met: Percent *not* met that week (use open triangles: △———△)
4. W. % Exc.: Percent excused that week (use closed triangles: ▲———▲)

LEVEL 3
D.L.S. OBSERVATIONAL SCHEDULE DATA SHEET
FIRST SHIFT
SCHEDULE #3

DATE:													
TIME	MET (√, X, OR E)	BEHAV (A, J, AI, i OR O)	OBSERV PYMNT	DCS		TIME	MET (√, X, OR E)	BEHAV (A, J, AI, I OR O)	OBSERV PYMNT	DCS			
9:20						12:55							
10:00						1:30							
11:10						2:15							
11:40						2:40							
12:45						2:55							
												Shift Total	DCS
Tot. Met													
Tot. Not Met													
Tot. Exc.													
Tot. Observ													
Tot. "A"													
Tot. "J"													
Tot. "AI"													
Tot. "I"													
Tot. "O"													
Tot. Observ Pymnt													

Figure 2-30

LEVEL 3
D.L.S. OBSERVATION SHEET
SECOND SHIFT
SCHEDULE #1

DATE:													
TIME	MET (√, X, OR E)	BEHAV (A, J, AI, I OR O)	OBSERV PYMNT	DCS		TIME	MET (√, X, OR E)	BEHAV (A, J, AI, I OR O)	OBSERV PYMNT	DCS			
3:45						6:35							
4:20						6:50							
5:20						7:20							
6:10						7:30							
6:15						8:55							
												Shift Total	DCS
Tot. Met													
Tot. Not Met													
Tot. Exc.													
Tot. Observ													
Tot. "A"													
Tot. "J"													
Tot. "AI"													
Tot. "I"													
Tot. "O"													
Tot. Observ Pymnt													

Figure 2-31

LEVEL 3
DAILY LIVING SCHEDULE ELIMINATION SCHEDULE SHEET

CONSECUTIVE WEEKS OF CRITERION REQUIRED			8	4	4	4
STEP	ENTRANCE TO B.E.P.	BASELINE (B)	TREATMENT (T)	ELIMINATION STEP 1 (E 1)	ELIMINATION STEP 2 (E 2)	ELIMINATION STEP 3 (E 3)
NUMBER OF D.L.S.'s REQUIRED/wk	---	---	7*	3	2	1
NAMES						

*Unless resident is engaging in a Saturday and/or Sunday Special

Figure 2-32

LEVEL 3
DAILY LIVING SCHEDULE DATA SHEET

DATE:						NAME:							
	WED.	THURS.	FRI.	SAT.	SUN.	MON.	TUES.						
Ap. Time (√ or X)													
Periods (√ or X)													
"A" (#)													
"J" (#)													
Ap. Comp (√ or X)													
Ap. Comp Paid													
DCS													
D.T. Met													
D.T. Not Met													
D.T. Exc.													
D.T. Observ													
D.% Met													
D.% N.Met													
D.% Exc.													
D.T. "A"													
D.T. "J"													
D.T. "AI"													
D.T. "I"													
D.T. "O"													
D.T. Pd.													
D. Crit.													
DCS													

Figure 2-33

LEVEL 3
DAILY LIVING SCHEDULE WEEKLY SUMMARY DATA SHEET

NAME:													
DATE													
STEP													
W.Ap. Comp													
W. % Ap. Comp													
W.T. Met													
W.T. N.Net													
W.T. Exc.													
W.T. Observ													
W. % Met													
W. % N. Met													
W. % Exc.													
W.T. "A"													
W.T. "J"													
W.T. "AI"													
W.T. "I"													
W.T. "O"													
W.T. Paid													
T.D. Crit.													
W. Crit.													
DCS													

Figure 2-34

LEVEL 3
HOUSEHOLD FINANCIAL MANAGEMENT PROGRAM

GENERAL STATEMENT

One of the skills necessary for independent living in the community is being able to manage household finances. In order to accomplish this task an individual must be able to budget money for food, clothing, housing, and other household expenses. Before an individual can successfully budget for these expenses, however, he/she must possess basic knowledge pertaining to menu planning, grocery shopping, and selecting and maintaining a residence. The Household Financial Management Program has been developed to help residents to acquire and utilize these skills.

PURPOSE

1. To teach money management skills
2. To teach household management skills
3. To help instill a sense of personal independence
4. To teach menu planning skills
5. To increase self-esteem
6. To help reduce stress resulting from financial issues
7. To teach skills needed to find a residence

PROCEDURE

I. General Policies
   A. Household Financial Management (HFM) classes are to be conducted for one hour, two days each week.
      1. Classes are to be held from 10:00 A.M.–11:00 A.M.
      2. Classes are to be held on Tuesdays and Fridays.
      3. Classes are to consist of verbal instruction, group discussion, *in vivo* training, and classroom and homework assignments.
   B. The HFM Program is divided into three units.
   C. A resident may only begin instruction with Unit I (NOTE: A resident may only begin Unit 1 at the beginning of the unit).
   D. A resident is to repeat a unit until he/she meets the criteria specified for the unit (exceptions may be made on an individual basis in Interdisciplinary Treatment Team Conferences).
   E. Individual programs based upon the specific needs of the resident may be developed which supersede the HFM Program.
II. Outline of HFM Program
   A. Unit 1: Menu Planning and Budgeting
      1. Unit 1 Sections
         a. Section 1: Development of a weekly menu
            (1) The basic four food requirements of a balanced diet
            (2) The minimum quantities needed in a balanced diet
            (3) Caloric needs of residents
         b. Section 2: Cost management of food for weekly menu
            (1) Bargain shopping
            (2) Factors to consider when choosing a shopping facility
            (3) Factors to consider when budgeting for food
            (4) Guidelines for planning a grocery shopping list
            (5) Guidelines for grocery shopping

2. Unit 1 Training Outline
3. Unit 1 Teaching Technique
4. Unit 1 Review
5. Unit 1 Criteria
6. Unit 1 Reinforcement
7. Unit 1 Data Collection
B. Unit 2: Living accommodations
 1. Unit 2 Sections
  a. Section 1: Various types of living accommodations
   (1) Factors to consider when choosing a residence (rental)
   (2) Types of residents available
  b. Section 2: Obtaining a residence (rental)
   (1) Means of locating a residence
   (2) Financial costs of residences
   (3) Leases, receipts, and security deposits
 2. Unit 2 Training Outlines
 3. Unit 2 Teaching Technique
 4. Unit 2 Review
 5. Unit 2 Criteria
 6. Unit 2 Reinforcement
 7. Unit 2 Data collection
C. Unit 3: Developing a Budget
 1. Unit 3 Sections
  a. Section 1: Factors to be considered when developing a monthly budget
  b. Section 2: Development of a monthly budget in an independent living situation
 2. Unit 3 Training Outline
 3. Unit 3 Teaching Technique
 4. Unit 3 Review
 5. Unit 3 Criteria
 6. Unit 3 Reinforcement
 7. Unit 3 Data Collection
III. Instructional Procedure
 A. Unit 1: Menu Planning and Budgeting
  1. Unit 1 Sections
   a. Section 1: Development of a weekly menu
   b. Section 2: Cost management of food for a weekly menu
  2. Unit 1 Training Outline
   a. Section 1: Development of a weekly menu
    (1) Menu Components
     (a) Basic four food requirements of a balanced daily diet
      i. Meat/poultry
      ii. Vegetables, fruits
      iii. Grains, bread, cereal
      iv. Dairy products
     (b) Quantities of basic four food requirements needed in a balanced diet
     (c) Caloric needs for residents
      i. Caloric needs to maintain weight
      ii. Caloric needs to lose weight
      iii. Caloric needs to gain weight
   b. Section 2: Cost management of food for weekly menu
    (1) Bargain shopping
     (a) What is a bargain?

LEVEL 3 HOUSEHOLD FINANCIAL MANAGEMENT PROGRAM

  (b) How to find bargains?
    i. Advertisements
    ii. Price—compare various stores
 (2) Factors to consider when choosing shopping facility
  (a) Convenience of shopping
  (b) Transportation costs
  (c) Variety and items available
  (d) Frequency of sales: store-advertised and newspaper-advertised bargains
  (e) Costs of items most frequently purchased
 (3) Factors to consider when budgeting for food
  (a) Amount earned
  (b) Special diet requirements
  (c) Convenience foods
  (d) Restaurants
  (e) Other living expenses
 (4) Guidelines for planning a grocery shopping list
  (a) Look for advertised bargains
  (b) Plan weekly menu
  (c) Check pantry and refrigerator for needed items
  (d) List food according to categories
 (5) Guidelines for grocery shopping
  (a) Plan menus for at least one week, preferably for same number of days between paydays (i.e., if paid monthly plan menu for one month, if paid weekly plan menu for 7 days).
  (b) Stick to grocery list.
  (c) Avoid impulse buying.
  (d) Never shop for groceries when hungry.
  (e) Write price next to item and keep running total as a means to help stay within your budget and for price comparison.
3. Unit 1 Teaching Technique
 a. Section 1: Development of weekly menu
  (1) Basic four food requirements of a balanced daily diet
   (a) The instructor and class are to discuss the basic four food requirements needed in a balanced diet.
   (b) The instructor is to present and discuss the Basic Four Food Requirements Chart. (Form HFM-BFFR) (See Table 2-2, p. 170)
   (c) The instructor and class are to review and discuss filmstrip entitled *You Are What You Eat* (New York: Communications in Learning, Inc., #339921) (Film is located in the Dietary Office).
   (d) The instructor and class are to discuss reasons for inclusion of the basic four foods in a daily menu.
   (e) Classroom Assignment 1-1 (HFM CA1-U1S1)
    i. Each resident is to list and categorize on the Daily Food Consumption Form (form HFM-DFC) (See Figure 2-35, p. 171), the meals and snacks he/she actually consumed during the preceding day (breakfast, lunch, supper, and snacks).
    ii. The instructor and class are to discuss and compare each resident's completed Daily Food Consumption Form.
    iii. The instructor and class are to discuss and compare each resident's completed Daily Food Consumption Form.
    iv. Each resident's Daily Food Consumption Form is to be given to the instructor at the end of the class period.

v. The instructor is to evaluate and record percent accurate completion (See Unit 1 Data Collection).
vi. The criterion for Classroom Assignment 1-1 is 75% accuracy.
vii. The assignment is to be returned to resident at the next class period.
viii. The instructor is to discuss the results of the assignment with the class.

(2) Quantities of basic four requirements needed in a balanced diet.
 (a) The instructor is to discuss quantities needed to meet minimum basic four food requirements utilizing the Basic Four Food Requirements Chart (Form HFM-BFFR) and the Basic Four Food Requirements Quantities Chart. (Form HFM-BFFRQ) (See Table 2-3, p. 172.)
 (b) The instructor and class are to collectively develop one complete daily menu (breakfast, lunch, supper), utilizing the Basic Four Food Requirements Chart and the Basic Four Food Requirements Quantities Chart.
 (c) The instructor is to randomly select residents to suggest food items to be included in the daily menu. Responses should include:
  i. Specification of meal for which food items is/are being suggested
  ii. Categorization of each food item
  iii. Needed quantity of each food item to meet minimum food requirements
 (d) The instructor and the class are to discuss the daily menu developed by the class
 (e) The instructor and class are to develop three complete daily menus (for three consecutive days) utilizing the Basic Four Food Requirements Chart *and* the Basic Four Food Requirements Quantities Chart
  i. The daily menus are to consist of breakfast, lunch, supper for each of the three days.
  ii. The instructor is to randomly select residents to suggest food items to be included in the menus. Responses should include:
   (i) Specification of meals for which each food item is being suggested
   (ii) Categorization of each food item utilizing the Basic Four Food Requirements Chart
   (iii) Needed quantity of each food item to meet minimum food requirements utilizing the Basic Four Food Requirements Quantities Chart
  iii. The instructor and class are to discuss the three daily menus collectively developed by the class.
 (f) Homework Assignment 1-1 (HFM HA1-U1S1)
  i. One Basic Four Food Requirements Chart and one Basic Four Food Requirements Quantities Chart is to be posted on the bulletin board in the Activity Room.
  ii. Each resident is to independently develop three complete daily menus utilizing the Basic Four Food Requirements Chart *and* the Basic Four Food Requirements Quantities Chart on the Menu Food Plan form. (See Figure 2-36, p. 173.)
  iii. The daily menus are to consist of breakfast, lunch, and supper for each of the three days.

iv. Each resident is to specify the meal for which each food item is being suggested on the Menu Food Plan form.
v. Each resident is to categorize each food item on the form, utilizing the Basic Four Food Requirements Chart.
vi. Each resident is to list needed quantity of each food item to meet minimum food requirements
vii. Each resident is to turn in assignment at the next class period.
viii. The instructor is to evaluate and record percent accurate completion (See Unit 1 Data Collection).
ix. The criterion for Homework Assignment 1-1 is 75% accuracy.
x. The assignment is to be returned to resident at the next class period.
xi. The instructor is to discuss the results of the assignment with the class.

(3) Caloric needs of residents
  (a) The instructor is to discuss caloric needs of resident with attention given to the following factors:
    i. Caloric needs to maintain weight
    ii. Caloric needs to lose weight
    iii. Caloric needs to gain weight
  (b) The instructor is to present and discuss a calorie chart.

(4) Classroom Assignment 1-2 (HFM CA2-U1S1)
  (a) Each resident is to develop three complete daily menus on the Menu Food Plan form without the aide of the Basic Four Food Requirements Chart *but* with the aide of a calorie chart.
  (b) Each resident is to specify the mean for which food item is being suggested.
  (c) Each resident is to categorize each food according to the Basic Four Food Requirements Chart.
  (d) Each resident is to list needed quantities of each food item to meet minimum food requirements.
  (e) Each resident is to list number of calories for each food item listed on his/her menu utilizing a calorie chart.
  (f) Assignments are to be turned in to the instructor at the end of the class.
  (g) The instructor is to evaluate and record percent accurate completion (See Unit 1 Data Collection).
  (h) The criterion for Classroom Assignment 1-2 is 75% accuracy.
  (i) The assignment is to be returned to resident at the next class period.
  (j) The instructor is to discuss the results of the assignment with the class.

(5) Classroom Assignment 1-3 (HFM CH3-U1S1)
  (a) The instructor and class are to collectively develop a seven day menu on the Menu Food Plan Form.
  (b) The menu is to consist of seven breakfast, seven lunch, and seven supper meals
  (c) Each resident is to state the quantity of each food serving listed on the menu without the aide of the Basic Four Food Requirements Chart.
  (d) Each resident is to categorize each food listed on the menu without the Basic Four Food Requirements Chart.
  (e) Each resident is to specify number of calories for each food serving listed on the menu utilizing a calorie chart.

(f) Assignment is to be turned in to the instructor at the end of the class.
(g) The instructor is to evaluate and record percent accurate completion (See Unit 1 Data Collection).
(h) The criterion for Classroom Assignment 1-3 is 75% accuracy.
(i) The assignment is to be returned to resident at the next class period.
(j) The instructor is to discuss the results of the assignment with the class.

(6) Homework Assignment 1-2 (HFM HA2-U1S1)
  (a) Each resident is to develop a weekly menu on the Menu Food Plan Form.
  (b) Each resident is to list the quantity of each food serving listed on his/her menu with the aide of the Basic Four Food Requirements Chart.
  (c) Each resident is to categorize each food listed on his/her menu with the aide of the Basic Four Food Requirements Chart.
  (d) Each resident is to list number of calories for each food serving listed on his/her menu with the aide of a calorie chart.
  (e) Assignment is to be turned in by 12:00 noon the following day to his/her assigned/alternate DCS.
  (f) The instructor is to evaluate and record percent accurate completion (See Unit 1 Data Collection).
  (g) The criterion for Homework Assignment 1-2 is 75% accuracy.
  (h) The assignment is to be returned to resident at the next class period.
  (i) The instructor is to discuss the results of the assignment with the class.

b. Section 2: Cost management of food for weekly menu
  (1) Factors to consider when bargain shopping
    (a) The instructor and class are to discuss bargain shopping with consideration given to the following factors:
      i. Do you like item on sale?
      ii. Amount of waste, i.e., bones, liquid, etc.
      iii. Distance of store from home
    (b) The instructor and class are to discuss how to find bargains.
      i. Newspaper
      ii. TV, radio
      iii. Friends
      iv. Price-compare various newspaper advertisements
  (2) Factors to consider when choosing a shopping facility
    (a) The instructor and class are to discuss the following factors when choosing a shopping facility:
      i. Convenience of shopping facility to home and/or work
      ii. Transportation costs
        (i) Do you own a car?
        (ii) If so, what is the cost of gas?
        (iii) What is the cost of public transportation (i.e., taxi, bus)?
        (vi) If walking, how are you going to transport groceries?
      iii. Variety and quality of items available
        (i) Does the store carry the preferred cuts and brands of meats?
        (ii) Are the fruits and vegetables fresh?
        (iii) Does the store carry specialty items?
      iv. How frequently are bargains advertised in the store and/or newspaper?
      v. What is the cost of items most frequently purchased?

(3) Factors to consider when budgeting for food
   (a) The instructor and class are to discuss the following factors when budgeting for food:
      i. Do you have special diet requirements?
      ii. Does your schedule require convenience foods?
      iii. If so, how costly are they?
      iv. How costly is eating out?
      v. What are your other living expenses?
      vi. Is the grocery allowance within 10% to 25% of net pay?
(4) Guidelines for planning a grocery shopping list
   (a) The instructor and the class are to discuss and collectively plan a grocery shopping list, utilizing the Menu Food Plan Form and the Grocery Shopping List Form (Form HFM-GSL). (See Figure 2-37, p. 174.) The following guidelines are to be used:
      i. Shopping for a seven day weekly menu shopping list.
      ii. Look for advertised bargains in newspaper.
      iii. Check pantry and refrigerator for needed items.
      iv. List food according to categories.
   (b) Classroom Assignment 1-4 (HFM CA4-U1S2)
      i. Each resident is to plan a seven day weekly menu shopping list, utilizing the Menu Food Plan Form and the Grocery Shopping List Form.
      ii. Each resident is to list food according to categories on the Menu Food Plan Form (meat, vegetables, dairy products, bread-cereal).
      iii. Each resident is to indicate number of meals the listed food item is to serve on the Grocery Shopping List Form.
      iv. Each resident is to list prices of desired food items advertised in newspaper on the Grocery Shopping List Form.
      v. Each resident is to list projected prices of desired food items not advertised in newspaper on the Grocery Shopping List Form.
      vi. Each resident is to total cost of all items.
      vii. Each resident's shopping list total is to be within 10% to 25% of a weekly *net* earning of $150.00.
      viii. The instructor is to evaluate and record percent accurate completion (See Unit 1 Data Collection).
      ix. The criterion for Classroom Assignment 1-4 is at least a 75% level of accuracy.
      x. The assignment is to be returned to resident at the next class period.
      xi. The instructor is to discuss the results of the assignment with the class.
(5) Fieldtrip Assignment 1-1 (HFM FTA1-U1S2)
   (a) The instructor and class are to plan a group dinner meal for the class.
   (b) The meal is not to cost more than $2.00 per person.
   (c) The meal is to include the basic four food requirements of a balanced meal.
   (d) The class is to prepare a shopping list by utilizing the Grocery Shopping List Form and by
      i. Looking for advertised bargains in the newspaper
      ii. Listing food according to categories utilizing the Menu Food Plan Form

158 PSYCHIATRIC UNIT PROCEDURES

- iii. Listing food costs as advertised in paper and store in which they are advertised
- (e) The class is to purchase the food. (The instructor is to arrange transportation, if necessary.)
- (f) The class is to prepare the food.
  - i. The instructor is to assign the various preparation tasks to residents.
  - ii. The instructor is to assign the various cooking tasks to residents.
  - iii. The instructor is to assign the kitchen cleanup tasks to residents.
  - iv. The class is to eat the meal.
  - v. The instructor is to evaluate and record percent participation (See Unit 1 Data Collection).
  - vi. The criterion for Fieldtrip Assignment 1 is at least a 75% level of participation.

4. Unit 1 Review
   a. Sections to be reviewed
      (1) Section 1: Development of a weekly menu
      (2) Section 2: Cost management of food for a weekly menu
   b. Teaching Technique
      The instructor and class are to review and discuss the sections of the unit.
5. Unit 1 Criteria
   a. Completion of each Unit 1 classroom assignment with *at least* a 75% level of accuracy.
   b. Completion of each Unit 1 homework assignment with *at least* a 75% level of accuracy
   c. Completion of the Fieldtrip Assignment with *at least* a 75% level of participation.
   d. Attendance at a minimum of 90% of the classes conducted on this unit (unless excused from class).
6. Unit 1 Reinforcement
   a. When a resident attends a class
      (1) Give him/her verbal praise
      (2) Give him/her a 10¢ token money payment
   b. When a resident appropriately completes a Unit 1 classroom assignment (*at least* 75% level of accuracy)
      (1) Give him/her verbal praise
      (2) Give him/her a 10¢ token money payment
   c. When a resident appropriately completes a Unit 1 homework assignment (*at least* 75% level of accuracy)
      (1) Give him/her verbal praise
      (2) Give him/her a 25¢ token money payment
   d. When a resident meets the Unit 1 criteria:
      (1) Give him/her verbal praise
      (2) Give him/her a 50¢ token money payment
7. Unit 1 Data Collection
   a. There is to be one Household Financial Management Program Unit 1 Data Sheet (See Figure 2-38, p. 175.) per resident.
   b. If a resident needs to repeat Unit 1 of the Household Financial Management Program, a new data sheet is to be used.
   c. The data sheet is to be kept in the resident's Individual Program Book.
   d. The class instructor and/or the staff member who evaluates an assignment is to record the data.
   e. Data to be recorded:

(1) Name: Record the name of the resident.
(2) Course: Record whether the resident is enrolled in Unit 1 of the Household Financial Management Program for the first, second, third, etc., time.
(3) Date: Record the date on which the resident attended a class, completed an assignment, etc.
(4) Class Attend.: Record either a check mark (✓), an *X,* or an *E.*
   (a) "✓": Record a check mark (✓) each time the resident attends a Household Financial Management Program Unit 1 Class (Also, record the date in the "Date" column and a slash (i.e., 1 = 1; 2 = 11; 3 = 111; 4 = 1111; 5 = 1111; etc.) in the "Total Number" row for each occurrence.)
   (b) *X:* Record an *X* each time a Household Financial Management Program class was conducted on Unit 1 and the resident did not attend. (Also, record the date in the "Date" column.)
   (c) *E:* Record an *E* when a Household Financial Management Program class was conducted on Unit 1 and the resident was excused from attending.
(5) Class. Assign. 1-1: Record the percent level of accuracy achieved by the resident on Unit 1 Classroom Assignment 1-1. Percent accuracy is determined by calculating the following:
   (a) Score one point for each meal for which food is listed (three possible points).
   (b) Score two points for each *category* (per meal) for which food is accurately categorized (24 possible points: two points × three meals × four categories).
   (c) Calculate total number of points earned by the resident (27 possible points).
   (d) Divide the total number of points earned by the total possible points (27). The resulting figure is the percent level of accuracy achieved.
(6) Home. Assign. 1-1: Record the percent level of accuracy achieved by the resident on Unit 1 Homework Assignment 1-1. Percent level of accuracy is determined by calculating the following:
   (a) Score one point for each meal for which food is listed (nine possible points: one point × three meals × three days).
   (b) Score two points for each *category* (per meal) in which food is accurately categorized (72 possible points: two points × three meals × four categories × three days).
   (c) Score two points for each *quantity* (per day and category) that is accurately specified (24 possible points: two points × three days × four categories)
   (d) Calculate total number of points earned by the resident (105 possible points: 9 + 72 + 24).
   (e) Divide the total number of points earned by the total possible points (105). The resulting figure is the percent level accuracy achieved.
(7) Class. Assign. 1-2: Record the percent level of accuracy achieved on Class Assignment 1-2. Percent level of accuracy is determined by calculating the following:
   (a) Score one point for each meal for which food is listed (nine possible points: one point × three meals × three days).
   (b) Score two points for each *category* (per meal) for which food is accurately categorized (72 possible points: two points × three meals × four categories × three days).

(c) Score two points for each *quantity* (per category and day) that is accurately specified (24 possible points: two points × three days × four categories).
(d) Score two points for each *number of calories* (per category and day) accurately specified (24 possible points: two points × three days × four categories).
(e) Calculate the total number of points earned by the resident (129 possible points: 9 + 72 + 24 + 24).
(f) Divide the total number of points earned by the total possible points (129). The resulting figure is the percent level of accuracy achieved.

(8) Class. Assign. 1-3: Record the percent level of accuracy achieved by the resident on Unit 1 Classroom Assignment 1-3. Percent level of accuracy is determined by calculating the following:
  (a) Score one point for each meal for which food is listed (21 possible points: one point × three meals × seven days).
  (b) Score two points for each *category* (per meal) for which food is accurately categorized. (168 possible points: two points × three meals × four categories × seven days).
  (c) Score two points for each *quantity* (per category and day) that is accurately specified (56 possible points: two points × four categories × seven days).
  (d) Score two points for each *number of calories* (per category and day) accurately specified (56 possible points: two points × seven days × four categories).
  (e) Calculate the total number of points earned by the resident (301 possible points: 21 + 168 + 56 + 56).
  (f) Divide the total number of points earned by the total possible points (301). The resulting figure is the percent level of accuracy achieved.

(9) Home Assign. 1-2: Record the percent level of accuracy achieved by the resident on Unit 1 Homework Assigned 1-2. Percent level of accuracy is determined by calculating the following:
  (a) Score one point for each meal for which food is listed (21 possible points: one point × three meals × seven days).
  (b) Score two points for each *category* (per meal) for which food is accurately categorized (168 possible points: two points × three meals × four categories × seven days).
  (c) Score two points for each *quantity* (per category and day) that is accurately specified (56 possible points: two points × four categories × seven days).
  (d) Score two points for each *number of calories* (per category and day) accurately specified (56 possible points: two points × seven days × four categories).
  (e) Calculate the total number of points earned by the resident (301 possible points: 21 + 168 + 56 + 56).
  (f) Divide the total number of points earned by the total possible points (301). The resulting figure is the percent level of accuracy achieved.

(10) Classroom Assignment 1-4: Record the percent level of accuracy achieved by the resident on Unit 1 Classroom Assignment 1-4. Percent level of accuracy is determined by calculating the following:
  (a) Score one point for each meal for which food is listed (21 possible points: one point × three meals × seven days).
  (b) Score one point for each *category* (per meal) for which food is accurately categorized (84 possible points: one point × three meals × four categories × seven days).

(c) Score two points for each price listed for each food item (168 possible points: two points × three meals × four categories × seven days).

(d) Score seven points if resident accurately totals the cost of all food items.

(e) Score twenty points if the total cost of all the food items is within 10% to 25% of weekly *net* earning of $150.00.

(f) Calculate the total number of points earned by the resident (300 possible points: 21 + 84 + 168 + 7 + 20).

(g) Divide the total number of points earned by the total possible points (300). The resulting figure is the percent level of accuracy achieved.

(11) Fieldtrip Assignment 1: Record the percent level of participation by the resident in the Unit 1 Fieldtrip Assignment 1. Percent level of participation is determined by calculating the following:

(a) Score 25 points if the resident assisted in preparing the shopping list. (25 points).

(b) Score 25 points if the resident assisted in shopping for food (25 points).

(c) Score 25 points if the resident assisted in preparation of food (25 points).

(d) Score 25 points if the resident assisted in clean-up of kitchen (25 points).

(e) Calculate total number of points earned by the resident (100 possible points).

(f) Divide the total number of points earned by the total possible points (100). The resulting figure is the percent level of participation.

(12) Staff: Record the initials of the staff member recording the data.

(13) Comments: Record any comments relevant to the recorded data.

(14) Total #✓s: Record a slash mark (i.e., 1 = 1, 2 = 11, 3 = 111, 4 = 1111, 5 = 1111, etc.) in the appropriate column each time the resident attends class and/or attempts an assignment. (Attempts are to be recorded whether the resident is successful *or* not successful.)

(15) Crit.: Record either a check mark (✓), X, or an L:

(a) "✓": Record a check mark (✓) in the appropriate column if the resident met the specified criterion for class attendance (crit. = 90%), a classroom assignment (crit. = 75%), a homework assignment (crit. = 75%), and/or the fieldtrip assignment (crit. = 75%).

(b) *X:* Record an X in the appropriate column if the resident did *not* meet the criterion for class attendance, a classroom assignment, a homework assignment, and/or the fieldtrip assignment.

(c) *L:* Record an L in the appropriate column if the resident met the specified criterion for a classroom assignment, a homework assignment, and/or the fieldtrip assignment but turned it/them in late.

(16) Unit 1 Crit.: Record either a check mark (✓) or an X:

(a) "✓": Record a check mark (✓) if the resident

  i. Attended *at least* 90% of the classes conducted on Unit 1 (excluding times when the resident was excused from class)

  ii. Completed each of the classroom assignments with *at least* a 75% level of accuracy

  iii. Completed each of the homework assignments with *at least* a 75% level of accuracy

iv. Participated in the fieldtrip assignment *at least* a 75% level of participation
    (b) *X:* Record an *X* if the resident did *not*
        i. Attend *at least* 90% of the classes conducted on Unit 1 (excluding times when the resident was excused from class).
        ii. Complete each of the classroom assignments with *at least* a 75% level of accuracy.
        iii. Complete each of the homework assignments with *at least* a 75% level of accuracy.
        iv. Participate in the fieldtrip assignment with *at least* a 75% level of participation.
B. Unit 2: Living Accommodations
    1. Unit 2 Sections
        a. Section 1: Various types of living accommodations (rental)
        b. Section 2: Obtaining a residence (rental)
    2. Unit 2 Training Outline
        a. Section 1: Various types of living accommodations (rental)
            (1) Factors to consider when choosing a residence (rental):
                (a) The various population sizes of communities (e.g., urban vs. rural areas) and living accommodations (e.g., small vs. large apartment complex)
                (b) The location of the residence
                (c) The type of neighbors available
                (d) The availability of transportation
                (e) Utilities
                (f) Services offered by the landlord
                (g) The physical condition of the facility
            (2) Types of residences available
        b. Section 2: Obtaining a residence (rental)
            (1) Means of locating a residence
            (2) Financial costs of residences
            (3) Leases, receipts, and security deposits
    3. Unit 2 Teaching Techniques
        a. Section 1: Various types of living accommodations
            (1) The instructor and class are to discuss advantages/disadvantages of various population sizes of communities (e.g., suburban vs. rural areas) and of living accommodations (e.g., small vs. large apartment complex).
            (2) The instructor and class are to discuss the following factors concerning selecting a residence:
                (a) The distance from employment
                (b) The distance from shopping areas
                (c) The distance from recreational facilities
                (d) The distance from church
                (e) The availability of transportation
                (f) Furnished versus unfurnished
                (g) Utilities
                    i. The types of utilities
                    ii. The cost of utilities
                    iii. Steps necessary to obtain utilities
                    iv. Deposits necessary to obtain utilities
                (h) Services offered by the landlord
                    i. Plumbing repairs
                    ii. Electrical repairs

LEVEL 3 HOUSEHOLD FINANCIAL MANAGEMENT PROGRAM

    iii. Replacement of fixture, flooring, etc.
    iv. Landscaping upkeep
    v. Painting
   (i) The physical condition of the facility
  (3) The instructor and class are to discuss the advantages/disadvantages of the following types of living accommodations:
   (a) Single room dwelling house
   (b) Boarding house
   (c) Furnished Apartment (furnished vs. not furnished)
   (d) Efficiency apartment
   (e) Trailer
   (f) Low income housing (sliding scale rent)
   (g) Subsidized independent living situation (e.g., mental health sponsorship)
 b. Section 2: Obtaining a living accommodation
  (1) The instructor and class are to discuss means of locating a residence:
   (a) Friends
   (b) Fellow workers
   (c) Advertisements in newspapers
   (d) Family
   (e) Real estate agent
  (2) The instructor and class are to discuss financial costs for renting a residence:
   (a) The amount of rent
    The amount of rent (not including cost of utilities) should not exceed ⅓ of monthly net salary.
   (b) The frequency of rent
    i. Monthly
    ii. Bi-monthly
    iii. Weekly
    iv. Daily
  (3) The instructor and class are to discuss leases, receipts and security deposits with consideration given to the following factors:
   (a) Leases
    i. What is a lease?
    ii. Information found in a lease:
     (i) Rate and amount of rent
     (ii) The duration of the lease
      ((i)) Thirty day notice by either party
      ((ii)) One year
     (iii) The terms of the lease
      ((i)) Responsibilities of the landlord (e.g., lawn care, plumbing utilities)
      ((ii)) Responsibilities of the renter (e.g., date rent is due, pets)
     (iv) Any additional agreements between the landlord and the renter (e.g., guests, parking)
   (b) Receipts
    i. What is a receipt?
    ii. Reasons for receipts:
     (i) Tax record
     (ii) Proof of payment
     (iii) Information found in a receipt
      ((i)) The current date

((ii)) The amount paid
((iii)) The signature of the individual receiving payment
((iv)) The name of the individual making payment
 (c) Security Deposits
  i. Definition of a security deposit:
   A specified amount of money required in addition to first rent payment.
  ii. Purpose of a security deposit:
   To cover cost to repair any damages to dwelling that were not the result of expected wear.
  iii. Amount of security deposit:
   Generally, a security deposit is equivalent to the rent amount for one month. However, there frequently is an additional charge if the renter has a pet(s).
  iv. Conditions necessary to receive a security deposit refund:
   (i) Renter must give advance notice of vacating the residence.
   (ii) The renter must leave the residence clean and undamaged.
   (iii) Additional conditions may be specified in rental lease.
(4) Classroom Assignment 2-5 (HFM CA5-U2S1)
 (a) Each resident is to compose a statement (written) describing his/her preferences and needs concerning a residence, and the factors to be considered when selecting a residence. The statement is to address at least the following:
  i. Population size of community and residence
  ii. Distance of residence from employment
  iii. Distance of residence from recreational facilities
  iv. Distance of residence from shopping areas
  v. Transportation
  vi. Furnished versus unfurnished
  vii. Utilities
  viii. Services offered by landlord
  ix. Physical condition of residence
 (b) Each resident's statement is to be given to the instructor at the end of the class period.
 (c) The instructor is to evaluate and record the percent accurate completion (See Unit 2 Data Collection).
 (d) The criterion for classroom Assignment 2-5 is at least a 75% level of accuracy.
 (e) The resident's assignment is to be returned to him/her at the next class period.
 (f) The instructor is to discuss the results of the assignment with the class.

4. Unit 2 Review
 a. Sections to be reviewed
  (1) Section 1: Various types of living accommodations (rental)
  (2) Section 2: Obtaining a residence (rental)
 b. Teaching Technique
  The instructor and class are to review and discuss the sections of the unit.
5. Unit 2 Criteria
 a. Completion of the Unit 2 classroom assignment with *at least* a 75% level of accuracy.
 b. Attendance at a minimum of 90% of the classes conducted on this unit (unless excused from class).

6. Unit 2 Reinforcement
   a. When a resident attends a class
      (1) Give him/her verbal praise
      (2) Give him/her a 10¢ token money payment
   b. When a resident appropriately completes the Unit 2 Classroom assignment (*at least* 75% level of accuracy)
      (1) Give him/her verbal praise
      (2) Give him/her a 10¢ token money payment
   c. When a resident meets the Unit 2 criteria
      (1) Give him/her verbal praise
      (2) Give him/her a 50¢ token money payment
7. Unit 2 Data Collection
   a. There is to be one Household Financial Management (HFM) Program Unit 2 Data Sheet per resident. (See Figure 2-39, p. 176.)
   b. If a resident needs to repeat Unit 2 of the Money Management Program, a new data sheet is to be used.
   c. The data sheet is to be kept in the resident's Individual Program Book.
   d. The class instructor and/or the staff member who evaluates an assignment is to record the data.
   e. Data to be recorded:
      (1) Name: Record the name of the resident.
      (2) Course: Record whether the resident is enrolled in Unit 2 of the HFM Program for the first, second, third, etc., time.
      (3) Date: Record the date on which the resident attended a class, completed an assignment, etc.
      (4) Class Attend.: Record either a check mark (✓), an *X*, or an *E*.
         (a) "✓": Record a check mark (✓) each time the resident attends a HFM Program Unit 2 class. (Also, record the date in the "Date" column and a slash (i.e., 1 = l; 2 = ll; 3 = lll; 4 = llll; 5 = ℍℍ; etc.) in the "Total Number" row, for each occurrence.)
         (b) *X:* Record an *X* each time a HFM Program class was conducted on Unit 2 and the resident did not attend. (Also, record the date in the "Date" column.)
         (c) *E:* Record an *E* when a HFM Program class was conducted on Unit 2 and the resident was excused from attending.
      (5) Class. Assign. 2-5: Record the percent level of accuracy achieved by the resident on Classroom Assignment 2-5. Percent level of accuracy is determined by calculating the following:
         (a) Score 10 points if population size preference is specified.
         (b) Score 10 points if distance of residence from employment is specified, *or* if resident indicates that this is not relevant because he/she will not be employed.
         (c) Score 10 points if distance of residence from recreational facility(ies) is specified.
         (d) Score 10 points if distance of residence from shopping area(s) is specified.
         (e) Score 10 points if means of transportation (i.e., bus, taxi, personal vehicle, etc.) is specified.
         (f) Score 10 points if furnished versus not furnished preference is specified.
         (g) Score 10 points if method of obtaining utilities is specified.
         (h) Score 10 points if the services offered by landlord are specified.
         (i) Score 10 points if the condition of residence is specified.

(j) Calculate the total number of points earned by the resident (90 possible points: 10 × 9).
(k) Divide the total number of points earned by the total possible points (90). The resulting figure is the percent accurately achieved.
(6) Staff: Record the initials of the staff member recording the data.
(7) Comments: Record any comments relevant to the recorded data.
(8) Total #✓s: Record a slash mark (i.e., 1 = 1; 2 = 11; 3 = 111; 4 = 1111; 5 = 1111, etc.) in the appropriate column each time the resident attends class and/or attempts an assignment. (Attempts are to be recorded whether the resident is successful or not successful.)
(9) Crit.: Record either a check mark (✓), an *X*, or an *L*:
   (a) "✓": Record each check mark (✓) in the appropriate column if the resident met the specified criterion for class attendance (crit. ≥ 90%) and/or the Unit 2 classroom assignment (crit. ≥ 75%).
   (b) *X*: Record an *X* in the appropriate column if the resident did *not* meet the specified criterion for class attendance and/or the Unit 2 classroom assignment.
   (c) *L*: Record an *L* in the appropriate column if the resident met the specified criterion for the Unit 2 classroom assignment (crit. ≥ 75%) but turned it in late.
(10) Unit 2 Crit.: Record either a check mark (✓) or an *X*:
   (a) "✓": Record a check mark (✓) if the resident
      i. Attended *at least* 90% of the classes conducted on Unit 2 (excluding times when the resident was excused from class)
      ii. Completed the Unit 2 classroom assignment with *at least* a 75% level of accuracy
   (b) *X*: Record a *X* if the resident did *not*
      i. Attend *at least* 90% of the classes conducted on Unit 2 (excluding times when the resident was excused from attending class)
      ii. Complete the Unit 2 classroom assignment with *at least* a 75% level of accuracy

C. Unit 3: Developing a budget
  1. Unit 3 Sections
     a. Section 1: Steps to be observed when developing a monthly budget
     b. Section 2: Development of a monthly budget in an independent living situation
  2. Training Outline
     a. Section 1: Steps to be observed when developing a monthly budget
        (1) Review spending habits
        (2) Determine month's needs and expenses
        (3) Develop first draft of budget
        (4) Review and adjust budget, if necessary
     b. Section 2: Development of a monthly budget in an independent living situation
        (1) Determining projected costs
        (2) Development of budget
  3. Unit 3 Teaching Technique
     a. Section 1: Factors to be considered when developing a monthly budget
        (1) The instructor and class are to discuss developing a budget with consideration given to the following factors:
           (a) Monthly expenses
              i. Rent (25% to 33.3% of net monthly income)
              ii. Food (10% to 25% of net monthly income)

iii. Transportation
    (i) Gas and oil for personal automobile
    (ii) Automobile repairs
    (iii) Public transportation
iv. Clothing
v. Toiletries
vi. Insurance
    (i) Health
    (ii) Life
    (iii) Automobile
vii. Loan Payments
    (i) Personal
    (ii) Automobile
    (iii) Credit cards
viii. Taxes
    (i) Property
    (ii) Income
    (iii) Other
ix. Household operating expenses
    (i) Telephone
    (ii) Utilities (e.g., electricity, gas, water)
    (iii) Supplies (e.g., cleaning supplies, light bulbs)
x. Entertainment
xi. Medical and dental expenses not covered by insurance
xii. Miscellaneous expenses
          (b) Monthly net pay (take-home pay)
    b. Section 2: Development of a monthly budget in an independent living situation
      (1) The instructor and class are to develop a monthly budget with consideration given to the factors discussed in Section 1.
      (2) The Monthly Budget Form (Form MM-MB) (See Figure 2-40, p. 177) is to be utilized to develop the budget.
      (3) Homework Assignment 3-3 (HFM HFM HA3-U3S3)
        (a) Each resident is to develop one monthly budget utilizing the Monthly Budget Form. (Form MM-MB, p. 177.)
        (b) An entry is to be made for every expense item on the Monthly Budget Form (Note: If there is no expense for a given item, the resident is to record a 0.
        (c) Each resident is to base his/her monthly budget on a monthly net income of $600.00.
        (d) Each resident is to turn in the completed assignment at the next class period.
        (e) The instructor is to evaluate the assignment and record the % accurate completion (See Unit 3 Data Collection section).
        (f) The criterion for the assignment is at least a 75% level of accuracy.
        (g) The evaluated assignment is to be returned to the resident.
        (h) The instructor is to discuss the results of the assignment with the resident.
4. Unit 3 Review
    a. Sections to be reviewed
      (1) Section 1: Steps to be observed when developing a monthly budget
      (2) Section 2: Development of a monthly budget in an independent living situation

168 PSYCHIATRIC UNIT PROCEDURES

    b. Teaching Technique
       The instructor and class are to review the sections of the unit.
5. Unit 3 Criteria
    a. Completion of the Unit 2 homework assignment with *at least* a 75% level of accuracy.
    b. Attendance at a minimum of 90% of the classes conducted on this unit (unless excused from class).
6. Unit 3 Reinforcement
    a. When a resident attends a class
       (1) Give him/her verbal praise
       (2) Give him/her a 10¢ token money payment
    b. When a resident appropriately completes the unit classroom assignment (*at least* 75% level of accuracy)
       (1) Give him/her verbal praise
       (2) Give him/her a 50¢ token money payment
7. Unit 3 Data Collection
    a. There is to be one Household Financial Management Program Unit 3 Data Sheet (See Figure 2-41, p. 178) per resident.
    b. If a resident needs to repeat Unit 3 of the Money Management Program, a new data sheet is to be used.
    c. The data sheet is to be kept in the resident's Individual Program Book.
    d. The class instructor and/or the staff member who evaluates an assignment is to record the data.
    e. Data to be recorded:
       (1) Name: Record the name of the resident.
       (2) Course: Record whether the resident is enrolled in Unit 3 of the HFC Program for the first, second, third, etc., time.
       (3) Date: Record the date on which the resident attended a class, completed an assignment, etc.
       (4) Class Attend.: Record either a check mark (✓), an *X* or an *E*.
          (a) "✓": Record a check mark (✓) each time the resident attends a HFM Program Unit 3 class. (Also, record the date in the "Date" column and a slash (i.e., 1 = 1; 2 = 11; 3 = 111; 4 = 1111; 5 = ̶1̶1̶1̶1̶1̶; etc.) in the "Total Number" row for each occurrence.)
          (b) *X:* Record an *X* each time a HFM Program class was conducted on Unit 3 and the resident did not attend. (Also, record the date in the "Date" column.)
          (c) *E:* Record an *E* when a HFM Program class was conducted on Unit 2 and the resident was excused from attending.
       (5) Home. Assign. 3-3: Record the percent level of accuracy achieved by the resident on Homework Assignment 3-3. Percent accuracy is determined by calculating the following:
          (a) Score 10 points if *Rent* expense is specified and it is within 25% to 33.3% of net monthly income ($600).
          (b) Score 10 points if *Food* expense is specified and it is within 10% to 25% of net monthly income ($600).
          (c) Score 10 points if expenses for a personal automobile (i.e., gas and oil, repairs), *and/or* expenses for public transportation are specified.
          (d) Score 10 points if *Clothing* expense is specified.
          (e) Score 10 points if *at least* one of the three types of *Household Operating Expenses* is specified.
          (f) Score 5 points if *Entertainment* expense is specified.
          (g) Score 5 points if *Total Expense* is accurately specified.

(h) Score 5 points if *Monthly Net Pay* is specified.
(i) Score 5 points if *Income Minus Expense* is specified.
(j) Score 20 points if *Income Minus Expense* is less than *Monthly Net Income.*
(k) Score 10 points if an entry (dollar amount *or* 0) is made for every item on the monthly Budget Form.
(l) Calculate the total number of points earned by the resident (100 possible points).
(m) Divide the total number of points earned by the total possible points (100). The resulting figure is the percent accurately achieved.

(6) Staff: Record the initials of the staff member recording the data.
(7) Comments: Record any comments relevant to the recorded data.
(8) Total #✓s: Record a slash mark (i.e., 1 = 1; 2 = 11; 3 = 111; 4 = 1111; 5 = 1111, etc.) in the appropriate column each time the resident attends class and/or attempts an assignment. (Attempts are to be recorded whether the resident is successful.)
(9) Crit.: Record either a check mark (✓), or X, or an *L:*
  (a) "✓": Record a check mark (✓) in the appropriate column if the resident met the specified criterion for class attendance (crit. ≥ 90%) and/or the Unit 3 Homework Assignment (crit. ≥ 75%).
  (b) X: Record an X in the appropriate column if the resident did *not* meet the specified criterion for class attendance and/or the Unit 3 homework assignment.
  (c) *L:* Record an L in the appropriate column if the resident met the specified criterion for the Unit 3 homework assignment (crit. ≥ 75%) but turned it in late.
(10) Unit 3 Crit.: Record either a check mark (✓) or an *X:*
  (a) "✓": Record a check mark (✓) if the resident
    i. Attended *at least* 90% of the classes conducted on Unit 3 (excluding times when the resident was excused from class)
    ii. Completed the Unit 3 homework assignment with *at least* a 75% level of accuracy.
  (b) *X:* Record an X if the resident did *not*
    i. Attend *at least* 90% of the classes conducted on Unit 3 (excluding times when the resident was excused from attending class)
    ii. Complete the Unit 3 homework assignment with *at least* a 75% level of accuracy

Table 2-2 Household Financial Management Program
Unit 1
Basic Four Food Requirements Chart
(Form HFM-BFFR)

MILK GROUP			MEAT GROUP		
Milk	Yogurt		Liver	Chicken	Fish
Evaporated Milk	Ice Cream		Beef	Turkey	Lamb
Cottage Cheese			Pork	Tuna	Bacon
Dry Milk					
Cheese			Beans	Eggs	
			Peanut Butter	Dry Peas	

VEGETABLE-FRUIT GROUP			BREAD-CEREAL GROUP	
Spinach	Greens	Broccoli	Bread	Flour
Tomatoes	Oranges	Grapefruit	Cereal	Macaroni
Carrots	Squash	Cauliflower	Rice	
Peas	Apples	Peaches	Whole Grain or Enriched	
Potatoes	Lettuce	Celery		

HOUSEHOLD FINANCIAL MANAGEMENT PROGRAM
UNIT 1
DAILY FOOD CONSUMPTION FORM
(FORM HFM-DFC)

NAME: DATE:

Meal	Foods/Liquids Consumed (A)	Foods/Liquids Left on Tray (B)	Quantity (A)	Quantity (B)	Snack	Quantity	Milk Group	Meat Group	Vegetable-Fruit Group	Bread Cereal Group	Number of Calories
Breakfast											
Lunch											
Supper											

Figure 2-35

Table 2-3
Household Financial Management Program
Unit 1
Basic Four Food Requirements Quantities Chart
(Form HFM-BFFRQ)

MILK GROUP (Two Servings)
(One serving = one cup)
Children under 9: 2 to 3 cups
Children 9–12: 3 cups or more
Teenagers: 4 or more cups
Adults: 2 or more cups

MEAT GROUP (Two or More Servings)
Two or 3 ounces of cooked lean meat, poultry, or fish equals one serving
Two eggs equals one serving
One cup cooked dry beans or peas equals one serving
Four tablespoons of peanut butter equals one serving

VEGETABLE-FRUIT GROUP (Four or More Servings)
One-half cup (raw or cooked) equals one serving
One portion such as a banana, potato, peach, etc., equals one serving

BREAD-CEREAL GROUP (Four or More Servings)
One slice of bread or one biscuit equals one serving
One ounce of ready-to-eat cereal equals one serving
One-half cup to 3/4 cup cooked cereal, grits, macaroni, rice, spaghetti, etc., equals one serving

HOUSEHOLD FINANCIAL MANAGEMENT PROGRAM
UNIT 1
MENU FOOD PLAN FORM
(FORM HFM-MFP)

NAME:	DATE:					
		Milk Group	Meat Group	Vegetable–Fruit Group	Bread Cereal Group	Number of Calories
Breakfast		Quantity				
Lunch						
Supper						
Snacks						

Figure 2-36

HOUSEHOLD FINANCIAL MANAGEMENT PROGRAM
UNIT 1
GROCERY SHOPPING LIST FORM
(FORM HFM-GSL)

NAME:			DATE:
FOOD ITEM	NUMBER OF MEALS	COST ADVERTISED IN NEWSPAPER	PROJECT COST
Total Cost of Newspaper Advertised Items			
Total Projected Costs			
Grand Total Cost			
Weekly Net Earning			$

Figure 2-37

HOUSEHOLD FINANCIAL MANAGEMENT PROGRAM DATA SHEET
UNIT 1
MENU PLANNING AND BUDGETING

NAME:										
DATE	CLASS ATTEND (√, X, or E)	CLASS ASSIGN. 1-1 (%)	HOME ASSIGN. 1-1 (%)	CLASS ASSIGN. 1-2 (%)	CLASS ASSIGN. 1-3 (%)	HOME ASSIGN. 1-2 (%)	CLASS ASSIGN. 1-4 (%)	FIELD ASSIGN. 1 (%)	STAFF	COMMENTS
Total # √s										
Crit. (√, X or L)										
Unit 1 Crit. (√ or X)										

Figure 2-38

HOUSEHOLD FINANCIAL MANAGEMENT PROGRAM DATA SHEET
UNIT 2
LIVING ACCOMODATIONS

NAME: COURSE:

DATE	CLASS ATTEND. (√, X, or E)	CLASS ASSIGN. 2-5 (%)	STAFF	COMMENTS
Total # √s				
Crit. (√, X, or L)				
Unit 2 Crit. (√ or X)				

Figure 2-39

HOUSEHOLD FINANCIAL MANAGEMENT PROGRAM
UNIT 3
MONTHLY BUDGET FORM
(FORM HFM-MB)

EXPENSES

Rent (25% to 33.33% of net pay) _____

Food (10% to 25% of net pay) _____

Transportation

    Gas and oil _____

    Automobile Repairs _____

    Public Transportation _____

Clothing _____

Toiletries _____

Insurance

    Health _____

    Life _____

    Automobile _____

Loan Payments

    Personal _____

    Automobile _____

    Credit Cards _____

Taxes

    Property _____

    Income _____

    Other _____

Household Operating Expenses

    Telephone _____

    Utilities (e.g., water, electricity) _____

    Supplies (e.g., cleaning supplies, light bulbs) _____

Entertainment _____

Medical and Dental Expenses Not Covered by
  Insurance _____

Miscellaneous Expenses _____

TOTAL EXPENSES _____

MONTHLY NET PAY _____

Monthly Net Pay _____

—Total Expense _____

Income Minus Expense _____

Figure 2-40

HOUSEHOLD FINANCIAL MANAGEMENT PROGRAM DATA SHEET
UNIT 3
DEVELOPING A BUDGET

NAME:				COURSE:
DATE	CLASS ATTEND. (√, X, or E)	HOME. ASSIGN. 3-3 (%)	STAFF	COMMENTS
Total # √s				
Crit. (√, X, or L)				
Unit 2 Crit. (√ or X)				

Figure 2-41

LEVEL 1, 2, AND 3 RECREATIONAL-LEISURE ACTIVITIES PROGRAM

GENERAL STATEMENT

Leisure time is a natural and vital component of everyone's daily routine. The manner in which an individual utilizes this time is often involved in the determination of a person's level of emotional adjustment and mental health. A well-adjusted individual is capable of engaging in a wide variety of activities in order to occupy his/her available time. These activities may vary according to a number of factors including the number of people necessary, the amount of time needed, the location and cost, the materials and/or equipment required, the need for supervision and/or training, and personal preference. Since the availability of these activities will necessarily vary, it is imperative that a person experience and be capable of engaging in a wide variety of activities in order to satisfactorily occupy his/her leisure time.

PURPOSE

1. To help develop socially acceptable behavior
2. To reduce the tensions acquired during the day
3. To reduce boredom
4. To help develop interest in a wide variety of activities
5. To help develop reinforcers in society
6. To help develop peer relationships
7. To help create activity-seeking behavior
8. To help create self-confidence in social situations
9. To increase active participation in social events
10. To increase decision-making behavior
11. To develop money management techniques
12. To help develop interpersonal skills
13. To increase self-esteem

TERMINAL OBJECTIVE

The terminal objective is to have the resident appropriately use his/her leisure time by engaging in a wide variety of recreational-leisure activities.

I. General Policies
   A. The Recreational-Leisure Activities Program is divided into five areas:
      1. On-Ward Activities (e.g., ping pong, card games, board games)
      2. On-Campus, Off-Ward Activities (e.g., dances, picnics)
      3. Off-Campus, Unescorted Activities (e.g., shopping trips, movies)
      4. Off-Campus, Escorted Activities (e.g., sightseeing trips, movies, shopping trips)
      5. Arts and Crafts
   B. Recreational/leisure activities may be organized by a Direct-Care Staff member (DCS) and/or residents with staff approval.
   C. Participation in *ward-wide* recreational activities is considered mandatory unless otherwise determined by the ward psychologist or nurse.
   D. This procedure is to be followed by residents in the token economy system as well as those not in the token economy system. Residents not in the token economy system are not required to make the prescribed token payments.
   E. For Level 3 residents, there is no token charge for the four (4) recreational activities required daily. (See *Level 3 Goal Orientation Procedure,* p. 134.)
   F. Individual programs (based on the needs of the resident), which supersede the Recreational-Leisure Activities Program, may be developed.

II. Behavioral Requirements
   A. Baseline Period (Beginning on the day that the resident enters the program)
      1. Absence of any restrictions placed on the resident on the ward from which he/she transferred that would preclude participation in the Recreational-Leisure Activities. The DCS in charge of the office on the day the resident enters the program is to determine if such restrictions were placed on the resident.
      2. Absence of any restrictions in effect as a function of inappropriate behavior such as stealing, aggression, and/or sexual misconduct that would preclude participation in recreational-leisure activities.
      3. The resident is to be prompted to participate but not required.
   B. Treatment Period (beginning on the Monday following the resident's Revised Rehabilitation Plan Review. (See Interdisciplinary Treatment Team Conferences Procedure, p. 12.)
      1. On-ward Recreational-Leisure Activities
         a. Absence of any restrictions in effect as a function of inappropriate behavior such as stealing, sexual misconduct, or agitation that would preclude participation in recreational-leisure activities.
         b. Any criteria specified in the resident's Individual Program are to be met.
      2. On-Campus, Off-Ward Recreational-Leisure Activities
         a. Self-Care Skills daily criterion is to be met for the day that the resident is requesting to participate in on-campus, off-ward recreational-leisure activities. (See *Self-Care Skills Program,* p. 41.)
         b. Absence of any restrictions in effect as a function of inappropriate behavior such as stealing, sexual misconduct, or agitation that would preclude participation in recreational-leisure activities.
         c. Any criteria specified in the resident's Individual Program are to be met.
      3. Off-Campus, Escorted Recreational-Leisure Activities
         a. Self-Care Skills daily criterion is to be met for the day that the resident is requesting to participate in off-campus, escorted recreational-leisure activities. (See *Self-Care Skills Program,* p. 41.)
         b. Absence of any restrictions in effect as a function of inappropriate behavior such as stealing, sexual misconduct, or agitation that would preclude participation in recreational-leisure activities.
         c. Any criteria specified in the resident's Individual Program are to be met.
      4. Off-Campus, Unescorted Recreational-Leisure Activities
         a. Self-Care Skills daily criterion is to be met for the day, and the seven days preceding the day that the resident is requesting to participate in off-campus, unescorted recreational-leisure activities. (See *Self-Care Skills Program,* p. 41.)
         b. The resident is to have had no legitimate complaints lodged by any personnel associated with the recreational-leisure activity and/or townspeople as a result of previous participation in an off-campus, unescorted recreational-leisure activity. If such a complaint was lodged, the resident is to be restricted from off-campus, unescorted recreational-leisure activities. The duration of this restriction is to be determined by a staff psychologist in consultation with treatment team members, and is to be based on the resident's inappropriate behavior during the off-campus unescorted recreational-leisure activity and on the resident's needs and treatment program.
         c. Absence of any restrictions in effect as a function of inappropriate behavior such as stealing, sexual misconduct, or agitation that would preclude participation in recreational-leisure activities.
         d. Any criteria specified in the resident's Individual Program are to be met.
      5. Arts and Crafts
         a. Self-Care Skills weekly criterion is to be met for the two weeks preceding initial participation in arts and crafts. (See *Self-Care Skills Program,* p. 41.)

b. Self-Care Skills daily criterion is to be met for the day that the resident is to participate in arts and crafts. (See *Self-Care Skills Program,* p. 41.)

c. Absence of any restrictions in effect as a function of inappropriate behavior such as stealing, sexual misconduct, or agitation that would preclude participation in recreational-leisure activities.

d. Any criteria specified in the resident's Individual Program are to be met.

III. Financial Requirements (for residents in the token economy system)

A. All token money bills are to be paid prior to participation in recreational-leisure activities.

B. For Level 3 residents only, there is no token charge for the four (4) recreational activities required daily. (See *Level 3 Goal Orientation Program,* p. 134.)

C. Token charges for recreational-leisure activities are as follows:
 1. On-Ward Recreational-Leisure Activities
    a. Games—10¢ per half-hour
    b. Television—10¢ per half-hour
    c. Record Player—10¢ per half-hour
    d. Radio—10¢ per half-hour
 2. On-Campus, Off-Ward Recreational-Leisure Activities—30¢
 3. Off-Campus, Off-Ward Recreational-Leisure Activities—50¢
 4. Outside Time
    Financial requirements for outside time are specified in the Outside Privileges Procedure (p. 191).
 5. Weekend Visit
    Financial requirements for weekend visits are specified in the Weekend Visits Procedure (p. 198).
 6. Escorted Shopping Trip, either alone or with other residents—50¢
 7. Unescorted Shopping Trip without other residents—50¢
 8. Unescorted Shopping Trip with other residents—40¢
    NOTE: 20¢ per hour is to be charged for each hour the resident is away past 5:00 P.M. on an unescorted shopping trip (either with or without other residents), which was previously approved by the ward psychologist or nurse.
 9. Other recreational-leisure activities, including arts & crafts, scheduled by staff and/or residents—token charge is to be determined by the ward psychologist or nurse.

IV. Financial Penalties

A. If a resident engages in a recreational-leisure activity without having first paid the required token charge (See Section III. C. above), he/she is to be charged double the required token charge.

B. Outside time—20¢ per half-hour is to be charged for each half-hour, or portion thereof, that the resident is late returning without a valid reason. (See *Outside Privileges Procedure,* p. 191.)

C. Weekend Visits—20¢ per hour (Levels 1 and 2) or 50¢ per hour (Level 3) is to be charged for each hour, or portion thereof, that the resident is late returning without a valid reason (See *Weekend Visits Procedure,* p. 198.)

D. Unescorted Shopping Trips either with or without other residents—50¢ per hour will be charged for each hour, or portion thereof, that the resident(s) is (are) away past 5:00 P.M. without a staff member's prior approval.

V. Data Collection

A. Follow the data collection procedures for the *Weekend Visits Procedure* (p. 198), *Outside Privileges Procedure* (p. 191), and *Goal Orientation Procedure* (Level 3 only, p. 134).

B. Arts and Crafts—The data collection procedure is to be developed on an individual basis by the Interdisciplinary Treatment Team and is to be based on the resident's individual needs and treatment program and specified in the resident's Individual Treatment Program.

182 PSYCHIATRIC UNIT PROCEDURES

LEVEL 1, LEVEL 2, AND LEVEL 3
JOB ASSIGNMENT PROCEDURE

GENERAL STATEMENT

The Job Assignment Procedure is designed to be a means by which residents in the Program may earn varying sums of additional financial rewards (token money) for specified on-ward work activities (housekeeping). The procedure is also designed to facilitate the development of responsibility in caring for the resident's own needs and living area, and to encourage good self-management and work habits.

PURPOSE

1. To increase feelings of self-worth
2. To help develop housekeeping skills
3. To obtain extra token money (residents in the Token Economy)
4. To help instill the concept of cleanliness
5. To help develop a sense of responsibility
6. To help develop pride in one's living area

PROCEDURE

I. General Policies
   A. Levels 1, 2, and 3
      1. This procedure is to be followed by all residents in the program, whether participating in the token economy or not. Residents in the token economy system are given token money payments or verbal praise for the completion of ward jobs, and the other residents receive verbal praise only for job completion.
      2. A resident may be restricted from earning token money for the completion of ward jobs (see Section III: Token Payments).
      3. After completing a job the resident is to notify his/her assigned Direct Care Staff (DCS) member.
      4. A resident may participate in the Job Assignment Program unless otherwise specified in his/her Individual Treatment Plan.
   B. Level 1
      1. Residents are to have assigned jobs unless otherwise specified in his/her Individual Treatment Plan.
      2. Each resident is to be given an initial job by his/her assigned DCS member immediately following the Revised Treatment Plan Review (see Interdisciplinary Treatment Team Conference Procedure, p. 12).
      3. Residents may be assigned additional jobs on an individual basis. Any additional jobs must be approved by the ward psychologist.
      4. Unless a specified time is stated on the Job List (See Section IV: Job List), assigned jobs are to be completed between 8–10 A.M. or 6–8 P.M., depending upon the shift responsible for monitoring a particular job.
      5. All jobs are to be completed each day, Monday through Friday.
      6. Before beginning a job the resident is to notify his/her assigned DCS.
      7. After completing a job the resident is to notify his/her assigned DCS to evaluate the work.
      8. Residents are to keep their assigned job(s) until that assignment is changed. Resident may request a job change at any time.
      9. All job changes must be approved by the ward psychologist.
   C. Level 2
      1. Ward jobs are to be assigned to a resident for a five-day period (Monday–Fri-

day) by his/her assigned/alternate 1st shift Direct-Care Staff (DCS) member, each Monday morning.
  a. A resident who does not have an Industrial Therapy (I.T.), Vocational Rehabilitation (V.R.), etc., job assignment for at least three hours/day, is to be assigned two ward jobs (to be completed daily).
  b. A resident who has a V.R., I.T., etc., job assignment for at least three hours/day and no more than six hours/day is to be assigned one ward job (to be completed daily).
 2. All ward jobs are to be completed during the following time periods:
   a. 9:00 A.M.–11:00 A.M.
   b. 1:00 P.M.–4:00 P.M.
   c. 6:00 P.M.–7:00 P.M.
 3. A resident in the token economy may request additional ward job assignments, but must meet specified criteria (See Section II: Behavioral Requirements) before he/she is to be paid (tokens) for more than two ward jobs/day.
D. Level 3
 1. Each resident is to select ward jobs on a daily basis.
  a. A resident who does not have an I.T., V.R., etc., job assignment for at least four hours/day is to select four ward jobs daily.
  b. A resident who has an I.T., V.R., etc., assignment for at least four hours/day and no more than six hours/day is to select two ward jobs daily.
 2. Ward jobs are to be scheduled on the resident's Daily Living Schedules. (See Goal Orientation Procedure, p. 134.)

II. Behavioral Requirements
 A. Baseline Period
  —None
 B. Treatment Period (Beginning on the Monday following the Revised Treatment Plan Review) (See Interdisciplinary Treatment Team Conferences Procedure, p. 12). There are no behavioral requirements for participation in the Job Assignment Procedure without token payments, unless specified on an individual basis and included in the treatment plan.

III. Token Payments (For resident in the token economy system)
 A. Residents in the token economy system may earn token money for satisfactorily completed jobs so long as there are no restrictions in effect as a result of inappropriate behavior (e.g., stealing, severe agitation, sexual inappropriateness) that would restrict token earning power.
 B. Any criteria specified in the resident's Individual Treatment Plan are to be met before tokens may be given.
 C. Token money payments are to be given at the completion of each job.
 D. Level 1
  1. Token payment is to be made as follows:
   a. If job is completed appropriately with no more than one prompt
    (1) Give the resident the full token payment specified for the job (See Level 1 Job List, Table 2-4, p. 185.)
    (2) Give the resident verbal praise
   b. If job is completed appropriate with two prompts
    (1) Give the resident half of the specified token payment (See Job List)
    (2) Give the resident verbal praise
   c. If job is not completed appropriately 30 minutes after the second prompt
    (1) Do not give the resident token payment
    (2) Do not give the resident verbal praise
    (3) Allow other residents to perform the job if they choose
   d. The resident is to be paid only if the job was completed with two prompts or fewer.

E. Level 2
   1. A resident in the token economy is to be paid for no more than two ward jobs per day until he/she meets two consecutive weeks of Self-Care Skills (S.C.S.) criteria. (See Self-Care Skills Procedure, p. 41.)
   2. As soon as a resident in the token economy meets two consecutive weeks of S.C.S. criteria, he/she may be paid for more than two ward jobs per day, provided that he/she has met daily S.C.S. criteria, and provided that there are no restrictions in effect as a function of inappropriate behavior (i.e., stealing, sexual misconduct, agitation).
   3. In order for a resident in the token economy to be paid for a ward job(s), he/she must have appropriately completed the job without any prompts.
   4. The amount of token money to be given for each ward job is specified on the Level 2 Job List. (See Table 2-5, p. 186.)
F. Level 3
   1. A resident in the token economy program is to be paid for the required ward jobs. (See Section I: General Policies, D. Level 3, p. 183.) prior to meeting the Self-Care Skills criterion for two consecutive weeks, if he/she indicates on his/her Daily Living Schedules (See Goal Orientation Procedures, p. 134.) the jobs he/she wishes to be paid for, by checking (✓) his/her choices.
   2. A resident in the token economy may be paid for more than four ward jobs/day after meeting two consecutive weeks of the S.C.S. criteria if
      a. He/she meets the daily S.C.S. criterion for the day
      b. There are no restrictions in effect as a function of inappropriate behavior, *and*
      c. He/she schedules the job(s) on his/her Daily Living Schedule
   3. In order for a resident in the token economy to be paid for a ward job(s), he/she must have appropriately completed the job without any prompts.
   4. The amount of token money to be given for each ward job is specified on the Level 3 Job List. (See Table 2-6, p. 187.)
IV. Job List (See Tables 2-4, 2-5, and 2-6, pp. 185, 186, and 187)
   A. There is to be one Job List for each program level (i.e., Level 1, 2, and 3).
   B. One copy of the Job List is to be filed in the front of each Job Assignment Chart, and on the bulletin board beside each of the DCS offices.
   C. The sheet is to contain
      1. The job number and a brief description of job
      2. Specification of token money payment for each job (NOTE: Token money payments may be different for some residents. When this occurs it is to be specified in the resident's individual treatment plan.)
V. Job Assignment Sheet (See Figure 2-42, p. 189.) (Levels 1 and 2 only)
   A. One Job Assignment Sheet is to be posted on the bulletin board by the DCS office on each ward for residents to read.
   B. The sheet is to be replaced weekly on Sunday night by 3d shift DCSs
   C. DCSs are to place a black check mark (✓) in the appropriate space when jobs are completed correctly, on time, and with no more than two prompts.
   D. If not completed according to criteria, place a red X and initials in space
VI. Job Assignment Data Sheet (See Figure 2-43, p. 190.)
   A. There is to be one Job Assignment Data Sheet per resident.
   B. The data sheet is to be located in the resident's Individual Program Book.
   C. The data sheet is to be completed by the DCS to whom the resident reports at the completion of a job.
   D. Data to be recorded
      1. Date—Record the date the job was completed.
      2. Job No.—Record the number of the job the resident completed

3. Outcome—Record a(n):
    "✓" if the job was completed appropriately
    X if the job was not completed appropriately
4. Prompts: Record the number of prompts the resident received.
5. Token Payment—Record the token payment given to the resident.
6. DCS—Record the initials of the DCS making the recordings.

Table 2-4 Level 1 Job List

JOB #	TOKENS	RESPONSIBLE SHIFT	JOB DESCRIPTION
1	20	1st	*Wipe chairs.* All vinyl chairs and sofas are to be wiped with a damp cloth. (Three residents may be assigned this job.)
2	10	1st	*Dust furniture and windowsills.* All furniture (other than vinyl chairs and sofas) is to be dusted with a dry cloth. All window sills on the main hall and alcoves are to be dusted. (Two residents may be assigned.)
3	20	1st	*Sweep Porch.* Resident is to sweep porch area and place refuse in trash can. (One resident assigned.)
4	20	1st	*Clean Bathroom Sinks.* All bathroom sinks are to be rinsed out and dried with a towel. This job should be completed between 2–2:30 P.M. (One resident assigned.)
5	20	1st	*Laundry to Ward.* Resident will assist staff in bringing clean laundry to ward. This job will be completed at 10:00 A.M. (Two residents assigned.)
6	10	1st and 2d	*Pick up magazines and cups on ward.* Resident will pick up and discard all empty cups on ward and place magazines in appropriate racks. This job is to be performed on both 1st and 2d shifts. (One resident assigned.)
7	10	1st and 2d	*Empty Garbage Cans.* Resident is to empty all ward garbage cans in the dumpster outside. Job is to be completed at 2:30 P.M. and 7:30 P.M. (Two residents assigned.)
8	20	1st and 2d	*Wash Garbage Cans.* Resident is to rinse out all ward garbage cans after they are emptied. Job is to be completed at 2:45 P.M. and 7:45 P.M. (Two residents assigned.)
9	20	1st and 2d	*Empty Ashtrays.* Resident is to empty all ashtrays following each smoking period throughout the day. (One resident assigned.)
10	20	1st and 2d	*Wash Ashtrays.* Resident is to wash and dry all ashtrays twice a day at 2:30 P.M. and 8:30 P.M. (One resident assigned.)
11	20	1st and 2d	*Clean Tables in Smoking Area.* Twice per day (11:30 A.M. and 4:30 P.M.) resident is to wipe all tables with a damp cloth. (One resident assigned.)
12	20	1st and 2d	*Sweep Smoking Room.* Twice per day (11:30 A.M. and 4:30 P.M.), resident is to sweep smoking area and place refuse in garbage can. (One resident assigned.)
13	10	1st	*Clean Porch Tables.* All tables on the porch are to be wiped with a damp cloth. (One resident assigned.)

Table 2-5 Level 2 Job List

JOB #	TOKEN WAGES	
		RESTROOM AREA
1	15	Sweep restroom
2	20	Clean Restroom and staff walls—mirrors
3	20	Clean sinks
		SHOWER ROOM
4	15	Sweep shower room and stalls
5	20	Clean shower room and stall walls
6	15	Clean bathtub
		BEDROOM HALL AREA
7	15	Dust mop bedroom hall
8	20	Wipe off bedroom hall baseboard brass with damp towel
9	15	Dust bedroom hall furniture and clean mirrors
10	5	Clean water fountain
		TV/SMOKING AREA
11	10	Dust mop TV/Smoking Area Hallway
12	10	Dust all furniture in TV/Smoking Area
13	10	Wash all vinyl furniture in TV/Smoking Area
14	20	Wipe off TV/Smoking area with damp towel
15	10	Spot clean and tidy up TV/Smoking Area
		BACK PORCH (Porch At HCT Office Window)
16	15	Sweep and straighten up back porch (Clean smokestands and ashtrays)
17	15	Wash benches and chairs on back porch
		SIDE PORCH
18	15	Sweep and straighten up side porch (Clean smokestands and ashtrays)
19	15	Wash benches and chairs on side porch
		SMOKESTANDS AND ASHTRAYS
20	15	Empty and wash all smokestands and ashtrays (1st shift)
21	15	Empty and wash all smokestands and ashtrays (2d shift)
		LAUNDRY ROOM
22	15	Sweep laundry room
23	15	Clean washer and dryer (inside and outside)
		ELEVATOR LOBBY
24	5	Dust mop elevator lobby
		MOP ROOM
25	15	Sweep mop room
		MISCELLANEOUS AREA
26	15	Empty all trash cans at 2:30 P.M.
27	15	Wash, dry and put paper towels in all trash cans at 2:30 P.M.
28	15	Empty all trash cans at 8:30 P.M.
29	15	Wash, dry, and put paper towels in all trash cans at 8:30 P.M.
30	15	Replace ward supplies (i.e., cups, paper towels, toilet paper, etc.)
31	25	Fold and neatly stack all linen (Laundry)
32	15	Sweep linen room
33	15	Sweep time-out room
34	15	Sweep storage room
35	10	Straighten up storage room

Table 2-6 Level 3 Job List

TOKEN WAGES	JOB#	
		RESTROOM AREA
15	1	Sweep and mop restroom
20	2	Clean Restroom and stall walls—mirrors
20	3	Clean commodes and sinks
		SHOWER ROOM
15	4	Sweep and mop shower room and stalls
20	5	Clean shower room and stall walls
5	6	Clean bathtub
		BEDROOM HALL AREA
10	7	Dust mop bedroom hall
20	8	Clean bedroom hall baseboard brass
10	9	Dust bedroom hall furniture and clean mirrors
25	10	Wash bedroom hall walls
5	11	Clean water fountain and tile walls
		OFFICE HALL AREA
10	12	Dust mop office hall
20	13	Clean office hall baseboard brass
5	14	Dust office hall furniture (clean mirrors-optional)
25	15	Wash office hall walls
		TV AREA
10	16	Dust mop dayroom
10	17	Dust all dayroom furniture
10	18	Wash all dayroom vinyl furniture
20	19	Clean dayroom baseboard brass
5	20	Spot clean and tidy up dayroom
20	21	Wash dayroom walls
		ACTIVITY ROOM
10	22	Dust mop activity room
10	23	Dust and/or clean all activity room furniture
20	24	Wash activity room walls
10	25	Clean activity room baseboard brass
5	26	Spot clean and tidy up activity room
		BACK PORCH (Porch At HCT Office Window)
15	27	Sweep and straighten up back porch (Clean smokestands and ashtrays)
15	28	Wash benches and chairs on back porch
		SMOKESTANDS AND ASHTRAYS
10	29	Empty and wash all smokestands and ashtrays in activity room
15	30	Empty and wash all smokestands and ashtrays in dayroom
10	31	Empty and wash all smokestands and ashtrays in hall
		LAUNDRY ROOM
15	32	Sweep and mop laundry room
15	33	Clean washer and dryer (inside and outside)

Table 2-6 Level 3 Job List (*continued*)

TOKEN WAGES	JOB#	
		ELEVATOR LOBBY
10	34	Sweep and mop laundry room
15	35	Wash walls in elevator lobby
15	36	Clean elevator lobby baseboard brass
		MOP ROOM
15	37	Sweep and mop, mop room
15	38	Wash mop room walls, rach and clean deep sink
		MISCELLANEOUS AREA
10	39	Sweep ramp
15	40	Empty all trash cans at 2:30 P.M.
15	41	Wash, dry, and put paper towels in all trash cans at 2:30 P.M.
15	42	Empty all trash cans at 8:30 P.M.
15	43	Wash, dry, and put paper towels in all trash cans at 8:30 P.M.
5	44	Replace ward supplies
25	45	Fold and neatly stack all linen (laundry)
15	46	Sweep and mop linen room
15	47	Sweep and mop time-out room
15	48	Sweep and mop storage (Recreation room)
10	49	Straighten up Recreation room

LEVEL 1 AND LEVEL 2 JOB ASSIGNMENT SHEET

NAME		JOB NO.	SHIFT		MON.	TUES.	WED.	THURS.	FRI.	

Figure 2-42

JOB ASSIGNMENT DATA SHEET (LEVELS 1, 2, AND 3)

DATE	JOB NUMBER	OUTCOME (√ or X)	PROMPTS	TOKEN PAYMENT	DCS	DATE	JOB NUMBER	OUTCOME (√ or X)	PROMPTS	TOKEN PAYMENT	DCS

Figure 2-43

LEVEL 1, LEVEL 2 AND LEVEL 3 OUTSIDE (ON-CAMPUS) PRIVILEGES PROCEDURE

GENERAL STATEMENT

All residents residing in the program are to be given the opportunity to go outside daily. Each resident is responsible for meeting the requirements to acquire and maintain outside privileges as defined in this procedure.

PURPOSE

1. To increase motivation
2. To increase exercise
3. To increase behaviorally appropriate activities
4. To help develop a sense of responsibility
5. To help develop time awareness
6. To broaden social contacts

PROCEDURE

I. General Policies
   A. Outside Privileges is defined as leaving the premises of the resident's treatment program (going outside) but not leaving the campus of the facility (this privilege is in addition to the outside time required by Clients' Rights—See Section II. *Mandatory Outside Time* of this procedure).
   B. Outside Privileges is to be followed by residents in the token economy system and residents not in the token economy system, with the exception that residents not in the token economy system are not required to make the prescribed token payments.
   C. There is to be a ten-minute grace period on the return time.
   D. Individual programs, based on the needs of the resident may be developed, which supersede the Outside Privileges Procedure
II. Mandatory Outside Time
   A. All residents, except those who are sick or unable, are to be taken outside as a group for at least 15 minutes each day (weather permitting).
   B. This 15 minute outing is to occur daily, usually following lunch.
   C. There is to be at least one male and one female Direct-Care Staff (DCS) member with the residents outside.
   D. Restriction from this activity requires written authorization from a mental health or mental retardation professional responsible for the formulation of the resident's treatment plan (G.S. 122-55. 2 (b) (d), 122-55.14 (b) (c)). "Mental health professional" is defined as any person with appropriate training or experience in the field of mental health care of the mentally ill or inebriate, including but not limited to physicians, psychiatrists, psychologists, social workers, and registered nurses (G.S. 122-36.h.p. 35)[1]
III. Earned Outside Time
   A. Time limits
      1. A resident may go outside as prescribed by Doctor's Orders (Ph.D. or M.D.).
      2. A resident may stay outside no longer than 60 minutes without reporting back to the ward.

---

[1] North Carolina Department of Human Resources. (1982). *North Carolina Mental Health, Mental Retardation, and Substance Abuse Laws.* Charlottesville, Virginia: The Michie Company.

3. The length of time outside and the frequency depends on
   a. The amount of token money he/she is willing to pay for the activity (if participating in the token economy)
   b. Whether the resident has fulfilled all behavioral and financial requirements and responsibilities

B. Outside time requests
   1. A resident wanting to go outside is to first obtain permission from his/her assigned or alternate DCS, unless specified otherwise in the resident's treatment plan.
   2. When a resident in the token economy program does *not* request outside time before going outside, he/she is to pay the financial penalty specified in the Financial Penalties Section (VI. A.) of this procedure.
   3. Upon returning to the building, the resident is to report to his/her assigned or alternate DCS.
   4. If a resident in the token economy program does *not* report in to the appropriate staff, he/she is to pay the financial penalty specified in the Financial Penalties Section (VI. C.) of this procedure.
   5. When a resident is late returning to the building (beyond the ten minute grace period) without a valid excuse, he/she is to be restricted to his/her treatment program area for the remainder of the day (except for 15 minute outside time required by Client Rights—See Section II of this procedure). Also, if the resident is in the token economy program he/she is to pay the financial penalty specified in the Financial Penalties Section (VI. A.) of this procedure.

IV. Behavioral Requirements
   A. Baseline Period
      1. Absence of any restrictions placed on the resident on the ward/program/facility from which he/she transferred that would preclude outside privileges. The DCS in charge of the office on the day the resident enters the program is to find out if such restrictions were placed on the resident.
      2. Absence of any restrictions in effect as a function of inappropriate behavior such as stealing, sexual inappropriateness, agitation, etc., that would preclude outside privileges.
   B. Treatment Period (beginning on the Tuesday following the Revised Treatment Plan Review—See Interdisciplinary Treatment Team Conferences Procedure, p. 12.)
      1. Self-Care Skills *daily* criterion is to be met for the day that the resident is requesting outside privileges. (See *Self-Care Skills Program,* p. 41.)
      2. Absence of any restrictions in effect as a function of inappropriate behavior such as stealing, sexual inappropriateness, agitation, etc., that would preclude outside privileges.
      3. Any criteria specified in the resident's Individual Treatment Plan are to be met.

V. Financial Requirements (for residents in the token economy system)
   A. All token bills are to be paid before a resident can purchase outside time.
   B. Any time a resident in the token economy wants to go outside, there is to be a token money financial charge.
   C. All token money payments for outside time are to be made in advance.
   D. Each 30 minutes outside costs 10¢ in token money.
   E. A resident may purchase as much outside time as desired.
   F. A resident may not purchase less than 30 minutes time and no more than 60 minutes at one time.
   G. A resident may return to the building before the amount of time purchased has expired. He/she may then go outside again if there is still time remaining. This process may continue until the amount of time purchased has expired.
   H. When the resident returns before his/her outside time has expired, any time spent inside is to be considered part of his/her outside time. For example, if a resident

purchases 60 minutes of time outside, but returns in 15 minutes and then goes back outside 10 minutes later, 25 minutes of the purchased hour have passed.
  I. A resident may purchase time outside, come back inside before the time has expired, and report to appropriate DCS that he/she is finished going outside for that time period.
  J. When a resident reports that he/she is finished going outside to the appropriate DCS, he/she may not use remaining purchased outside time.
VI. Financial Penalties (for resident in the token economy system)
  A. When a resident does *not* request outside time before going outside, he/she is to be charged 20¢ in token money for each half-hour outside.
  B. When a resident is late beyond the ten minute grace period, he/she is to be charged for an additional hour (20¢ in token money) for each half-hour.
    1. Any time beyond the ten minute grace period is to be considered a half-hour
    2. Any time beyond the first half-hour is to be considered a second half-hour, etc.
  C. When a resident returns within the ten minute grace period but does not report in to the appropriate DCS within the ten minute grace period, he/she is to be charged a 20¢ token money penalty.
VII. Appropriate Behavior During Outside Privileges
  A. All other treatment areas (including other areas within the building) are off-limits unless the resident is given permission in advance. In addition, residents may not loiter in the lobby area of any building on the campus.
    1. If the resident is in specified off-limits area without permission, give him/her one verbal warning. (Document this in a progress note in the resident's chart.)
    2. If the resident repeats this behavior, he/she is to be restricted from outside privileges as defined in this procedure for 2–7 days. The duration of this restriction is to be determined on an individual basis by the psychologist (record this information on the Outside Privileges Data Sheet and the Individual Restriction Data Sheet).
  B. The resident is not to engage in inappropriate sexual behavior.
    1. If the resident engaged in inappropriate sexual behavior while outside, he/she is to be restricted from outside privileges, as defined in this procedure, for 2–7 days.
    2. The duration of the restriction is to be determined on an individual basis by the psychologist.
    3. Record the appropriate information on the Outside Privileges Data Sheet and the Individual Restriction Data Sheet.
  C. Leaving the campus is to be allowed only when the resident is given special permission. When a resident leaves the hospital grounds without special permission, follow the Elopement Procedure. (See Elopement Procedure, p. 215.)
VIII. Instructions to Residents
  A. Before the resident goes outside, tell him/her
    1. The amount of time allowed outside
    2. The specified areas which are considered off-limits unless special permission is given
    3. That leaving the campus is not permitted
    4. Any individual rules or requirements
    5. That he/she may come back into the building and go outside again as many times as desired during the time allowed outside period, which is not to exceed 60 minutes for any one period
    6. That he/she must report back to his/her assigned DCS at least every 60 minutes
    7. That he/she is to report to his/her assigned DCS when no more time is desired outside during the allowed period
    8. That once he/she reports in, no more time will be allowed outside during the time period (unless additional time is purchased)

194 PSYCHIATRIC UNIT PROCEDURES

        9. That he/she must report in (to his/her assigned DCS) by the end of the time period
- IX. Outside Privileges Data Sheet (See Figure 2-44, p. 196.)
  - A. There is to be one Outside Privilege Data Sheet per resident.
  - B. The data sheet is to be located in the resident's Individual Program Book.
  - C. The data are to be recorded by the DCS who gives the resident permission to leave and who signs him/her in.
  - D. Data to be recorded
    1. Date—Record the date each day the activity is engaged in.
    2. Time Out—Every time the resident leaves his/her treatment area as a function of participating in this activity, record the time he/she left.
    3. Reg. payment—Record the amount of token money the resident paid for outside time (excluding financial penalties).
    4. Time in—Every time the resident returns to the ward and reports in as a function of participating in this activity, record the time he/she returned.
    5. Time late—Record the number of minutes late in returning.
    6. Add. payments—Record the financial penalties paid by the resident.
    7. Appro.—Place a check mark (✓) in this column if the resident's behavior was appropriate. (i.e., checked in, not late, followed all outside behavior rules, etc.). If the resident's behavior was not appropriate place an *X* in this column and specify the inappropriate behavior in the "comments" section of the data sheet.
    8. Total payment—Record the total amount of token money the resident paid (regular payment + financial penalties).
    9. DCS—Record the initials of the DCS recording data.
    10. Comments—Record any reports obtained by the staff or others concerning the resident's behavior while engaging in the activity, (i.e., lateness, not following any of the outside behavior rules).
- X. Outside Privilege Weekly Data Sheet (See Figure 2-45, p. 197.)
  - A. There is to be one data table per resident.
  - B. The data table is to be kept in the resident's Individual Program Book.
  - C. The data table is to be completed on a weekly basis every Monday evening.
  - D. The data table is to be completed by the 3d shift DCSs.
  - E. Record the following data
    1. Date—Record the date on which the weekly data are being recorded.
    2. Freq. of act.—Record the total number of times the behavior was engaged in by the resident during that week.
    3. Total time used—Calculate the total amount of time the resident used during that week by
       - a. Determining the number of minutes between signed out and *signed in* for each occurrence of the activity on each day of the week
       - b. Adding the calculated lapse of time for each occurrence of the activity for each day during the week
       - c. Recording the resulting figure
    4. Total time purchased—Calculate the total time purchased (in minutes) during that week by
       - a. Adding together the regular time purchased and any additional time purchased as a result of returning late
         - (1) To calculate the regular time purchased add any regular payments for the week and multiply this figure by 3.
         - (2) To calculate the late time purchased, add up the number of minutes late for each occurrence of the activity for each day during the week (from the "Time Late" column).

5. Num. times appropriate—Calculate the total number of times the activity was engaged in appropriately by the resident during that week by adding up the total number of times the behavior was engaged in appropriately.
6. Total payments—Record the total amount paid by the resident for this activity for the week by summing the "Total Payment" column on the Data Sheet for the week.
7. DCS—Record the initials of the DCS making the weekly calculations and recording on the Weekly Data Table.

OUTSIDE PRIVELEGES DATA SHEET

DATE	TIME OUT	REG. PAYMENT	TIME IN	TIME LATE	ADD. PAYMENT	APPRO. (√) (X)	TOTAL PAYMENT	DCS	COMMENTS

Figure 2-44

OUTSIDE PRIVILEGES WEEKLY DATA SHEET

DATE	FREQ. OF ACT	TOTAL TIME USED	TOTAL TIME PURCH.	NUM TIMES APP.	TOTAL PAY-MENTS	DCS	DATE	FREQ. OF ACT	TOTAL TIME USED	TOTAL TIME PURCH.	NUM TIMES APP.	TOTAL PAY-MENTS	DCS

Figure 2-45

LEVEL 1, LEVEL 2, AND LEVEL 3
WEEKEND VISITS
PROCEDURE

GENERAL STATEMENT

Visiting a family member or a friend for a weekend or longer is a privilege most adults have in our society. Before an individual can engage in such a visit, however, there are usually several behavioral and financial prerequisite responsibilities. First, the individual needs to find out if he/she is welcome. Second, the individual needs to have the amount of money needed for travel and other expenses. Third, the individual needs to have "free days" available for the trip. The residents of the program are given the privilege of weekend or extended visits. However, just as individuals living in the community must typically fulfill several behavioral and financial prerequisite responsibilities, so must individuals in the program.

PURPOSE

1. To enable residents to experience a variety of environmental situations
2. To increase the probability of treatment generalization
3. To help develop and/or maintain positive social interactions
4. To involve the family in the rehabilitation of the resident
5. To increase social awareness
6. To help prevent the "institutionalization" of residents
7. To increase motivation for improvement

PROCEDURE

I. General Policies
   A. This procedure is to be followed by residents in the token economy system and residents not in the token economy system, with the exception that residents not in the token economy system are not required to make the prescribed token payments.
   B. A weekend is defined as any two consecutive days in which work is not required.
   C. Typically a weekend is to be Saturday and Sunday.
   D. Weekends other than Saturday and Sunday are to be allowed only when prior approval is given by the Unit Director.
   E. A resident must submit a request for a visit two days in advance of the visit.
   F. A weekend begins at 5:00 P.M. the evening prior to the first day off (i.e., Friday, if Saturday is first day off).
   G. A weekend ends at 8:00 P.M. of the last day off (i.e., Sunday, if the weekend is Saturday and Sunday).
   H. Time changes may be obtained at the discretion of psychology or nursing staff for valid reasons.
   I. All reasons for time changes are to be listed in the comments section on the Weekend Visits Data Sheet. (See Figure 2-46, p. 202.)
   J. There is to be a 30 minute grace period on the return time.
   K. A resident is to be allowed to take the entire or any part of a weekend.
   L. Whenever a resident leaves the hospital grounds, a Doctor's order (Ph.D. or M.D.) *must* be obtained.
   M. Individual programs based on the needs of the resident may be developed, which supersede the Weekend Visits Procedure.
II. Behavioral Requirements
   A. Baseline Period
      1. Absence of any restrictions placed on the resident on the ward from which he/she transferred that would preclude a weekend visit.

2. Absence of any severe agitation (as defined in the Agitation Procedure, p. 206) on the day of departure and the preceding seven days.
3. Absence of any stealing on the day of departure and the preceding seven days.
4. Absence of any sexually inappropriate behavior on the day of departure and the preceding seven days.
5. Absence of any program restrictions for inappropriate behavior that would preclude a weekend visit.

B. Treatment Period (beginning on the Monday following the Revised Treatment Plan Review; See Interdisciplinary Treatment Team Conference Procedure, p. 12.)
1. Self-Care skills weekly criterion is to be met for the week preceding the weekend visit.
2. Absence of any severe agitation on the day of departure and the preceding seven days.
3. Absence of stealing on the day of departure and the preceding seven days.
4. Absence of any sexually inappropriate behavior on the day of departure and the preceding seven days.
5. Absence of any restrictions for inappropriate behavior that would preclude a weekend visit.
6. Any criteria specified in the resident's Individual Treatment Plan Program are to be met.
7. If there was a home report from the resident's last visit (if applicable) indicating that he/she engaged in inappropriate behavior and/or created a major problem(s) during the visit, he/she may be restricted from Weekend Visits. The duration of this restriction is to be based on the inappropriate behavior engaged in, the resident's needs and treatment program, and his/her behavior and treatment outcomes since the last visit.
8. Completion of the Resident's Questionnaire for Home Visits for the last visit (See Section V).
9. Leaving the ward before 5:00 P.M. requires prior approval by the program psychologist and/or nurse.

C. There are no behavioral requirements for a weekend visit (as defined in this procedure) for major religious and national holidays (e.g., Christmas, New Year, Easter, Thanksgiving), other than the absence of indicants of dangerous behavior such as severe agitation or suicidal behavior. Visits during the holiday periods may extend beyond two consecutive days (this is determined by the Interdisciplinary Treatment Team).

III. Financial Requirements (for resident's in the token economy system)
A. During the baseline period, there are no financial requirements (token charges) for a weekend visit.
B. There are no financial requirements for a weekend visit (as defined in this procedure) for major religious and national holidays (e.g., Christmas, New Years, Easter, Thanksgiving). Visits during holiday periods may extend beyond two consecutive days (this is determined by the Interdisciplinary Treatment Team).
C. All token money bills are to be paid before leaving on a weekend visit.
D. Token Payment for visit day(s)
1. Level 1 and Level 2: 50¢ (token money) is to be paid in advance for each visit (full or partial).
2. Level 3: $1.50 (token money) is to be paid in advance for each visit day (full or partial).
E. If a resident desires to leave earlier than the specified time (i.e., 5:00 P.M.), or return later than the specified time (i.e., 8:00 P.M.)
1. He/she is to obtain permission from the program psychologist and/or nurse
2. He/she is to pay the *additional* token charges:
   a. Level 1 and Level 2: 10¢ (token money) for each additional hour
   b. Level 3: 30¢ (token money) for each additional hour

IV. Financial Penalties (for residents in the token economy system)
   A. Visit time taken, but not paid for (any time period exceeding the specified time limit and the 30 minute grace period)
      1. One to 60 minutes past grace period is to be considered an hour.
      2. Sixty-one minutes to 120 minutes past grace period is to be considered two hours, etc.
      3. Token payment for extended visit time
         a. Level 1 and Level 2: Each extended visit hour is to cost an additional 20¢ (token money).
         b. Level 3: Each extended visit hour is to cost an additional 50¢ (token money).
   B. The resident's assigned or alternate Direct-Care Staff (DCS) member may eliminate the token payment for returning late, if answers to the following questions warrant an elimination:
      1. Did the resident notify the staff prior to the scheduled arrival time?
      2. Was the reason for being late valid?
      3. How late was the resident?
      4. How frequently has the resident been late in the past?
   C. When the late payment is eliminated, the reason is to be specified in the comments section of the Weekend Visit Data Sheet. (See Figure 2-46, p. 202.)
V. Resident's Questionnaire For Home Visits (See Table 2-48, p. 204.)
   A. To be completed by the resident immediately upon returning to the ward.
   B. There is to be one questionnaire completed per visit.
   C. The resident is to be given assistance when necessary.
   D. The completed questionnaire is to be located in the resident's Individual Program Book.
VI. Family's Questionnaire For Home Visits (See Table 2-49, p. 205.)
   A. To be completed by the individual(s) visited
   B. A DCS is to give the questionnaire to the resident.
      1. Place the questionnaire in an envelope.
      2. Instructions for the individual to be visited are to be typed or written on the envelope.
      3. The questionnaire is to be given to the resident when he/she leaves for a home visit.
      4. Give the resident instructions:
         a. Tell him/her that the person being visited is to complete the questionnaire.
         b. The completed questionnaire is to be placed in the envelope and *sealed* by the person who completed it.
   C. The completed questionnaire is to be returned to the ward in the sealed envelope.
   D. One questionnaire is to be completed for each home visit.
   E. The completed questionnaire is to be located in the resident's Individual Program Book.
VII. Weekend Visit Data Sheet (See Figure 2-46, p. 202.)
   A. There is to be one Weekend Visit Data Sheet per resident.
   B. The data sheet is to be located in the resident's Individual Program Book.
   C. The data are to be recorded immediately.
   D. The resident's assigned or alternate DCS is to record the data
   E. Data to be recorded:
      1. Date—Record the date on which the weekend visit began.
      2. Time left—Record the time the resident left for the weekend visit.
      3. Regular payments—Record the amount of token money paid by the resident for the weekend visit (including token payments made for approved early departures and late returns, but excluding token payments for returning late without approval).
      4. Date returned—Record the date on which the resident returned from the weekend visit.

5. Time returned—Record the time of day that the resident returned from the weekend visit.
6. Resident's Visit Quest.—Record either a check mark (✓) or an X
   a. Record a check mark (✓) if the resident completed and turned in the Resident's Visit Questionnaire.
   b. Record an X if the resident did *not* complete and/or did *not* turn in the questionnaire.
7. Family Visit Quest.—Record either a check mark (✓) or an X
   a. Record a check mark (✓) if the Family's Visit Questionnaire is completed by the person visited and turned in to a staff member.
   b. Record an X if the questionnaire is not completed and/or not turned in.
8. Add. payment—Record the amount of additional token money paid by the resident for the visit (e.g., late fee).
9. DCS—Record the initials of the DCS recording the data.
10. Comments—Record any comments concerning the home visit (e.g., condition on return, extensions of time approved, approved early leave).

VIII. Week-End Visit Weekly Data Sheet (See Figure 2-47, p. 203.)
   A. There is to be one Weekend Visit Data Table per resident.
   B. The table is to be kept in the resident's Individual Program Book.
   C. The table is to be completed on the first of each month.
   D. The third shift is to complete the table.
   E. Record the following data:
      1. Date—Record the date on which the weekly data are being recorded.
      2. Freq. of visits—Record how often that month the resident actually made a visit.
      3. Freq. met. crit.—Record how often that month the resident met the criteria for a weekend visit.
      4. # Weeks—Record the number of weekends the resident had available for visits given that all criteria had been met.
      5. Freq. of time—Record how often the resident met the specified time requirements (exclude those times the resident had valid reasons for being late from total figure).
      6. Freq. of time valid—Record how often the resident had valid reasons for extending the time limit.
      7. Amt. of time late—Record the total number of minutes late without a valid reason.
      8. Freq. of quest. appro.—Record the number of completed questionnaires turned in.
      9. Freq. of quest. inappro.—Record the number of questionnaires that were not completed or were not turned in.
      10. DCS—Record the initials of the DCS recording the data.

WEEKEND VISIT DATA SHEET

DATE	TIME LEFT	REGULAR PYMNT.	DATE RETURNED	TIME RETURNED	RESI-DENT'S VISIT QUEST.	FAMILY VISIT QUEST.	ADD PYMNT.	DCS	COMMENTS

Figure 2-46

WEEKEND VISITS WEEKLY DATA SHEET

DATE	FREQ. OF VISITS	FREQ. MET CRIT.	# WEEKS	FREQ. OF TIME	FREQ. OF TIME VALID	AMT. TIME LATE	FREQ. QUEST APPRO.	FREQ. QUEST INAPPRO.	DCS		

Figure 2-47

RESIDENT'S QUESTIONNAIRE FOR HOME VISITS

1. Did you enjoy yourself on your visit?_____
2. Did you become upset at any time during your visit?_____
   If so, please explain_____
   _____
   _____

3. Did you attend any social functions while on visit?_____
   If so, please (1) specify the activity(ies), (2) specify any problems, and (3) who suggested the activity_____
   _____
   _____

4. Have you noticed any changes in your relationship with your family or friend(s) since the last visit?_____
   _____
   _____

5. Were there any annoying habits or behaviors which you felt are in need of change?___
   If so, please specify and explain_____
   _____
   _____

6. Did you take your medication appropriately?_____
7. Did you sleep well?_____
8. Did you take care of your own personal needs, i.e., bathing, brushing your teeth, cleaning your own room, etc.?_____
   If not, please specify what was not done and why it was not done _____
   _____
   _____

9. Did you offer to help in any of the home duties?_____
10. Do you feel that the program has been of any benefit to you?_____
    Please explain your answer_____
    _____
    _____

RESIDENT'S NAME_____
NAME OF PERSON VISITED_____
DIRECT-CARE STAFF MEMBER_____
DATE_____

Figure 2-48

FAMILY'S QUESTIONNAIRE FOR HOME VISITS

1. Did your visitor enjoy himself or herself? _____
2. Did your visitor become upset at any time during the visit? _____
   If so, please explain _____
   _____
   _____

3. Did the visitor attend any social functions while at home? _____
   If so, please (1) specify the activity(ies), (2) specify any problems, and (3) who suggested the activity _____
   _____
   _____

4. Have you seen any changes in the visitor since the last visit? _____
   _____
   If so, please explain _____
   _____
   _____

5. Were there any annoying habits or behaviors which you felt are in need of change? _____
   If so, please specify and explain _____
   _____
   _____

6. Did your visitor take his or her medication appropriately? _____
7. Did your visitor sleep well? _____
8. Did your visitor take care of his or her own personal needs, i.e., bathing, brushing teeth, cleaning own room, etc? _____ If not, please specify what was done and how he/she reacted _____
   _____
   _____

9. Did your visitor help, or offer to help, in home duties? _____
10. Do you feel that the program/unit has been any benefit to either you and your family or to the visitor? _____
    Please explain your answer _____
    _____
    _____
    _____

VISITOR'S NAME _____
NAME OF FAMILY MEMBER (OR FRIEND) _____
DIRECT-CARE STAFF MEMBER _____
DATE _____

Figure 2-49

LEVEL 1, LEVEL 2, AND LEVEL 3 AGITATION PROCEDURE

GENERAL STATEMENT

At one time or another, all people become agitated. The manner in which the agitation is expressed varies between individuals, as well as within the same individual. Of major importance to both society and the individual who is agitated is the manner in which the agitation is expressed. Basically, there are two ways of dealing with feelings of agitation—the rational approach and the irrational approach. Most people try to cope with their problems in the most objective, rational manner possible. Only when one's emotions are under control can the irrational approach give way to the rational-objective approach. The typical outcomes of using the irrational approach are (1) negative short-term interactions; (2) increased negative long-term interactions; (3) immediate gratification or release of negative feelings, (4) counter agitation. By using the rational-objective approach to agitation the typical outcomes are (1) positive short-term interactions, or at least a higher probability of them; (2) a higher probability of positive long-term interactions; (3) solving the cause of the agitation and perhaps developing a corrective measure; (4) a release of tensions resulting in a more beneficial self-concept, i.e., "I did this myself, and I did it right."

PURPOSE

1. To increase positive interactions, both short and long term
2. To develop socially acceptable means of dealing with one's agitated feelings
3. To safeguard property
4. To safeguard individuals from harm (psychological and physical)
5. To create a "cooling-off period"
6. To develop a positive self-concept

PROCEDURE

I. General Policies
  A. All residents of Levels 1, 2, and 3 are required to follow the Agitation Procedure unless specified otherwise in an individual program.
  B. The Agitation Procedure is put into effect the moment the resident enters the program.
  C. There are two types of agitation
    1. Mild agitation
      a. Verbal threats to do bodily harm to oneself or others
      b. Verbal threats to do harm to property
      c. Screaming which can be heard at a distance of 30 feet
      d. Cursing, defined as words that refer to a sexual or elimination process or are religious in nature, used by themselves or in combination with other words, expressing disrespect or contempt for someone or something.
      e. Verbal statements implying obstruction of another's movements
      f. Unusual and/or abrupt movements, pacing and verbal behavior (unusual is defined for each resident)
    2. Severe agitation
      a. Causing damage to property
      b. Approaching another individual with hand(s) clenched into fist(s) or with a solid object in a raised, slashing or jabbing motion, or a combination of both
      c. Physically preventing movement of another
      d. Refusal to remove hands from another's body after being asked
      e. Damage to self or others

f. Running away from a situation of supervision. Physical coercion required by staff to stop and/or return the individual
D. Always record a progress note when the agitation occurs.
E. Always record a brief note in the Ward Daily Log (Date, Name, Behavior, "See Progress Note", Direct-Care Staff (DCS) member) when agitation occurs.
F. Whenever any agitation procedure is used, the program psychologist is to be notified as soon as possible.
G. Time-out (T.O.) procedure
  1. The T.O. room is to be used (unlocked room).
  2. The resident is to comply with 15 minutes of continuous calm behavior in the T.O. room.
  3. The time is restarted any time the resident becomes agitated (e.g., yelling or banging on the door).
  4. The door is to be closed, *but never locked.*
  5. A staff member is to be within 30 feet of the T.O. room at all times to insure resident safety.
  6. Immediately following time-out, a staff member is to discuss the incident and the purpose of time-out with the resident.
  7. If the resident is in time-out at bedtime
    a. Request that the resident go to his/her bedroom
    b. The resident is not to return to time-out the following morning. If agitation occurs after bedtime, follow appropriate Agitation Procedure for the degree or type
H. Seclusion Procedure
  1. The seclusion room is to be used as needed (locked room).
  2. Follow institution-wide seclusion policy.
  3. If possible explain the reason for seclusion to the resident.
  4. Before locking the resident in the seclusion room, check to see that he/she has no matches or lighter, or any object with which he/she could harm him/herself, others, or hospital property.
  5. Anytime a resident is secluded, there should be a mattress in the seclusion room.
  6. The resident is to remain in seclusion for 30 continuous minutes of calm behavior.
  7. Any interruption of the 30 minutes of calm behavior restarts the clock.
  8. If the resident is in seclusion at bedtime
    a. He/she is to remain in seclusion until criteria are met
    b. If asleep when criteria are met
      (1) Leave door closed but unlocked
      (2) If he/she awakens give resident choice of
        a. Going to bed
        b. Remaining in seclusion room with door unlocked
      (3) Write a progress note in the resident's chart to reflect reason he/she remained in seclusion room beyond the required period.
  9. The resident must be checked at least once every 15 minutes to assure personal safety. As little attention as possible, consistent with safety, should be given to the resident during these checks to reduce the probability of reinforcing inappropriate behavior. When behavior has been appropriate for two consecutive 15 minute intervals, the resident may be released from seclusion.
  10. Allow bathroom privileges and fluids every hour during the day (given DCS judgment on safety).
  11. At night, allow bathroom privileges every three hours, or when necessary (given DCS judgment on safety).

12. When agitated, allow the resident fluids every two-three hours during the day and every three hours at night (if awake).
    a. The resident, if he/she desires, is to be given fluids in the seclusion room, served in a paper cup.
    b. Observe resident while consuming fluids.
13. Residents in seclusion are to be served all meals unless he/she presents a clear and imminent danger to self, others, and/or property.

I. Restraints
  1. Restraints are to be used in accordance with all established institutional policies.
  2. The use of restraints is considered a last resort in cases where severe agitation poses an immediate threat of self-injury.
  3. A psychologist and/or nurse is to be present whenever restraints are applied.

J. Incident Diary Procedure (Level 3 only) See Figure 2-50, p. 211.)
  1. After the resident returns to a calm state, he/she will be requested, *but not required,* to complete an Incident Diary, consisting of
     a. Descriptive statement—30 or more words describing the incident and the feelings experienced by the resident
     b. Antecedents—the possible reason(s) why the resident became agitated, e.g., something that he/she or another person may have said or done
     c. Consequences—the result and/or effect of the incident
     d. Alternative behavior—two or more positive behaviors that could have been engaged in instead of the behavior that actually occurred
  2. If the resident refuses to complete the Incident Diary, prompt every 30 minutes for two hours or until he/she completes it appropriately, whichever occurs first.
  3. DCS may assist the resident in completing the Incident Diary.
  4. If and when the Incident Diary is completed, DCS is to review and discuss it with the resident.

II. Mild Agitation Procedure
  A. On first occurrence of the day
     1. Tell resident what is wrong and ask him/her to stop the inappropriate behavior (oral warning)
     2. Explain future consequence (i.e., time out)
     3. Ask resident if he/she wants to talk
     4. Write a progress note in the resident's chart
  B. On any additional occurrence of Mild Agitation the same day
     1. Level 1, 2, and 3: Follow Time-out procedure
     2. After Time-out (Level 3 only)
        a. Request that the resident complete the Incident Diary
        b. If he/she refuses, prompt every 30 minutes for the rest of the day or until he/she completes the Incident Diary appropriately
        c. DCS may assist the resident in completing the Incident Diary
        d. If and when the Incident Diary is completed, DCS is to review and discuss it with the resident
  C. If a resident becomes severely agitated while the Mild Agitation Procedure is being employed, move immediately to Severe Agitation Procedure (III below).

III. Severe Agitation Procedure
  A. When a resident engages in severe agitation (See I, C, 2, above) place him/her on Ward Restriction for two to seven consecutive days (the actual duration being specified by the program psychologist within 48 hours).
  B. Whenever physical aggression occurs, examine the resident for evidence of physical injury after the completion of the Severe Agitation procedure.
  C. On first occurrence of Severe agitation on any day
     1. Ask the resident to stop the inappropriate behavior (oral warning)

2. The resident is to be prevented from harming him/herself, others or property
3. As little physical contact and force should be used as is necessary for the situation
4. Attempt to calm the resident by discussing the problem or incident with him/her
5. If the resident becomes calm:
   a. Levels 1 and 2—Implement no further contingencies
   b. Level 3
      (1) Ask the resident to complete the Incident Diary. (See Figure 2-50, p. 211.)
      (2) If the resident refuses, prompt every 30 minutes for two hours or until the Diary is appropriately completed, whichever occurs first.
      (3) DCS may assist the resident in completing the diary.
      (4) When the Diary is completed, DCS is to review and discuss it with the resident.
D. Following any additional occurrences of Severe Agitation the same day
   1. The resident is to be prevented from harming him/herself, others, or property
   2. As little physical contact and force should be used as is necessary for the situation
   3. Follow the seclusion procedure immediately
   4. After seclusion (Level 3 only)
      a. Request the resident to complete the Incident Diary (See Figure 2-50, p. 211.)
      b. If the resident refuses, prompt every 30 minutes for two hours or until he/she completes the Incident Diary appropriately, whichever occurs first
      c. DCS may assist the resident in completing the Incident Diary
      d. If and when the Incident Diary is completed, a DCS is to review and discuss it with the resident

IV. Data Collection
   A. There is to be one Agitation Data Sheet for each resident.
   B. Each occurrence or addition of agitation is to be recorded on a new line.
   C. Data to be recorded on the Agitation Data Sheet: (See Figure 2-51, p. 212.)
      1. Name: Record the name of the resident.
      2. Date: Record the date only for those days on which agitation occurred.
      3. Time began: Record the time that the agitation was first observed and dealt with.
      4. Time ended: Record the time that the resident completed the agitation procedure.
      5. Type: Record the type of agitation and each occurrence of agitation (the type may or may not change that day; in either event record a 1 for mild agitation and a 2 for severe agitation).
      6. Oral Warn: Record either a check mark (✓) or an X
         1. Record a check mark (✓) when an oral warning was given.
         2. Record an X when an oral warning was *not* given.
      7. Diary (Level 3 only): Record a check mark (✓) or an X
         a. Record a check mark (✓) if the resident appropriately completed the diary.
         b. Record an X if the resident did *not* complete the diary or did not complete it appropriately.
      8. Disc: Record either a check mark (✓) or an X
         a. Record a Check mark (✓) if the resident discussed the incident.
         b. Record an X if the resident did *not* discuss the incident.
      9. T.O.:
         a. If the resident was placed in time-out, record
            (1) The time he/she was placed in time-out
            (2) The time he/she came out of time-out
         b. If the resident was *not* placed in time-out, record an X.

10. Secl:
    a. If the resident was placed in seclusion record
        (1) The time he/she was placed in seclusion
        (2) The time he/she came out of seclusion
    b. If the resident was *not* placed in seclusion, record an *X*.
11. Res:
    a. If restraints were used, record
        (1) The time the use of restraints began
        (2) The time the use of restraints ended
    b. If restraints were *not* used, record an *X*
12. PRN:
    a. If PRN medication was given, record the time of its administration.
    b. If PRN medication was *not* given, record an *X*.
13. DCS: Record the initials of the DCS recording the data.
14. Psy: Record the initials of the psychologist reviewing the data.

D. All data are to be recorded.
E. No columns are to be left blank.

INCIDENT DIARY

Name: _____ Date: _____

Description: (Write a general description of the incident and your feelings concerning the incident.) _____

_____
_____
_____
_____
_____
_____

Antecedents: (What did you and/or someone else do that may have caused the incident?)

_____
_____
_____
_____
_____

Consequences: (What happened as a result of the incident? Were there any effects on you and/or anyone else? If so, what were they?) _____

_____
_____
_____

Alternative Behaviors: (What are two or more possible things you could have done instead of what actually occurred?)

1. _____
_____
2. _____
_____
3. _____
_____
4. _____
_____

Figure 2-50

AGITATION DATA SHEET

DATE	TIME BEGAN	TIME ENDED	TYPE 1=MILD 2=SEV.	ORAL WARN. √=YES X=NO	DIARY √=YES X=NO	DISC. √=YES X=NO	T-O (TIME OR "X")	SECL. (TIME OR "X")	RES. (TIME OR "X")	PRN (TIME OR "X")	DCS	PSY.

Figure 2-51

LEVEL 1, LEVEL 2, AND LEVEL 3 SMOKING POLICY

GENERAL STATEMENT

Many people do not enjoy tobacco or any of its by-products (e.g., inhalation of smoke, the odor of burning tobacco, eyes affected by smoke, the potential fire hazards). At the same time, those who do enjoy smoking should be allowed to engage in that behavior. In order to accommodate both groups, many facilities (e.g., theaters, department stores, schools) are designating special locations designed for smokers.

PURPOSE

1. To reduce the probability of fire
2. To allow nonsmokers, areas that are free from smoke
3. To allow smokers, areas where smoking is permissable

PROCEDURE

I. General Policies
    A. Smoking is forbidden at any time in
        1. Bedrooms
        2. Bathrooms
        3. Other areas as specified on each level
    B. Smoking is permitted
        1. Level 1
            a. Once each hour
            b. Only in the designated smoking room
        2. Levels 2 and 3
            a. At any time
            b. In any area other than those designated as "no smoking" areas
            c. In an area occupied by other residents *only* if prior permission to smoke is obtained from the other residents
    C. Smoking Abuse
        1. Borrowing cigarettes from others
        2. Stealing cigarettes from others
        3. Scavenging cigarettes—i.e., smoking a cigarette that has been partially used by another resident or that has been discarded by another resident
        4. Putting cigarettes out on the floor
        5. Dropping ashes on the floor and not cleaning the ashes up *immediately*
        6. Burning furniture
        7. Smoking in no smoking areas
        8. Smoking in areas requiring permission and not having obtained that permission

II. Penalties for Smoking Abuse
    A. When the resident engages in borrowing, stealing, scavenging, putting cigarettes out on the floor, or dropping ashes on the floor without immediately cleaning them up
        1. He/she is *not* to have free access to cigarettes for the remainder of that day and the next day
        2. Levels 1 and 2
            a. Allow the resident one cigarette at the end of each meal period and one at 8:30 P.M.
            b. Allow smoking only in a designated smoking area.

3. Level 3
    a. Allow resident to smoke only once every two hours.
    b. Allowed cigarettes are to be smoked while standing by an ashtray, away from others.
    c. Residents are not to interact with others while smoking.
4. Any smoking violation during a smoking restriction is to extend restriction for the next day only (not cumulative).

B. When the resident burns furniture with a cigarette, or smokes in a no smoking area
1. He/she is *not* to have free access to cigarettes for the remainder of that day and the next *seven days*
2. Levels 1 and 2
    a. Allow the resident one cigarette at the end of each meal period and one at 8:30 P.M.
    b. Allow smoking only in a designated smoking area.
3. Level 3
    a. Allow resident to smoke only once every two hours.
    b. Allowed cigarettes are to be smoked while standing by an ashtray away from others.
    c. Residents are not to interact with others while smoking.
4. Any smoking violation during a smoking restriction period is not to extend the restriction beyond seven consecutive days from the day of the violation.
5. When a resident is placed on smoking restriction for three or more consecutive days, he/she is to have one day subtracted from his/her total smoking restriction period for every 2 consecutive days that he/she does not violate the Smoking Policy.

C. When the resident is on one of the above smoking restrictions (A or B above) and he/she engages in cigarette smoking off the ward, he/she may be restricted to the ward for the remainder of the smoking restriction period. This is to be determined on an individual basis by the program psychologist.

LEVEL 1, LEVEL 2, AND LEVEL 3 ELOPEMENT POLICY

GENERAL STATEMENT

An effective therapeutic program requires willing participation and genuine cooperation. Thus, it is necessary that each resident of the program be an active willing participant in his/her treatment program. Elopement usually indicates a desire to terminate active participation in the program but no matter what the reason, elopement abruptly interrupts treatment. With frequent elopements, the continuity of treatment is so disturbed that progress is impossible. Furthermore, frequent elopements are a sure indication that the resident does not want to be in the program and that he/she is not an active, willing participant.

PURPOSE

1. To give the resident an opportunity to willingly participate and cooperate in an active treatment program
2. To help develop in the resident, responsibility for active, willing participation in his/her therapeutic program
3. To give the resident the opportunity to voluntarily leave the program.

PROCEDURE

I. General Policies
   A. Elopement is defined as leaving the grounds of the facility without explicit written or oral permission from facility personnel.
   B. Steps for staff to take when an elopement occurs:
      1. Notify the Unit Director immediately.
      2. Notify the program psychologist immediately.
      3. Notify nurse on duty immediately.
      4. Notify campus security immediately.
      5. Recheck ward, building, and grounds. If resident is not found in a short period of time, the nurse on duty is to notify
         a. Resident's family
         b. Sheriff's Department in resident's home county (if resident is judicially committed)
      6. Record the appropriate data on the Individual Elopement Data Sheet. (See Section III.)
      7. Write a progress note in the individual's chart concerning the incident, the actions taken, and the reasons for the actions.
      8. When elopements extend beyond midnight, the resident is to be placed on unauthorized absence status.
      9. When elopements occur after 5:00 P.M. on Monday through Friday, on weekends, or on holidays, the nurse on duty is to notify (in addition to the individuals specified in 1-4 above) the Administrative Officer and the Clinical Administrative Officer on-call.
      10. When elopements extend beyond 72 hours
         a. If the resident is a voluntary resident, he/she is to be discharged
         b. If the resident is judicially committed, he/she is to remain on unauthorized absence status
      11. If and when the eloper returns to the ward, complete a body inspection for injuries and document findings in the resident's chart.

216 PSYCHIATRIC UNIT PROCEDURES

II. Consequences of Elopement
   A. Voluntary Resident—Upon a voluntary resident's return to the facility, thoroughly explain to him/her the following two alternatives and allow him/her to choose one:
      1. Discharge from the facility
      2. Continued participation in the program
   B. Judicially Committed Resident—upon a judicially committed resident's return to the program, he/she is to continue his/her participation in the program from which he/she eloped, *or* intrafacility transfer is to be implemented (if indicated).
   C. Repeated Elopements—Any elopement following a three-day "cooling off" period from the last elopement and within 30 days of the last elopement, may result in immediate initiation of an intrafacility transfer *or* discharge from the facility.
III. Individual Elopement Data Sheet (See Figure 2–52, p. 217.)
   A. There is to be one Individual Elopement Data Sheet kept in each resident's Individual Program Book.
   B. Data concerning elopement(s) are to be recorded by the Direct-Care Staff (DCS) member who first observes the absence of the resident and by the DCS who is on duty when the resident returns to the ward.
   C. Data to be recorded:
      1. Date—The date on which the elopement began
      2. Nurse—The name of the nurse to whom the elopement was reported
      3. Psych.—The name of the psychologist to whom the elopement was reported
      4. Campus Security—The name of the campus security officer to whom the elopement was reported
      5. Time Left—The time when the resident's absence was first noticed
      6. Time Return—The date and time of the resident's return to the program
      7. Returned by—The name of the person (if any) who brought the resident back to the program
      8. Phys. Cond.—The type of physical condition the resident was returned in by recording an *A*, a *C*, or an *E*.
         a. *A*—as good as when left
         b. *C*—some abrasions
         c. *E*—major physical problems
      9. Unauth. Absence—Record either a check mark (✓) or an *X*.
         a. If the individual was placed on unauthorized absence status record a check mark (✓)
         b. If the individual was *not* placed on unauthorized absence status, record an *X*
      10. Disch.—Record either a check mark (✓) or an *X*.
         a. If the resident was discharged, record a check mark (✓).
         b. If the resident was *not* discharged, record an *X*.
      11. Intrafacil. transfer—Record either a check mark (✓) or an *X*.
         a. Record a check mark (✓) if an intrafacility transfer was initiated.
         b. Record an *X* if an intrafacility transfer was *not* initiated.
      12. DCS—Record the initials of the DCS who first observed the resident's absence and the initials of the DCS who observed the return of the resident and recorded the required data.
      13. Comments—Record any unusual conditions, such as intoxication, etc.

INDIVIDUAL ELOPEMENT DATA SHEET

DATE	NURSE	PSYCH.	CAMPUS SECUR.	TIME LEFT	TIME RETURN	RETURN-ED BY	PHYS. COND. A, C, OR E	UNAUTH. ABSENCE √ = YES X = NO	DISCH. √ = YES X = NO	INTRA. FACIL. TRANS. √ = YES X = NO	DCS LEFT	DCS RET.	COMMENTS

Figure 2-52

LEVELS 1, 2, AND 3
DISCHARGE PREPARATION GROUP
Barbara Myers and Sam DePew

GENERAL STATEMENT

As residents approach discharge from the hospital it is important that they be informed of the placement options available to them. One important decision that they must make is whether they can manage themselves independently in the community, or if they will require some structure and supervision. They will also need some knowledge of available community resources (i.e., Department of Social Services, Health Department, Mental Health Center, etc.). For those residents who have made a decision concerning their discharge placement it would be advantageous to help them explore any questions, fears, or reservations they may have concerning this change in their living situation. The Discharge Preparation Group has been formed to meet these needs.

PURPOSE

1. To assist residents in making a smooth transition from the hospital to community living
2. To decrease residents' anxiety during the discharge transition
3. To educate residents about placement alternatives and community resources
4. To increase the probability of successful placement

PROCEDURE

I. General Format
    A. All Discharge Preparation Groups are to be led by a unit social worker.
    B. Separate groups are to be conducted for each of the three program levels (i.e., Levels 1, 2, and 3).
    C. All groups are to be coeducational.
    D. Each Discharge Preparation Group is to consist of a minimum of three residents.
    E. Scheduling
        1. Groups are to be formed on an as needed basis.
        2. Groups are to meet once per week.
        3. The group for each program level is to meet in the program's activity room.
II. Group Selection
    A. Residents who are within 8–10 weeks of discharge are to be referred to the appropriate social worker for placement in a group.
    B. Referrals are to be made by the resident's Interdisciplinary Treatment Team.
    C. Residents referred should be capable of meaningful participation and group interaction.
    D. Participation in group sessions is to be voluntary.
III. Predischarge Screening
    A. Following referral, each resident is to meet individually with his/her social worker.
    B. During the screening interview the following information is to be collected:
        1. Resident's preferences for placement
        2. Specific questions/problems concerning placement
        3. Degree of family support
        4. Extent of financial resources
IV. Content of Group Sessions
    A. First Session
        1. Introduction of group members
        2. Explain purpose and scope of group sessions.
        3. Discuss feelings concerning placement.

B. Second Session
   1. Discuss types of discharge placement alternatives.
   2. Discuss finances
   3. Discuss problems and concerns regarding discharge.
   4. Clarify earlier issues
C. Third Session
   1. Discuss community resources (with emphasis placed on Mental Health Center component).
   2. Provide residents with a list of community resources and services offered by each community agency.
   3. Discuss medication education (invite nursing personnel to participate in session).
   4. Discuss and clarify any issues related to sessions one through three.
D. Fourth Session
   1. Plan community visit(s) appropriate to the needs of group members.
   2. Discuss any outstanding issues.
   3. Schedule Exit Screening session (See Section V: *Exit Screening* below)
V. Exit Screening
   A. Following completion of Discharge Preparation Group sessions, the social worker is to meet individually with each resident.
   B. Social worker is to confirm discharge plans and tentative date of discharge with each resident.
   C. Social worker is to assess resident's discharge readiness:
      1. Determine if any significant questions remain pertaining to placement.
      2. Determine if resident has any particular concerns regarding placement.
VI. Data Recording
   A. Progress Notes
      1. Social worker is to write regular monthly progress notes that include the following:
         a. Resident's progress in group
         b. Concerns of resident and family
         c. Results of exit interview
      2. Social worker is to write other progress notes as required to describe any major problems or significant events.
   B. Discharge Preparation Group Data Sheet (See Figure 2-53, p. 221.)
      1. There is to be one Discharge Preparation Group Data Sheet for each resident participating in the Discharge Preparation Group.
      2. The data sheet is to be located in the resident's Individual Program Chart.
      3. Data to be recorded:
         a. Name: Record the name of each resident participating in the Discharge Preparation Group.
         b. Hospital #: Record the hospital number of each resident participating in the Discharge Preparation Group.
         c. Program Level: Record the program level (i.e., Level 1, 2, or 3) of the resident.
         d. Ward: Record the ward number of the resident.
         e. Social Worker: Record the name of the social worker conducting the Discharge Preparation Group.
         f. Date of Interview: Record the date of the Predischarge screening interview.
         g. Resident's Initial Preference Discharge Placement: Record the resident's initial preference for discharge placement.
         h. Group Sessions:
            (1) Dates: Record the date of each group session (whether the resident attended or not).

(2) Attendance: Record whether or not the resident attended the group session (Yes or No).

(3) If No, State Reason: If resident did not attend, explain why not.

i. Community Visits:

(1) Date of Visit: Record the date of the visit to the community.

(2) Type of Facility Visited: Record the type of facility visited.

(3) Address/Phone/Contact: Record the address and telephone number of the facility visited and the name of the contact person at the facility.

j. Date of Exit Screening Interview: Record the date of the Exit Screening Interview.

k. Final Discharge Placement Plans: Record the final discharge placement plans of the resident.

l. Discharge Dates:

(1) Projected: Record the date projected by the resident's Interdisciplinary Treatment Team for discharge.

(2) Actual: Record the actual date resident is discharged from the hospital.

DISCHARGE PREPARATION GROUP DATA SHEET

NAME: _____ HOSPITAL # _____

Program Level _____ Ward _____

Social Worker: _____ Date of Interview _____

Resident's Initial Preference Discharge Placement: _____
_____

Why? _____
_____

Comment _____
_____

GROUP SESSIONS:

Dates	Attendance (Yes/No)	If No, State Reason
1.		
2.		
3.		
4.		
5.		
6.		

COMMUNITY VISITS:

Date of Visit	Type of Facility Visited	Address/Phone #/Contact
1.		
2.		
3.		
4.		

Date of Exit Screening Interview: _____

Final Discharge Placement Plans: _____

DISCHARGE DATES:

1. Projected _____
2. Actual _____

Figure 2-53

HALFWAY HOUSE PROCEDURES

HALFWAY HOUSE POLICIES

GENERAL STATEMENT

The transition from institutional to independent living is often difficult for the psychiatric resident. Unlike most institutions which have rules and policies that greatly limit the independence and the range of decisions required of the resident, independent living allows much greater freedom and, consequently, a much wider array of personal responsibilities. To make the move toward increased freedom less stressful and to improve the resident's chances of success, a gradual transition is needed. The Halfway House Policies procedure attempts to systematically reduce the restrictions on the resident to a level more closely approximating the natural environment.

PURPOSE

1. To develop self-control and self-reliance
2. To gradually increase resident's freedom and responsibility
3. To develop independent living skills

PROCEDURE

I. General Policies
   A. House Facilitator (HF)
      1. All activities of the Halfway House are to be supervised by a HF.
      2. Any decisions made by the residents may be vetoed by a HF.
      3. The HFs are to inform the Halfway House Director whenever a resident decision is vetoed.
   B. Resident government (See Halfway House Therapeutic Community Procedure, p. 253.)
      1. Residents are to meet at least once per week to discuss issues related to the Halfway House.
      2. Leaders are to be elected monthly by the residents.
      3. New rules or policies may be enacted by majority vote.
      4. Decisions concerning house rules or policies shall stand unless vetoed by an HF.
   C. Admissions
      1. Male and female residents are to be admitted to the Halfway House.
      2. All residents are to enter the program voluntarily.
      3. Prior to Halfway House admission, all residents are to meet established admissions criteria.
   D. Dismissal
      1. Recommendation for dismissal may be initiated by an HF, a treatment team, or a director.
      2. The director must approve all dismissals.
      3. The following behaviors may result in dismissal (See policies below for further specification):
         a. Refusal to attend scheduled activities
         b. Inappropriate sexual behavior
         c. Frequent or severe agitation
         d. Use or possession of alcohol or illicit drugs
         e. Possession of weapons (mandatory dismissal)
         f. Frequent or serious disregard of established rules and policies

II. Rules and Procedures
   A. House hours
      1. Curfew
         a. Monday through Thursday—11:00 P.M.
         b. Friday and Saturday—1:00 A.M.
         c. Extended hours
            (1) Are to be approved by HF in advance
            (2) Are not to exceed 3:00 A.M.
      2. Overnight leaves
         a. Require prior approval of HF
         b. Are to be requested at least two hours in advance of departure
         c. Are not to be granted after 9:00 P.M.
      3. Bedtime
         a. Residents may retire at their own discretion.
         b. Residents may be asked to retire if causing a disturbance after being asked to be quiet.
         c. Bedtime restrictions may be imposed for health reasons if approved by treatment team.
      4. Sign in/Sign out Log Book
         a. Whenever leaving the Halfway House, residents are to record the following in the Log Book:
            (1) Name
            (2) Date
            (3) Time of departure
            (4) Destination
         b. When returning to the Halfway House, residents are to record in the Log Book
            (1) Name
            (2) Date
            (3) Time of return
      5. House keys
         a. Each resident is to be issued a house key.
         b. If key is lost, resident is to be charged $10.00 and a new key is to be issued.
         c. If key is lost a second time, resident is to be charged $15.00 and not issued a replacement key for at least 30 days.
   B. Visitors
      1. Residents may have visitors as long as visitors follow all established policies and rules.
      2. Visitation hours
         a. Weekdays: Visitors are not permitted in the House after 10:00 P.M.
         b. Weekends (Friday and Saturday): Visitors are not permitted in the House after 11:00 P.M.
      3. Visitors of the opposite sex in resident's rooms
         a. Must obtain prior approval of HF
         b. Must leave door open
         c. May not remain in room after 9:00 P.M.
   C. Self-Care Skills (See Halfway House Self-Care Skills Procedure, p. 234.)
      1. Each resident is to maintain his/her living area as specified in the Halfway House Self-Care Skills Procedure (p. 234).
      2. Appropriate dress is to be maintained at all times (Dress code is to be formulated by residents through the Resident Government).
   D. Drug/Alcohol use
      1. Alcohol is not permitted on the premises of the Halfway House at any time.
      2. Possession or use of illicit drugs is not permitted.

3. Inebriation is strongly discouraged.
4. Possession of alcohol on premises, the possession or use of illicit drugs, or repeated episodes of inebriation are grounds for dismissal from the Halfway House.

E. Sexual behavior
1. Appropriate sexual behavior required at all times.
   a. Defined generally as behavior compatible with community standards.
   b. May be more specifically defined by Resident Government or HFs, as the need arises.
2. Flagrant or repeated sexually inappropriate behavior is grounds for dismissal.

F. Aggression (See Halfway House Agitation Procedure, p. 270.)
1. All forms of aggression, whether verbal or physical, are prohibited.
2. Any incident of physical aggression or repeated episodes of verbal aggression are grounds for dismissal.

G. Possession of weapons
1. Residents may not possess firearms, or knives with blades longer than three inches.
2. Any resident found with such a weapon is to be immediately dismissed.

H. Smoking
1. Living room and recreation areas
   a. Permitted at all times
   b. Residents are to use ashtrays at all times.
2. Bedrooms
   a. Permitted only while seated in a chair or standing
   b. Never permitted in bed
   c. Each resident is to maintain a watercan in his/her bedroom for the disposal of cigarettes.
3. Smoking in dining areas is permitted only with the permission of everyone in the room.
4. Violation of smoking rules may result in restriction of smoking privileges.

I. Miscellaneous rules
1. Residents may operate motor vehicles if properly licensed and insured.
2. No pets are allowed in the Halfway House except as approved by the HFs and all residents of the Halfway House.
3. Each resident is responsible for preparation of his/her own meals unless participating in group meals. (See Halfway House Meals Procedure, p. 241.)
4. Each resident is to participate in the maintenance and cleaning of the House as specified in the Worksharing Procedure (p. 263).

HALFWAY HOUSE INTERDISCIPLINARY TREATMENT TEAM CONFERENCES PROCEDURE

Purpose

These policies and procedures have been formulated to specify the responsibility for constructing, monitoring, implementing, and updating individualized treatment plans for residents in the Halfway House. Treatment plans are combinations of therapies and programs designed by the Halfway House Treatment Team, to ensure progress in the area of skill deficits, and to reduce behavioral and emotional problems.

A Treatment Team shall be established to evaluate each resident's needs, plan an individualized treatment plan to meet identified needs, and to periodically review the resident's response to his/her treatment plan and revise the plan accordingly. This plan shall be based on an evaluation of the needs of the individual resident. The objective shall be described in behavioral terms that permit progress to be assessed. The plan shall provide for implementation, continuing assessment, and revisions as necessary.

The regular review process ensures the appropriate modification of the treatment plan, so that the resident may move from one level of achievement to another within the program, and out of the facility when he/she is ready.

Composition of the Interdisciplinary Treatment Team

Members of the team shall be selected from the following areas, as appropriate to the resident's needs. This includes those staff persons providing on-going services to the residents, as well as staff utilized on a consultant, or as needed basis.

A. Staff persons utilized on an on-going basis include:
   1. Halfway House Director
   2. Halfway House Facilitators (HFs)
   3. Vocational Rehabilitation Counselor
B. Staff persons utilized on a consultant, or as needed basis include:
   1. Physician
   2. Direct-Care Staff (DCS) from Level 1, 2, or 3
   3. Special Education Teacher
   4. Community Mental Health Clinic Staff

Ordinarily, the Treatment Team will include the Halfway House Director, HFs and the Vocational Rehabilitation Counselor. The HFs shall serve as team facilitators to implement the resident's treatment plan between regularly scheduled re-evaluation sessions by the team. The H.H. Director shall approve the treatment plan (and any revisions) in writing, and shall be responsible for the overall adequacy of the plan. Duties of the Interdisciplinary Treatment Team: Members of the Treatment Team shall be responsible for

1. Comprehensive evaluation of each resident as a basis for planning programming and management upon admission to the Halfway House.
2. Design and implementation of an individualized treatment plan to effectively meet the needs of the resident.
3. Regular review, evaluation, and revision, if necessary, of the resident's treatment plan.
4. Assuring movement of the resident from one level of achievement to another within the Halfway House Program through training, rehabilitation, and placement.
5. Providing an array of those services that will enable the resident to develop to his/her maximum potential.
6. Assuring that the resident's rights are protected.

226 HALFWAY HOUSE PROCEDURES

ADMISSIONS

Individuals accepted into the Halfway House are to begin residency on Mondays.

THE INITIAL TREATMENT PLAN REVIEW

Within 96 hours of the resident's admission to the Halfway House, the Treatment Team shall meet to determine the resident's needs for further testing and evaluation. The written results of this meeting shall include:

1. A review of the resident's social, educational, psychological, medical, and other pertinent histories.
2. An indication of what resources (e.g., family, guardians, or other contacts from the resident's home environment) are to participate in treatment or continue to be involved with the resident.
3. Initial goals for treatment and preliminary anticipated outcomes.
4. Discussion of any individual problems and baselines needed.
5. Listing of resident's personal strengths.
6. The names, titles, and functions of all persons participating in the treatment (Treatment Team present), and the signature of the H.H. Director and a HF.

The resident must attend the Initial Treatment Plan Review. Attendance of the resident's family or surrogates, and other persons designated as necessary contributors to the treatment plan, shall be requested by a member of the Treatment Team, provided that prior consent is obtained from the resident.

THE REVISED TREATMENT PLAN

Within 14 days of the Initial Treatment Plan Review, the Treatment Team shall meet to devise a written, detailed rehabilitation plan to be entered in the resident's record. The plan shall be based upon observations and a diagnosis or evaluation of the resident's behavior. The plan must provide for the resident's attainment of maximum independence in areas of skill deficits; a plan to minimize significant inappropriate behavior and emotional problems; and provisions to deal with any problems the resident may have with his/her family, or with the community (when possible). The plan shall include:

1. A detailed description of the resident's intellectual and emotional state, including a description of his behavior at the time the plan is prepared, along with a statement of any specific treatment or rehabilitation needs.
2. A detailed description of the nature of the recommended individual counseling, behavior therapy, family counseling, or any other form of treatment constituting part of the rehabilitation plan.
3. The names and titles of persons who will be responsible for furnishing any of these forms of treatment or rehabilitation.
4. A clear, concise statement of the elements of behavior that have been defined as problems, and that the plan is designed to treat; the short-range, and long-range treatment goals, with a projected time table for their attainment.
5. The names, titles, and functions of all members of the Treatment Team present, and the signature of the H.H. Director and a HF.

Additionally, the Revised Treatment Plan shall be directed at reviewing the appropriateness of the resident's placement into the Halfway House.

Prior to the meeting of the Treatment Team, all necessary evaluations shall be completed. The results of these evaluations shall be in the resident's Individual Program Book.

When any staff designated to attend the Revised Treatment Plan Review cannot attend, he/she is to summarize in writing, any evaluations, comments, or other pertinent information and place this summary in the resident's Individual Program Book prior to the review.

The resident must attend the Revised Treatment Plan Review. Attendance of the resident's family or surrogates, and other persons designated as necessary contributors to the treatment plan, shall be requested by a member of the Treatment Team, provided that prior consent is obtained from the resident.

Treatment Plan Reviews

Within four to six weeks from the date of the Revised Treatment Plan, and once every four to six weeks thereafter, unless otherwise indicated in the resident's individual program, the treatment plan shall be reviewed by the resident's Treatment Team to appraise his/her progress toward achieving the objectives specified by the plan, and to update the plan, if necessary. Progress shall be assessed on the basis of program data as interpreted by the Treatment Team. The meeting shall include:

1. Assessment of the resident's progress.
2. Necessary changes, additions, or deletions in the resident's Treatment Plan.
3. Changes, additions, or deletions shall include procedures and goals.
4. A detailed description of the nature of the changes and/or additions to the resident's treatment plan.
5. The names and titles of persons who will be responsible for furnishing any of these additional forms of treatment or rehabilitation.
6. A clear, concise statement of the elements of behavior that have been defined as additional problems, and that the revised treatment plan is designed to treat, along with the short-term and long-term treatment goals for each problem.
7. The names, title, and functions of all members of the Treatment Team present, and the signature of the H.H. Director and a HF.

Members of the Treatment Team who are not able to attend these reviews are to summarize in writing, any evaluations, comments, or other pertinent information and place this summary in the resident's Individual Program Book prior to the review.

The resident must attend the reviews. Attendance of the resident's family or surrogates, and other persons designated as necessary contributors to the treatment plan, shall be requested by a member of the Treatment Team, provided that prior consent is obtained from the resident.

Special Reviews

When needed, a member of the Treatment Team may request a special review of particular components of the resident's treatment plan. Special reviews are to be conducted immediately following the occurrences of potentially harmful behaviors that have no programs, individual or house-wide, and that adequately consequate the behavior. Attendance at Special Reviews shall consist of

1. Halfway House Director or on-call psychologist
2. Halfway House Facilitator(s) (HF)
3. Any other staff members who observed the occurrence of the target behavior and/or who can contribute information concerning the behavior

Discharge Conferences

These conferences are to take place prior to discharge from the Halfway House and placement into the community, and should include consideration of the following:

1. Overall progress of the resident toward goals set in the Halfway House program.
2. The current needs of the resident including services and therapies.
3. The suitability of the proposed placement environment for providing these services and therapies.
4. The suitability of the proposed placement from the perspective of the resident's family and/or surrogate (when applicable).
5. Plans for follow-up with the resident and family.
6. The names, titles, and functions of the persons participating in this staffing, and the signature of the H.H. Director and a HF.

Staff participation in this review is to consist of the resident's Treatment Team. Members of the Treatment Team, who are not able to attend these reviews, are to summarize in writing, any evaluations, comments, or other pertinent information, and place this summary in the resident's Individual Program Book prior to the review.

The resident must attend this review. Attendance of the resident's family or surrogates, and other persons designated as necessary contributors to this review, shall be requested by a member of the Treatment Team, provided that prior consent is obtained from the resident.

Documentation and Dissemination of the Treatment Plan Review Results

The resident's Individual Program Book shall be used to document the results of the evaluations on which the treatment plan is based; to specify the components of the treatment plan with the program goals stated in behavioral terms; to report the progress of the resident toward the goals as progress is assessed in Treatment Plan Reviews; to document review proceedings, and any modification of the treatment plan and goals in light of the resident's response; and to provide a means of communication among all persons contributing to the resident's treatment plan. Individual program procedures and data sheets shall also be placed in the resident's Individual Program Book.

All components of the Initial Treatment Plan and the Revised Treatment Plan, including the review of the appropriateness of the resident's placement into the Halfway House, and statement of the resident's prognosis, must be entered in the resident's record within 30 days of admission to the Halfway House. Thereafter, progress notes on the resident's response to his/her program shall be recorded in the resident's Individual Program Book with sufficient frequency to enable an evaluation of its efficiency. Once a week, a HF shall record a progress note in the resident's Individual Program Book describing therapeutic outcomes for the week. Progress notes must be made whenever a resident engages in any behavior requiring special attention of staff (e.g., aggression, elopement).

Reports of Treatment Plan Reviews which evaluate the program, and the progress and status of the resident, shall also be entered. The results of all evaluations and reviews shall be interpreted in action terms to the direct-care staff and special services staff responsible for implementing the resident's program, and to the parents or their surrogates when appropriate. Also, when appropriate, the results of reviews shall be interpreted to the resident, and the resident is to receive a copy of each new treatment plan formulated during reviews. Data on individual programs and observations shall be recorded on the appropriate data sheets in the resident's program book.

Procedure

I. Scheduling of Reviews
   A. Initial Treatment Plans, Revised Treatment Plans, and Treatment Plan Reviews shall be conducted on Thursday evenings (7:30 P.M.).
      1. The HFs shall
         a. Prepare a schedule of reviews on a weekly basis. This schedule shall be completed on the Monday preceding the Thursday on which reviews are to take place

b. Ensure that for each resident the Initial Treatment Plan is formulated within three days of admission to the Halfway House; that the Revised Treatment Plan is formulated within 14 days of the Initial Treatment Plan; and that each plan is reviewed monthly, and as needed
c. Submit a weekly schedule of reviews to the H.H. Director and ensure that all Treatment Team Members are informed of the residents schedule to be reviewed
d. Provide for notification of parents, as designated by the resident, of treatment plan reviews at least 48 hours prior to these reviews and place a written record of this notification in the resident's Individual Program Book

II. Entry of Results of Reviews into the Resident's Individual Program Book
   A. Preparation of the written report of reviews shall be the responsibility of the HFs. The person(s) preparing the report and the H.H. Director must sign the report.
   B. The report must be written, typed, and placed into the resident's Individual Program Book.
   C. Results of reviews shall be approved and entered into the resident's Individual Program Book within one week of the review.
   D. Any individual programs resulting from reviews shall be written, along with the necessary data sheets, and any other forms, by the HFs.
   E. The HFs shall prepare and place these individual programs in the resident's Individual Program Book by the Tuesday following the review.
   F. Results of emergency or special reviews shall be written, approved, and placed in the appropriate locations the same day as the review.

HALFWAY HOUSE
INDIVIDUAL PROGRAM BOOK PROCEDURE

GENERAL STATEMENT

Each resident in the Halfway House has his/her own idiosyncracies, strengths, weaknesses, and individuality. Accordingly, the development of individual treatment programs is necessary in order to implement a workable treatment package. The Individual Program Book has been developed for the purpose of having an organized record of the treatment programs, contracts, data, and other materials and information pertinent to the treatment of each resident in the Halfway House.

PURPOSE

1. To develop individualized programs for specified individual problems
2. To encourage each resident to participate in the development of his/her treatment plan
3. To develop a contractual agreement between the staff and the resident
4. To develop a reciprocal relationship
5. To foster a sense of responsibility
6. To recognize the person as an individual
7. To clearly state the responsibilities of the staff and the resident

PROCEDURE

I. General Policies
   A. Each resident is to have his/her own Individual Program Book.
   B. All materials pertaining to that resident are to be kept in his/her Individual Program Book.
   C. Each resident, prior to entering the Halfway House, is to complete the following:
      1. Read the Halfway House Information Handbook.
      2. Sign the necessary contracts.

II. Contents of the Individual Program Book
   A. Contractual agreements between the staff and the resident.
   B. A copy of all evaluations, test results, letters, etc., from any source relating directly to the resident.
   C. Treatment Programs
   D. Data and graphs

III. Individual Programs
   A. General information and policies
      1. All programs *must* be written.
      2. All programs *must* be agreed upon by the staff and resident.
      3. All programs require the signature of the resident on the program and on the program agreement. (See Figure 3-1, p. 233.)
      4. Before a program can be started, Steps 1 through 3 must be completed.
      5. A copy of each program is to be
         a. Given to the resident
         b. Given to Halfway House Program Director
         c. Placed in the resident's Individual Program Book
      6. Any program may be negotiated, renegotiated, or cancelled at any time by agreement between the resident and his/her Interdisciplinary Treatment Team.
      7. All programs are to be determined during
         a. Interdisciplinary Treatment Team Conferences (See Halfway House Interdisciplinary Treatment Team Conference Procedure, p. 225.)
         b. Special Reviews

IV. Specific Information and Policies
   A. All individual programs are to be developed with the resident present.
   B. Each behavior is to be operationally defined.
   C. When possible, baseline data are to be collected prior to the initiation of a treatment program.
   D. Each problem behavior is to be coded, beginning with 1, 2, 3, ...N.
   E. Each program developed for each behavior is to be given a number, 1, 2, 3, ...N.
   F. When a program is developed, an Individual Treatment Agreement (See Figure 3-1, p.233) is to be completed before the program is begun. The agreement is to include the
      1. Resident's name
      2. Problem number
      3. Target behavior
      4. Behavioral definition
      5. Beginning Date
      6. Resident's Signature
      7. House Facilitator's (HF) signature
      8. Halfway House Director's Signature
   G. New or modified programs for the same behavior
      1. New or modified programs for the same behavior are to receive a new program number.
      2. New or modified programs are to be recorded on the same Individual Treatment Agreement.
      3. Any components of the previous program that are still in effect are to be transferred to the new program.
      4. Once a new or modified program has been written, cancel all previous programs for that behavior.
   H. All staff members are to
      1. Commit the programs to memory
      2. Initial each program after reading it
   I. Programs are to be typed and are to begin on Tuesdays.
V. Example of an Individual Treatment Agreement and an Individual Program
   A. John Doe has not been interacting with other residents in the Halfway House. John has stated that he would like to talk to other people more but he is uncomfortable around people.
   B. During an Interdisciplinary Treatment Team Conference a decision was made to begin a baseline on John Doe's verbal interactions with others.
      1. Verbal interaction defined as any time he is observed talking to another individual.
      2. The behavior is to be observed on a 30 minute variable-interval (VI 30′) observation schedule.
   C. Verbal interaction is the target behavior. Since it is the sixth target behavior for John Doe it has been numerically coded as "Problem Number 6."
   D. All programs relating to Verbal Interactions are to be assigned a Program Number.
      1. The first program is to be Program Number 1.
      2. The last program is to be Program Number N.
   E. Treatment Program 1
      1. Name: John Doe
      2. Problem Number: 6
      3. Target Behavior: Verbal Interactions
      4. Program Number: 1
      5. Beginning Date: 7/13/83
      6. Program
         a. Give verbal praise every time resident is observed engaging in verbal interactions with another individual during a variable-interval observation.

F. The Individual Treatment Agreement is completed before the initiation of the program. The agreement includes
   1. Name: John Doe
   2. Problem Number: 6
   3. Target Behavior: Verbal Interactions
   4. Behavioral Definition: Any time he is observed talking to another individual during a variable-interval observation
   5. Program Number: 1
   6. Beginning date: 7/13/83
   7. Resident's Signature: John Doe
   8. HF Signature: Tom Smith
   9. Psychologist's Signature: William Jones

INDIVIDUAL TREATMENT AGREEMENT

I, _____ , have read or have had read to me the treatment program(s) specifically designed for me. I do agree to comply with the program(s) as specified. However, I reserve the right to cancel or renegotiate my agreement at any time. I further understand that the staff also reserves the right to alter my contract as long as it is in writing and I agree to the changes.

PROBLEM NUMBER: _____   TARGET BEHAV(S): _____

BEHAV. DEFINITION: _____

Program 1

Beginning Date _____ Ending Date _____

Resident: _____

HF: _____

Psychologist: _____

Program 4

Date _____

Resident: _____

HF: _____

Psychologist: _____

Program 2

Date: _____

Resident: _____

HF: _____

Psychologist: _____

Program 5

Date: _____

Resident: _____

HF: _____

Psychologist: _____

Program 3

Date: _____

Resident: _____

HF: _____

Psychologist: _____

Program 6

Date: _____

Resident: _____

HF: _____

Psychologist: _____

Figure 3-1

HALFWAY HOUSE
SELF-CARE SKILLS MAINTENANCE PROCEDURE

GENERAL STATEMENT

By the time an individual becomes a member of the Halfway House community, he/she is engaging in the necessary self-care skills expected by society. However, those entering the house community may be leaving a very highly structured environment, and entering an environment with an emphasis on self-control. This transition may result in some disorganization. By maintaining the same self-care skills criteria as in the Level 3 program with a rapid fading program, the disorganization should be limited. With the continued exposure to the basic procedures outlined for each self-care skill, the maintenance of these skills will be facilitated.

PURPOSE

1. To help ensure the maintenance of the basic self-care skills
2. To further an individual's awareness of him/herself
3. To further develop a positive self-concept
4. To help ensure maintenance of good personal hygiene
5. To help increase self-control behaviors

TERMINAL OBJECTIVE

The terminal objective is to have the resident perform his/her self-care skills with the proficiency specified in the Level 3 programs for each skill, without supervision, for at least two months and until discharged.

PROCEDURE

I. General Policies
  A. Self-care skills include all skills specified in the Level 3 Self-Care Skills Program. (See p. 41.)
  B. The only consequence for not completing self-care skills appropriately is prompts.
  C. Should prompts be required frequently, or if behaviors are not engaged in appropriately, individualized programs will be developed during Treatment Team Conferences.
  D. Frequent prompts is defined as
    1. More than two prompts during any one week
    2. One or more prompts for Self-medication during one week
  E. Appropriateness is determined by the same criteria specified in the Level 3 Self-Care Skills Program with the following changes:
  1. Bedroom Area Preparation
    a. Each resident's bedroom floor is to be mopped and furniture dusted at least once a week. The resident is to inform a house facilitator (HF) he/she has mopped the floor. A HF is to then inspect the floor.
    b. Sheets are to be changed once a week. The resident is to inform a HF when he/she has changed his/her sheets. The HF is to then inspect the bed for fresh linen.
    c. There are to be no stripped bed inspections.
  2. Wake-up Procedure
    a. The Sleep procedure does not include naps.
    b. The Therapeutic Community (See the *Therapeutic Community Procedure,* p. 253) is to specify a time by which resident's are to be awake (Monday through Saturday).

c. HFs are not to awaken a resident unless he/she is not awake by the specified time in which case a HF is to prompt him/her to wake up).
3. Dental Hygiene
   a. Residents are to keep a supply of plaque pills.
   b. After completing brushing, the resident is to chew another plaque pill and then have his/her teeth inspected for plaque.
4. Shower
   a. Observation of each behavior in the behavioral chain of showering (i.e., lathering, rinsing, etc.) is *not* required.
   b. Observation of indicants of showering (i.e., getting into shower, etc.) is required every other day.
5. Locker
   a. To include the resident's closet and night stand
   b. Omit procedure on locker day. (See Level 3 Locker Procedure, p. 75.)
   c. Randomly choose either the morning (following wake-up) or evening (after supper) for evaluations.
6. Medication—Follow Step IV Method (See Level 3 Self Medication Procedure, p. 79.)
7. Meals
   a. Omit evaluation for appropriate appearance and clean hands preceding meal. These two evaluations are to occur unobtrusively during the meal.
   b. One unobtrusive time sample is to be taken per resident per meal (five seconds per sample).

II. Evaluations
   A. Self-care skills evaluations are to begin immediately upon a resident's arrival at the Halfway House.
   B. Evaluations are to be made according to the following schedule:
      1. Stage 1
         a. HF is to randomly choose four days per week for each self-care skill for evaluations.
         b. Randomly chosen evaluation days are to be marked on the resident's self-care skills data sheet.
         c. Continue this stage until the resident has met the self-care skills weekly criterion for one week (as specified in the Level 3 Self-Care Skills procedure).
      2. Stage 2
         a. Two evaluations per week
         b. HF is to randomly choose two days per week for each self-care skill for evaluation.
         c. Randomly chosen evaluation days are to be marked on the resident's self-care skills data sheet.
         d. Continue this stage until the resident has met the self-care skills weekly criterion for one week (as specified in the Level 3 Self Care Skills procedure).
      3. Stage 3
         a. One evaluation per week
         b. HF is to randomly choose one day per week (for each self-care skill) for evaluation.
         c. The randomly chosen evaluation day is to be marked on the resident's self-care skills data sheet.
         d. The criterion for this stage consists of the resident obtaining all scores of 1 on one weekly evaluation.
      4. Stage 4
         a. One evaluation bi-weekly
         b. HF is to randomly choose one day per two weeks (for each self-care skill for evaluation).

236 HALFWAY HOUSE PROCEDURES

   c. The randomly chosen evaluation day is to be marked on the resident's self-care skills data sheet.
   d. The criterion for this stage consists of the resident obtaining all scores of 1 on the one bi-weekly evaluation.
  5. Stage 5
   a. One evaluation per month
   b. HF is to randomly choose one day per month (for each self-care skill) for evaluation.
   c. The randomly chosen day is to be marked on the resident's self-care skills data sheet.
   d. The criterion for this stage consists of the resident obtaining all scores of 1 for each self-care skill on the one monthly evaluation.
  6. Stage 6
   Discontinue evaluations
  7. Whenever a resident falls below criteria for any self-care skill, he/she is to begin the self-care skills program from the beginning with daily evaluations (i.e., Stage 1), unless otherwise determined on an individual basis. (Stage regressions are to be determined in Treatment Team Conferences.)
  8. Evaluations of weekly behaviors (i.e., wet mopping, dusting, changing linen) are to be completed weekly until one month after the Self-Care Skills Elimination Program has been completed.
 C. Evaluation Elimination Schedule Sheet (See Figure 3-2, p. 238.)
  1. There is to be one Evaluation Elimination Schedule Sheet Displayed in the Halfway House office.
  2. Record the following on the sheet:
   a. Names—Record the resident's name in the column depicting the elimination stage he/she is currently in.
   b. Date—Record the date on which the resident was placed into the current elimination stage.
   c. When the resident moves from one elimination stage to another, draw a single line through his/her name in the previous stage.
III. Self-Care Skill Data Sheet and Self-Care Skills Criterion Data Sheet
 A. Self-Care Skills Data Sheet (See Figure 3-3, p. 239.)
  1. There is to be one Self-Care Skills Data Sheet per resident
  2. The Self-Care Skills Data Sheet is to be located in the resident's Individual Program Book.
  3. Data to be recorded:
   a. Date—Record the date for that day.
   b. Stage—Record the evaluation stage the resident is currently in.
   c. Bedroom Area; Dental Hygiene; Shower; Locker; Medication; Meals—For each skill record the single score the resident obtained for that day (either a 1, 2, or 3 score).
   d. HF—Record the initials of the house facilitator making the recordings.
 B. Self-Care Skills Criteria Data Sheet (See Figure 3-4, p. 240.)
  1. There is to be one Self-Care Skills Criteria Data sheet per resident.
  2. The data sheet is to be located in the resident's Individual Program Book.
  3. Each Saturday evening the HF is to
   a. Record the date for the last day of the week that data were collected (this should always be the date for the Saturday—the day this recording is being done)
   b. Record the Evaluation Stage the resident is currently in
   c. For each self-care skill
    (1) Record the average for the week by summing the scores for the week for the skill and dividing by the number of days on which a score was obtained

(2) Record whether the resident met the criterion for each self-care skill
   (a) If the resident did meet the criterion for a self-care skill place a check mark (✓) in the appropriate column.
   (b) If the resident did *not* meet the criterion for the self-care skill, place an X in the appropriate column.
   (c) Stage crit.:
      1. If the resident did meet the criterion for his/her evaluation stage
         a. Place a check mark (✓) in the appropriate space
         b. Enter his/her name in the column for the next stage on the Evaluation Elimination Schedule Sheet and draw a single line through his/her name in the previous stage
      2. If the individual did *not* meet the criterion for his/her elimination stage, place an X in the appropriate space.
   (d) HF—Record the initials of the house facilitator making the weekly recordings on the Self-Care Skills Criteria Data Sheet.

HALFWAY HOUSE EVALUATION ELIMINATION SCHEDULE FOR SELF-CARE SKILLS

	DAILY EVALUATION	2 EVAL. PER WEEK	1 EVAL. PER WEEK	1 EVAL. BI-WEEKLY	1 EVAL. PER MONTH	NO EVAL.
DATE						

Figure 3-2

HALFWAY HOUSE
SELF-CARE SKILLS DATA SHEET

DATE	STAGE	BEDROOM AREA BED/MOP/DUST	DENTAL HYGIENE	SHOWER WASH SHAMPOO	LOCKER	MEDI-CATION	MEALS	HF	COMMENTS

Figure 3-3

HALFWAY HOUSE
SELF-CARE SKILLS CRITERIA DATA

Date:	BED. AREA	DEN. HYG.	SHOWER	LOCKER	MEDIC.	MEALS	STAGE	STAGE CRIT.	HF
Average (Mean)									
Criteria									
Date:									
Average (Mean)									
Criteria									
Date:									
Average (Mean)									
Criteria									
Date:									
Average (Mean)									
Criteria									
Date:									
Average (Mean)									
Criteria									
Date:									
Average (Mean)									
Criteria									

Figure 3-4

HALFWAY HOUSE
MEALS PROCEDURE

GENERAL STATEMENT

Having the ability to purchase food items, and organize and prepare meals is extremely important for independent and successful living. The acquisition, development, and/or maintenance of such skills increases the probability of the individual succeeding in the community once he/she leaves the hospital or Halfway House. Individuals receive training in menu preparation, food purchasing, and similar topics while in the Level 3 Program at the academic level and, to a limited extent, at the applied level. This instruction, however, does not guarantee that the individual will engage in these activities successfully in the community. The Meals Procedure has been designed to enable the individual to practice and develop these skills along with the preparation and cooking of food in a semi-structured environment. In addition, the procedure is designed to facilitate the development of appropriate social skills and cooperation with the other occupants of the Halfway House.

PURPOSE

1. To develop meal preparation skills (e.g., cooking, cleaning, etc.)
2. To help develop menu planning skills
3. To help develop independent living
4. To help develop social skills
5. To help develop dependability
6. To help develop money management abilities
7. To increase self-esteem
8. To help develop problem solving skills
9. To help develop organizational skills
10. To help develop cooperation

TERMINAL OBJECTIVE

The terminal objective is to have the resident prepare his/her own meals without the supervision of the House-Facilitators (HFs). This is to include the planning, organizing, cooking of meals, and the cleaning of the kitchen after meals.

PROCEDURE

I. General Policies
   A. All residents residing in the Halfway House are to participate in the Meals Program.
   B. Residents are to purchase their own food.
   C. There are to be two breakfast preparation periods:
      1. Monday-Friday
         a. 6:00–6:30 A.M.
         b. 6:30–7:00 A.M.
      2. Saturday and Sunday
         a. 10:00–10:30 A.M.
         b. 10:30–11:00 A.M.
   D. There are to be three lunch preparation periods:
      1. 11:30–12:00 noon
      2. 12:00–12:30 P.M.
      3. 12:30–1:00 P.M.

E. There are to be five periods during which residents are to sign up for the use of the stove:
   1. 4:40–5:00 P.M.
   2. 5:05–5:25 P.M.
   3. 5:30–5:50 P.M.
   4. 5:55–6:15 P.M.
   5. 6:30–6:40 P.M.
F. Residents are to sign up for breakfast, lunch, and supper meal periods the evening preceding the meals.
G. Anyone missing his/her scheduled meal preparation period and still wishing to prepare a meal is to do so during the half-hour following the last scheduled meal period (unless the kitchen is not available). The resident is not to be permitted to use the kitchen beyond this time (to prepare breakfast, lunch, or supper) unless he/she has a valid reason for missing the scheduled meal preparation period.
H. Specific conflicts and problems are to be handled on an individual basis.
I. Residents may invite guests for a meal (excluding breakfast).
   1. The resident is to sign-up to use the kitchen during the last meal period.
   2. Only when the residents and the house schedule permits (i.e., no scheduled meeting, or required activities that conflict with the meal).
   3. The resident is to follow the procedure described below. (See Section III.)
J. Residents may have separate meals.
K. Group meals may be planned.
L. Residents may use the kitchen during times other than the scheduled meal periods for snacks.

II. Meal Preparation Sign-Up Sheets (See Figures 3-5, 3-6, and 3-7, pp. 249, 250, 251.)
  A. The Meal Preparation Sign-Up Sheet is to be posted on the bulletin board.
  B. Each resident is to sign-up for meals (breakfast, lunch, supper) on the evening preceding the meal. Meals (snacks) during times other than breakfast, lunch, and supper periods are to be recorded sometime *before* the meal, but not necessarily during the preceding evening
  C. Breakfast
     1. Each resident is to sign-up for a meal preparation period for breakfast.
     2. No more than five residents are to sign-up for the same meal preparation period unless a group meal is planned.
     3. The resident is to indicate on the sheet whether the meal is to be an individual or group meal.
        a. When an individual meal is planned
           (1) The resident is to place a check mark (✔) in the "Individual Meal" column
           (2) The resident is to list the food he/she intends on preparing (before the meal)
        b. When a group meal is planned
           (1) The group is to choose some code (e.g., number, letter, symbol), and each member of the group is to place this group code in the "Group Meal Code" column
           (2) Each resident participating in a Group Meal is to record his/her meal job in the "Group Job" column (See Section IV: Group Meal Preparation Jobs)
           (3) Each resident is to record the food that he/she is contributing to the meal, prior to the meal
           (4) Each resident or group (when a group meal is planned) is responsible for his/her/their own food preparation, cooking, etc.
  D. Lunch
     1. Each resident is to sign-up for a meal preparation period for lunch on the evening preceding the meal but not sooner than 6:30 P.M.

2. No more than four residents are to sign-up for each of the three lunch preparation periods, unless a group meal is planned.
3. Each resident is to list the foods he/she intends on preparing (or is contributing to a group meal).
4. The resident is to indicate on the sheet whether the meal is to be an individual, group, or guest meal (guest meals only during last meal period unless special permission is given by a house facilitator (HF)).
   a. When an individual meal is planned, the resident is to place a check mark (✓) in the Individual Meal column.
   b. When a Group Meal is planned
      (1) The group is to choose some code (e.g., a number, letter, symbol), and each member of the group is to place this group code in the "Group Meal Code" column.
      (2) Each resident participating in a Group Meal is to record his/her meal job in the "Group Job" column. (See Section IV.)
      (3) The food each resident is contributing to the group meal is to be recorded prior to the meal.
   c. When a Guest Meal is planned the resident(s) is/are to place the number of guests expected in the "# Guests" column
5. Each resident or group (when a group meal is planned) is responsible for his/her/their own food preparation and cooking, cleaning, etc.

E. Supper
   1. Each resident is to sign-up for a stove-use period on the evening preceding the meal.
   2. No more than two residents are to sign-up for each of the five stove-use periods (except for group meals—See "Group Meals" below).
   3. Each resident is to list the foods he/she intends on preparing (or is contributing to a group meal).
   4. The resident is to indicate on the sheet whether the meal is to be an individual, group, or guest meal (guest meals only during the last meal period unless special permission is given by a HF).
      a. When an individual meal is planned, the resident is to place a check mark (✓) in the "Individual Meal" column.
      b. When a Group Meal is planned
         (1) The group is to choose some code (e.g., a number, letter, symbol), and each member of the group is to place this group code in the "Group Meal Code" column.
         (2) Each resident participating in a Group Meal is to record his/her meal job in the "Group Job" column. (See Section IV.)
         (3) The food each resident is contributing to the group meal is to be recorded prior to the meal.
      c. When a Guest Meal is planned, the resident(s) is/are to place the number of guests expected in the "#Guests" column.
   5. Each resident or group (when a group meal is planned) is responsible for his/her/their own food preparation and cooking, cleaning, etc.

III. Meals Preparation Method
   A. Breakfast
      1. Individual Meals
         a. Each resident is responsible for his/her own food preparation and cooking, cleaning, etc.
         b. Any utensils used for food preparation and/or cooking are to be washed before the resident begins eating.
         c. Any mess made by the resident (e.g., on stove, counter) is to be cleaned before the resident begins eating.

d. All dishes, silverware, etc., used by the resident are to be washed, dried, and put away after the resident finishes eating.
e. The resident is responsible for returning the kitchen and the dining room to the same condition they were in prior to the meal (e.g., sweeping the floor, wipe off table).
2. Group Meals
   a. Each member of the group is to contribute food for the meal.
   b. The group is responsible for food preparation and cooking, cleaning, etc.
   c. Allocation of duties is to be determined by the group and recorded on the Meal Preparation Sign-Up Sheet.
   d. Any utensils used for food preparation and/or cooking are to be washed before the group begins eating.
   e. Any mess made by the group (e.g., on the stove, counter) is to be cleaned before the group begins eating.
   f. All dishes, silverware, etc., used by the group are to be washed, dried, and put away after the group finishes eating.
   g. The group is responsible for returning the kitchen and the dining room to the same condition they were in prior to the meal (e.g., sweep floor, wipe off table).

B. Lunch
1. Individual Meals: The procedure prescribed for individual breakfast meals is to be observed. (See Sec. III, A.1.)
2. Group Meals: The procedure prescribed for group breakfast meals is to be observed. (See Sec. III, A.2.)
3. Meals with a guest
   a. Meals with a guest are to be scheduled during the last meal period.
   b. Scheduling of meals with guests:
      (1) The resident is to sign-up for the meal period on the evening preceding the meal.
      (2) On the day of the meal, if the last period has not been scheduled by someone else, a resident may use that period for a guest meal. This scheduling is to be done by phone or in-person and is to be recorded on the sign-up sheet and approved by an HF.
   c. Each resident is responsible for his/her own food preparation and cooking, cleaning, etc. (guest(s) may help).
   d. Any utensils used for food preparation and/or cooking are to be washed before eating begins (guest(s) may help).
   e. Any mess made (e.g., on stove, counter) is to be cleaned before eating begins (guest(s) may help).
   f. All dishes, silverware, etc., are to be washed, dried, and put away after eating is concluded (guest(s) may help).
   g. The resident is responsible for returning the kitchen and the dining room to the same condition they were in prior to the meal (e.g., sweep floor, wipe off table).

C. Supper
1. Individual Meals
   a. Each resident is to sign-up for a stove-use period on the evening preceding the meal.
   b. No more than two residents are to sign-up for the same stove-use period (one resident per stove).
   c. Stove-use periods are the time periods during which the resident is actually using the stove, and do not include food preparation (e.g., seasoning, mixing) eating, dishwashing, and cleaning time periods.
   d. Each resident is to begin preparing food (e.g., seasoning, mixing) prior to the stove-use period for which he/she signed up.

2. No more than four residents are to sign-up for each of the three lunch preparation periods, unless a group meal is planned.
3. Each resident is to list the foods he/she intends on preparing (or is contributing to a group meal).
4. The resident is to indicate on the sheet whether the meal is to be an individual, group, or guest meal (guest meals only during last meal period unless special permission is given by a house facilitator (HF)).
   a. When an individual meal is planned, the resident is to place a check mark (✓) in the Individual Meal column.
   b. When a Group Meal is planned
      (1) The group is to choose some code (e.g., a number, letter, symbol), and each member of the group is to place this group code in the "Group Meal Code" column.
      (2) Each resident participating in a Group Meal is to record his/her meal job in the "Group Job" column. (See Section IV.)
      (3) The food each resident is contributing to the group meal is to be recorded prior to the meal.
   c. When a Guest Meal is planned the resident(s) is/are to place the number of guests expected in the "# Guests" column
5. Each resident or group (when a group meal is planned) is responsible for his/her/their own food preparation and cooking, cleaning, etc.

E. Supper
1. Each resident is to sign-up for a stove-use period on the evening preceding the meal.
2. No more than two residents are to sign-up for each of the five stove-use periods (except for group meals—See "Group Meals" below).
3. Each resident is to list the foods he/she intends on preparing (or is contributing to a group meal).
4. The resident is to indicate on the sheet whether the meal is to be an individual, group, or guest meal (guest meals only during the last meal period unless special permission is given by a HF).
   a. When an individual meal is planned, the resident is to place a check mark (✓) in the "Individual Meal" column.
   b. When a Group Meal is planned
      (1) The group is to choose some code (e.g., a number, letter, symbol), and each member of the group is to place this group code in the "Group Meal Code" column.
      (2) Each resident participating in a Group Meal is to record his/her meal job in the "Group Job" column. (See Section IV.)
      (3) The food each resident is contributing to the group meal is to be recorded prior to the meal.
   c. When a Guest Meal is planned, the resident(s) is/are to place the number of guests expected in the "#Guests" column.
5. Each resident or group (when a group meal is planned) is responsible for his/her/their own food preparation and cooking, cleaning, etc.

III. Meals Preparation Method
   A. Breakfast
      1. Individual Meals
         a. Each resident is responsible for his/her own food preparation and cooking, cleaning, etc.
         b. Any utensils used for food preparation and/or cooking are to be washed before the resident begins eating.
         c. Any mess made by the resident (e.g., on stove, counter) is to be cleaned before the resident begins eating.

d. All dishes, silverware, etc., used by the resident are to be washed, dried, and put away after the resident finishes eating.
e. The resident is responsible for returning the kitchen and the dining room to the same condition they were in prior to the meal (e.g., sweeping the floor, wipe off table).

2. Group Meals
   a. Each member of the group is to contribute food for the meal.
   b. The group is responsible for food preparation and cooking, cleaning, etc.
   c. Allocation of duties is to be determined by the group and recorded on the Meal Preparation Sign-Up Sheet.
   d. Any utensils used for food preparation and/or cooking are to be washed before the group begins eating.
   e. Any mess made by the group (e.g., on the stove, counter) is to be cleaned before the group begins eating.
   f. All dishes, silverware, etc., used by the group are to be washed, dried, and put away after the group finishes eating.
   g. The group is responsible for returning the kitchen and the dining room to the same condition they were in prior to the meal (e.g., sweep floor, wipe off table).

B. Lunch
   1. Individual Meals: The procedure prescribed for individual breakfast meals is to be observed. (See Sec. III, A.1.)
   2. Group Meals: The procedure prescribed for group breakfast meals is to be observed. (See Sec. III, A.2.)
   3. Meals with a guest
      a. Meals with a guest are to be scheduled during the last meal period.
      b. Scheduling of meals with guests:
         (1) The resident is to sign-up for the meal period on the evening preceding the meal.
         (2) On the day of the meal, if the last period has not been scheduled by someone else, a resident may use that period for a guest meal. This scheduling is to be done by phone or in-person and is to be recorded on the sign-up sheet and approved by an HF.
      c. Each resident is responsible for his/her own food preparation and cooking, cleaning, etc. (guest(s) may help).
      d. Any utensils used for food preparation and/or cooking are to be washed before eating begins (guest(s) may help).
      e. Any mess made (e.g., on stove, counter) is to be cleaned before eating begins (guest(s) may help).
      f. All dishes, silverware, etc., are to be washed, dried, and put away after eating is concluded (guest(s) may help).
      g. The resident is responsible for returning the kitchen and the dining room to the same condition they were in prior to the meal (e.g., sweep floor, wipe off table).

C. Supper
   1. Individual Meals
      a. Each resident is to sign-up for a stove-use period on the evening preceding the meal.
      b. No more than two residents are to sign-up for the same stove-use period (one resident per stove).
      c. Stove-use periods are the time periods during which the resident is actually using the stove, and do not include food preparation (e.g., seasoning, mixing) eating, dishwashing, and cleaning time periods.
      d. Each resident is to begin preparing food (e.g., seasoning, mixing) prior to the stove-use period for which he/she signed up.

e. The resident's food is to be prepared (e.g., seasoned, mixed) by the time his/her stove-use period begins.

f. Each resident is responsible for his/her own food preparation and cooking, cleaning, etc.

g. Any utensils used for food preparation and/or cooking are to be washed before the resident begins eating.

h. Any mess made by the resident (e.g., on stove, counter) is to be cleaned before the resident begins eating.

i. All dishes, silverware, etc., used by the resident are to be washed, dried, and put away after the resident finishes eating.

j. The resident is responsible for returning the kitchen and dining room to the same condition they were in prior to the meal (e.g., sweep floor, wipe off table).

2. Group Meals

a. Each member of the group is to contribute food to the meal, and/or the group may decide to collect money from the members and purchase items for the meal.

b. The group is responsible for its own food preparation and cooking, cleaning, etc.

c. Allocation of duties is to be determined by the group and recorded on the Meal Preparation Sign-Up Sheet (by each resident in the group).

d. A stove-use period is the time period during which the group is actually using the stove and does not include food preparation (e.g., seasoning, mixing) eating, dishwashing, and cleaning time periods.

e. The cook is to begin preparing foods (e.g., seasoning, mixing) prior to the stove-use period for which they signed up.

f. The group's food is to be prepared (e.g., seasoned, mixed) by the time the group's stove-use period begins.

g. Any utensils used for food preparation and/or cooking are to be washed before the group begins eating.

h. Any mess made by the group (e.g., on stove, counter) is to be cleaned before the group begins eating.

i. All dishes, silverware, etc., used by the group are to be washed, dried, and put away after the group finishes eating.

j. The group is responsible for returning the kitchen and dining room to the same condition they were in prior to the meal (e.g., sweep floor, wipe off table).

k. When two or three residents are having a group meal, they may sign up for one or two consecutive stove-use period(s) (on the same stove), or one stove-use period using both stoves, depending on the type of meal planned (i.e., if a meal is planned that requires only 20 minutes of cooking time, residents should sign-up for one stove-use period, thus leaving the other stove available for another resident or group. Or if a meal is planned that requires more than 20 minutes but less than 40 minutes of cooking time, residents may sign up for two consecutive stove-use periods).

l. When four or five residents are having a group meal, they may sign-up for one, two, or three consecutive stove-use period(s) using one stove, or they may sign-up for one stove-use period using both stoves, depending on the type of meal planned (i.e., length of cooking time needed and complexity of meal).

m. When six, seven, or eight residents are having a group meal, they may sign-up for one, two, or three consecutive stove-use periods using one stove, or they may sign up for one or two consecutive stove-use period(s) using both stoves, depending on the type of meal planned (i.e., length of cooking time needed and complexity of meal).

n. When nine residents are having a group meal, they may sign-up for one, two, three, or four consecutive stove-use period(s) using one stove, or they may sign up for one, two, three, or four consecutive stove-use period(s) using both stoves, depending on the type of meal planned (i.e., length of cooking time needed and complexity of meal).
o. Whenever five or more residents are planning a group meal, all their cooking is to be completed by 6:15 P.M., unless special arrangements have been made with a HF.
p. The smallest possible number of stoves and stove-use periods are to be used for group meals.

3. Meals with a guest
   a. Scheduling of meals with guests
      (1) The resident is to sign-up for the meal period on the evening preceding the meal.
      (2) On the day of the meal, if the last period has not been scheduled by someone else, a resident may use that period for a guest meal. This scheduling is to be done by phone or in-person and is to be recorded on the sign-up sheet. If done by phone, the scheduling is to be approved by a HF.
   b. Meals with a guest are to be scheduled during the last meal period.
   c. If, when it is time to *prepare* the meal, no one has signed up for the immediately preceding stove-use period, the resident may use this period. This change is to be recorded on the Meal Preparation Sign-Up Sheet.
   d. The resident is responsible for his/her own food preparation and cooking, cleaning, etc. (guest(s) may help).
   e. Stove-use periods are the time periods during which the resident is actually using the stove and they do not include food preparation (e.g., seasoning, mixing) eating, dishwashing, and cleaning time periods.
   f. The resident is to begin preparing food (e.g., seasoning, mixing) prior to the stove-use period during which he/she will be cooking (guest(s) may help).
   g. The food is to be prepared (e.g., seasoned, mixed) by the time the stove-use period begins.
   h. Any utensils used for food preparation and/or cooking are to be washed before eating begins (guest(s) may help).
   i. Any mess made (e.g., on the stove, counter) is to be cleaned before eating begins (guest(s) may help).
   j. All dishes, silverware, etc., are to be washed, dried, and put away after eating is concluded (guest(s) may help).
   k. The resident is responsible for returning the kitchen and dining room to the same condition they were in prior to the meal (e.g., sweep floor, wipe off table, etc.).

D. Unscheduled Meals (Snacks)
   1. Residents are to use kitchen during times other than the scheduled meal periods for snacks.
   2. The procedure prescribed for lunch is to be followed (see Section III, B), with the exception that sign-up sheets and evaluations are not required.

IV. Group Meal Preparation Jobs
   A. Cook responsibilities
      1. Prepare and cook the group meal.
      2. Clean up any mess made (e.g., on the stove, counter, floor).
   B. Server responsibilities
      1. Remove food from preparation containers and place in serving bowls.
      2. Place food on table.
      3. Place pots, pans, etc., that were used for food preparation in sink to be washed.

C. Table Setter responsibilities
   1. Set the table for the group.
   2. Remove dishes, silverware, etc., from the table at the completion of the meal and place them in the sink in the kitchen to be washed.
   3. Wipe off dining room table.
D. Dishwasher responsibilities
   1. As the cook is finished using pots, pans, etc., for cooking, the dishwasher is to wash, dry, and put them away.
   2. Wash, dry, and put away all dishes, silverware, etc., at the end of a meal.
E. Data Recorder responsibilities
   1. Record all data as specified (See Section V: Kitchen and Dining Room Evaluations) on the Kitchen and Dining Room Evaluation Sheet. (See Figure 3-8, p. 252.)
   2. Turn the data sheet into the HF before beginning food preparation.
   3. Correct any inappropriate items (e.g., dirty dishes, mess on table, unswept floor) recorded on the evaluation sheet for the group's meal period.
F. When five residents sign up for a group meal, the job assignments are to follow the procedures delineated above (A through E).
G. When only four residents sign up for a group meal, the table setter and the data recorder positions are to be combined to form one position.
H. When only three residents sign up for a group meal
   1. The table setter and the data recorder positions are to be combined to form one position
   2. The dishwasher and the server positions are to be combined to form one position
   3. The cook's responsibilities are to remain the same
I. When only two residents sign-up for a group meal, both residents are equally responsible for all jobs.

V. Kitchen and Dining Room Evaluation Data Sheet (See Figure 3-8, p. 252.)
   A. The kitchen and dining room are to be evaluated before each meal preparation period using the Kitchen and Dining Room Evaluation Data Sheet
   B. Kitchen evaluations are to be done by the resident Data Recorder (for each group meal), prior to beginning food preparation but subsequent to the completion of the specified tasks (e.g., cleaning stove, counter, sweeping floor) by the resident in the preceding meal preparation period.
   C. The resident evaluator(s) is (are) to give the Kitchen and Dining Room Evaluation Data Sheet(s) to the HF immediately following the completion of the evaluations.
   D. After the last meal preparation period (for each meal), a HF is to evaluate the kitchen and dining room.
   E. During each evaluation (whether by a resident evaluator *or* HF), the resident evaluator(s) from the preceding meal is (are) to be present.
   F. When an evaluation is made and the kitchen and/or dining room is/are found to be inappropriate (as specified by the Kitchen and Dining Room Evaluation Data Sheet), the evaluator is to
      1. Inform an HF
      2. Inform the resident evaluator(s) from the preceding meal preparation period

VI. Data Collection
   A. There is to be one Kitchen and Dining Room Evaluation Data Sheet per evaluator.
   B. The kitchen and dining room are to be evaluated after each meal preparation period by a resident evaluator.
   C. After the last meal preparation period (for same meal), a HF is to evaluate the kitchen and the dining room.
   D. Data to record:
      1. Date: Record the current date.
      2. Meal: Record the meal during which the evaluation is occurring (either breakfast, lunch, or dinner).

3. Meal Period: Record the meal period during which the evaluation is occurring.
4. Table: Record either a check mark (✓) or an X.
   a. Record a check mark (✓) if the table has been cleared and wiped clean.
   b. Record an X if the table has *not* been cleared and/or wiped clean.
5. Counter: Record either a check mark (✓) or an X.
   a. Record a check mark (✓) if the counters have been cleared and wiped clean.
   b. Record an X if the counters have *not* been cleared and/or wiped clean.
6. Dishes: Record either a check mark (✓) or an X.
   a. Record a check mark (✓) if the dishes have been washed and put away.
   b. Record an X if the dishes have *not* been washed and/or put away.
7. Pots and pans: Record either a check mark (✓) or an X.
   a. Record a check mark (✓) if the pots and pans have been washed and put away.
   b. Record an X if the pots and pans have *not* been washed and/or put away.
8. Sink: Record either a check mark (✓) or an X.
   a. Record a check mark (✓) if the sink has been cleared and wiped clean.
   b. Record an X if the sink has *not* been cleared and/or wiped clean.
9. Stove #1: Record either a check mark (✓) or an X.
   a. Record a check mark (✓) if stove #1 has been cleared and wiped clean.
   b. Record an X if stove #1 has *not* been cleared and/or wiped clean.
10. Stove #2: Record either a check mark (✓) or an X.
    a. Record a check mark (✓) if stove #2 has been cleared and wiped clean.
    b. Record an X if stove #2 has *not* been cleared and/or wiped clean.
11. Floor: Record either a check mark (✓) or an X.
    a. Record a check mark (✓) if there are no particles or spills on the floor.
    b. Record an X if there are particles and/or spills on the floor.
12. Leftovers: Record either a check mark (✓) or an X.
    a. Record a check mark (✓) if all leftovers have been placed in appropriate containers or wrapping and put away.
    b. Record an X if all leftovers have *not* been placed in appropriate containers or wrapping and/or put away.
13. Appliances: Record either a check mark (✓) or an X.
    a. Record a check mark (✓) if all appliances have been turned off, wiped clean, and returned to original storing place or position.
    b. Record an X if all appliances have *not* been turned off, wiped clean, and/or not returned to original storing place or position. Record the name of the appliance(s) and the specific problem(s) in the comments column.
14. Evaluator: Record the initials of the resident who made the evaluation.
15. Comments: Record any comments.

MEAL PREPARATION SIGN-UP SHEET
BREAKFAST

DATE:				
MEAL PERIODS		INDIV. MEAL	GROUP MEAL CODE	GROUP JOB
6:00-6:30 (Sat. & Sun. Only: 10:00-10:30)	Name: Food:			
	Name: Food:			
	Name: Food:			
	Name: Food:			
	Name: Food:			
6:30-7:00 (Sat. & Sun. Only: 10:00-11:00)	Name Food:			
	Name: Food:			
	Name: Food:			
	Name: Food:			
	Name: Food:			

Figure 3-5

MEAL PREPARATION SIGN-UP SHEET
LUNCH

DATE:				
MEAL PERIODS		INDIV. MEAL	GROUP MEAL CODE	GROUP JOB
11:30–12:00	Name: Food:			
	Name: Food:			
	Name: Food:			
	Name: Food:			
12:00–12:30	Name: Food:			
	Name: Food:			
	Name: Food:			
	Name: Food:			
12:30–1:00	Name: Food:			#Guests
	Name: Food:			
	Name: Food:			
	Name: Food			

Figure 3-6

MEAL PREPARATION SIGN-UP SHEET
SUPPER

DATE:										
	STOVE 1					STOVE 2				
STOVE-USE PERIODS		INDIV. MEAL	GROUP MEAL CODE	GROUP JOB	# GUESTS		INDIV. MEAL	GROUP MEAL	GROUP JOB	# GUESTS
4:40-5:00	Name: Food:				//////	Name: Food:				//////
5:05-5:25	Name: Food:				//////	Name: Food:				//////
5:30-5:50	Name: Food:				//////	Name: Food:				//////
5:55-6:15	Name: Food:				//////	Name: Food:				//////
6:20-6:40	Name: Food:					Name: Food:				

Figure 3-7

KITCHEN AND DINING ROOM EVALUATION DATA SHEET

DATE:		COMMENTS:
Meal:		
Meal Period:		
Table:		
Counter:		
Dishes:		
Pots & Pans:		
Sink:		
Stove #1:		
Stove #2:		
Floor:		
Leftovers:		
Appliances:		
Evaluator:		
DATE:		COMMENTS:
Meal:		
Meal Period:		
Table:		
Counter:		
Dishes:		
Pots & Pans:		
Sink:		
Stove #1:		
Stove #2:		
Floor:		
Leftovers:		
Appliances:		
Evaluator:		

Figure 3-8

HALFWAY HOUSE THERAPEUTIC COMMUNITY

GENERAL STATEMENT

A very critical aspect of independent community living is being able to make decisions. Before a decision can be made, an individual must synthesize all the known details, and then develop a plan of action. Most institutionalized individuals have either (1) never had these skills, (2) lost these skills through lack of use, or (3) learned new, maladaptive decision-making processes. Institutionalized people typically make few decisions, inasmuch as staff members usually make decisions for them. The Therapeutic Community in the Halfway House enables residents to gain experience in rational decision-making. In addition to the decision-making process, residents gain experience in creating and implementing policies. A therapeutic community becomes a learning mechanism for decision-making, for appreciation of policies, and for appreciation of the feelings of others.

PURPOSE

1. To foster self-reliance
2. To help develop a positive self-concept
3. To help create and/or develop decision-making skills
4. To learn what is necessary in making decisions and policies that govern oneself and others
5. To learn to appreciate enforcement difficulties
6. To develop an acceptance of the world and to make changes in the world through the proper means

PROCEDURE

I. General Policies
   A. Every resident in the Halfway House is to be a member of the Therapeutic Community and is to have the opportunity to be actively involved in the community.
   B. A new Halfway House resident is to be given an orientation to the house and its rules by the elected Orientation House Representative.
   C. Membership in the Therapeutic Community is to begin the moment a resident begins living in the Halfway House.
   D. The Therapeutic Community is to choose a name for the community (by majority rule).
II. By-Laws
   A. Time, Day, and Frequency of Community Meetings
      1. There is to be one community meeting per week.
      2. Special emergency meetings are to be called when a majority of the community so decides, or when a house-facilitator (HF) decides to call a meeting.
      3. Meetings are to be held every Monday evening.
      4. All meetings are to begin at 7:00 P.M. or as determined by the Therapeutic Community.
   B. Administrative Offices
      1. All elected offices are to be for a two month duration (special committees are exceptions).
      2. A resident may not serve more than one consecutive term for the same office.
      3. Criteria for holding office:
         a. One month as member of community
         b. Active participation in all programs (i.e., individual, group, community)

c. Continued positive change toward meeting all criteria
d. Attendance at 90% (or more) of all meetings
e. Elected by majority rule
4. Elected offices and responsibilities
   a. Group leader
      (1) Lead meetings
      (2) Select speakers
      (3) Organize special meetings
      (4) Keep agenda posted
      (5) Select committees whenever necessary
   b. Assistant group leader
      (1) Replace the group leader when necessary
      (2) Assist the group leader
   c. Secretary
      (1) Record the minutes of the meetings
      (2) Submit minutes to a HF to be typed
      (3) Distribute typed minutes to the residents
   d. Orientation Leader
      (1) Introduce new members to the rules and policies (with HF)
      (2) Assist new members in their adjustment to the facility
      (3) Answer questions relating to all aspects of the facility
   e. Special committees
      (1) To be developed as needed
      (2) Members to be volunteers or selected by group leader, if necessary
      (3) Length of time for membership to be determined at time of conception
5. Impeachment: A resident may be removed from office
   a. By majority rule of the Therapeutic Community
   b. For not maintaining program criteria
   c. For infringements of Halfway House Rules and Policies
   d. For attending less than 90% of meetings without valid excuses
C. Voting Powers
   1. One person, one vote (including officers)
   2. The majority of entire community membership must pass rulings.
   3. HF has veto power and tabling power.
D. Attendance is required of all members of the community (exceptions by prior approval of HF).
E. Agenda
   1. Posted each Monday evening by the Group Leader for the next group meeting
   2. To contain any old business which needs to be dealt with at the next meeting
   3. To have available space for any new items for discussion
   4. To include
      a. Date item listed
      b. New or old item
      c. Name of resident listing item
F. HF is to
   1. Record all data as specified
   2. Review, correct, or modify (if needed) the minutes recorded by the resident secretary
   3. Have secretary type minutes
   4. Assist resident secretary if needed
G. Topics to be discussed
   1. Household problems
   2. Household programs

3. Individual problems
4. Individual programs
5. Group problems
6. Event planning
7. Grievances
H. Any new policies, procedures, or rules formulated and implemented by the Therapeutic Community are to be typed and
 1. Posted on the bulletin board in the Halfway House
 2. Filed with the *Halfway House Rules and Policies*

III. Data Collection
 A. File one copy of the minutes of each Therapeutic Community Meeting in the Halfway House Office.
 B. File one copy in the Halfway House Office of any rules, procedures, etc., that are formulated, approved, and implemented.
 C. Therapeutic Community Data Sheet (See Figure 3-9, p. 257.)
  1. There is to be one copy of the Therapeutic Community Data Sheet for each month.
  2. Data are to be recorded by the HF present at the meeting.
  3. Data are to be recorded within 48 hours after the meeting.
  4. Record the following data:
   a. Date-Record the date of the meeting.
   b. Leader-Record the name of the group leader (i.e., group leader or assistant group leader).
   c. Names-Record the names of the residents present at the meeting.
   d. Elections-When elections occur, record the names of elected officials and the office to which they were elected.
   e. Topics discussed-Record the major topics discussed in the meeting.
   f. Topics approved:
    1. Title-Record the title of the topic, procedure, rule, etc., that is approved and to be put into action.
    2. Date-Record the effective date of the topic, procedure, rule, etc.
   g. HF-Record the initials of the house-facilitator recording the data.
 E. Individual Therapeutic Community Data Sheet (See Figure 3-10, p. 258.)
  1. There is to be one Individual Therapeutic Community Data Sheet per resident.
  2. The data sheet is to be kept in the resident's Individual Program Book.
  3. Data are to be recorded by the HF present at the Therapeutic Community Meeting.
  4. Data are to be recorded within 48 hours after the meeting.
  5. Data to record:
   a. Name—Record the name of the resident.
   b. Date—Record the date of the meeting (record the date of the meeting whether the resident attended the meeting or not).
   c. Attendance
    1. Record a check mark (✓) if the resident attended the meeting.
    2. Record an *E* if the resident did *not* attend the meeting (with an excused absence).
    3. Record an *X* if the resident did *not* attend the meeting (*without* an excused absence).
   d. Office—Record the name of the office currently held by the resident (if any). This is to include committee participation and special assignments.
   e. New office—If a resident is elected to an office or given a committee or special assignment, record the name of the position and its effective date.
   f. Freq. of comments—Record the frequency of comments made by the resi-

dent during the meeting. (A comment must be at least three seconds long and made while the resident has the floor.)

g. Freq. of suggestions—Record the frequency of suggestions made by the resident during the meeting. (A suggestion must be at least three seconds long and made while the individual has the floor.)

h. HF—Record the initials of the house-facilitator recording the data.

i. HF comments—Record any comments of significance pertaining to the resident.

THERAPEUTIC COMMUNITY DATA SHEET

DATE	LEADER	NAMES	ELECTIONS	TOPICS DISCUSSED	TOPICS APPROV.				
					TITLE	DATE	HF		

Figure 3-9

INDIVIDUAL THERAPEUTIC COMMUNITY DATA SHEET

DATE	ATTENDANCE	OFFICE	NEW OFFICE		FREQ. COMMENTS	FREQ. SUGGESTIONS	HF	HF COMMENTS
			POSIT.	DATE				

Figure 3-10

HALFWAY HOUSE
RESIDENT PAYMENTS AND RENT PROGRAM

GENERAL STATEMENT

A major component of the institutionalized resident's rehabilitation process involves the development of self-sufficiency in a wide variety of personal and social areas (e.g., self-care skills, money management, education, problem solving). In the development of self-sufficiency, it is important for a resident to be able to utilize his/her money to its best advantage (e.g., allocations for rent, food, and other basic necessities). The Halfway House Resident Payments and Rent Program is designed to facilitate the goal of self-sufficiency in the area of money management. At the academic and at the applied level, money management training begins in the institution (Levels 1, 2, and 3). Further intense applied training is conducted, however, upon entry into the Halfway House. Once in the Halfway House, the resident is given the necessary applied training in paying rent, purchasing food, and budgeting for other basic needs. Thus, the resident will be able to apply the skill acquired during money management training received in the institution.

TERMINAL OBJECTIVE

The terminal objective is to have the resident become financially independent within the Halfway House via paying rent, purchasing food, and taking care of other basic necessities.

I. General Policies
   A. All residents residing in the Halfway House are to participate in the program.
   B. All residents are to observe the policies and guidelines specified unless an individual program specifies otherwise.
   C. The Resident Payments and Rent Program is divided into four consecutive steps.
   D. Residents not observing the guidelines specified in this procedure are to be dealt with on an individual basis.
   E. Payments given to residents and the rent collected from residents are to be based upon gross outside incomes. (See Table 3-1, p. 261.)
   F. The resident is to be given a receipt for each financial transaction with the Halfway House.
   G. A $30.00 security deposit is required of each resident.
   H. Charges for utilities (e.g., electricity, water) are included in rent payments.
II. Steps
   A. Step 1
      1. Residents are to be accepted into the Halfway House on Monday mornings.
      2. As soon as the new resident becomes oriented and moved into the Halfway House, he/she is to be given his/her specified payment. (See Table 3-1, p. 261.)
      3. The Halfway House facilitator (HF) is to then collect the amount of rent specified in Table 3-1.
      4. The resident is to be allowed to keep up to 6% of his/her payment for spending money.
      5. The HF is to take the resident to a bank to open up a checking account.
      6. The HF is *not* to open the checking account for the resident; he/she is to do it alone.
      7. The HF is to then take the resieent to a grocery store, so he/she can purchase food and supplies to last until the upcoming Friday.
      8. The HF is to supervise the purchasing and *not* actually do the shopping for the resident.

B. Step 2
   1. The following Friday morning the resident is to be given his/her specified payment. (See Table 3-1, p. 261.)
   2. This payment is to be made by check (made out to the resident).
   3. On Saturday morning the HF is to then collect the amount of rent specified. (See Table 3-1.)
   4. If the resident is not going to be there on Saturday, the rent is to be paid Friday afternoon or evening.
   5. The rent payment may be made by check or cash.
   6. The HF is to remind the resident to purchase groceries and any needed supplies to last for one week.
   7. Step 2 is to continue until the resident successfully purchases food and supplies and pays rent for four consecutive weeks.
C. Step 3
   1. Same as Step 2 except the resident is required to pay the amount of rent specified on Table 3-1, on a biweekly basis.
   2. Rent is to be collected on Saturday mornings.
   3. If the resident is not going to be there on the Saturday that rent is due, the rent is to be paid on the preceding Friday afternoon or evening.
   4. Step 3 is to continue until the resident successfully purchases food and supplies and pays rent for six consecutive weeks while in this step.
D. Step 4
   1. Same as Step 2 and 3 except the resident is to be required to pay the same amount of rent specified on Table 3-1 on a monthly basis.
   2. Rent is due on the first day of each month and *must* be paid by the fifth day of the month.
   3. When the resident is late paying rent, he/she is to be charged a late fee equaling 4% of the amount of rent.
   4. Step 4 is to continue until the resident is discharged from the Halfway House, unless it is decided in an Interdisciplinary Treatment Team Conference that due to a resident's negligence, he/she should be placed back into a lower step.
III. Payment Adjustments
Whenever a resident acquires an outside job or when there is a salary change for an outside job, payments from the Halfway House and rent are to be adjusted according to the Sliding Scale (Table 3-1).
IV. Residents Payments and Rent Data Sheet (RPRDS) (See Figure 3-11, p. 262.)
   A. There is to be one RPRDS per resident.
   B. The data sheet is to be located in the resident's Individual Program Book.
   C. Data are to be recorded by the staff member, who gives the resident the payment and/or collects the rent.
   D. Data to be recorded:
      1. Payment Date—Record the date on which the resident was paid.
      2. Payment Amnt.—Record the amount given to the resident.
      3. Rent step—Record the rent step the resident is currently in.
      4. Rent Date—Record the date on which the resident paid rent.
      5. Rent Amnt.—Record the amount paid by the resident.
      6. Late Fee—Record the late fee paid (when applicable).
      7. HF—Record the initials of the HF recording the data.

Table 3-1 Halfway House Resident Payments and Rent Program Sliding Scale

GROSS OUTSIDE INCOME		PAYMENTS TO RESIDENTS	RENT	
Weekly	*Monthly*	*Weekly*	*Weekly*	*Monthly*
$ 0–9	$ 0–36	$70.00	$24.50	$98.00
$10–19	$40–76	$65.00	$25.00	$100.00
$20–29	$80–116	$60.00	$27.50	$110.00
$30–39	$120–156	$55.00	$29.50	$118.00
$40–49	$160–196	$50.00	$31.00	$124.00
$50–59	$200–236	$45.00	$32.50	$130.00
$60–69	$240–276	$40.00	$33.75	$135.00
$70–79	$280–316	$35.00	$35.50	$142.00
$80–89	$320–356	$25.00	$35.50	$142.00
$90–99	$360–396	$15.00	$35.50	$142.00
$100–109	$400–436	$10.00	$37.50	$150.00
$110–119	$440–476	$ 0.00	$37.50	$150.00
$120–129	$480–516	$ 0.00	$38.75	$155.00
$130–139	$520–556	$ 0.00	$41.25	$165.00
$140–149	$560–596	$ 0.00	$43.75	$175.00
$150–159	$600–636	$ 0.00	$46.25	$185.00
$160–169	$640–676	$ 0.00	$48.75	$195.00
$170–179	$680–716	$ 0.00	$52.50	$210.00
$180–189	$720–756	$ 0.00	$55.00	$220.00
$190–199	$760–796	$ 0.00	$57.50	$230.00
$200–209	$800–836	$ 0.00	$61.25	$245.00

RESIDENT PAYMENTS AND RENT DATA SHEET

PAYMT. DATE	PAYMT. AMNT.	RENT STEP	RENT DATE	RENT AMNT.	LATE FEE	HM INIT.	PAYMT. DATE	PAYMT. AMNT.	RENT STEP	RENT DATE	RENT AMNT.	LATE FEE	HM INIT.

Figure 3-11

HALFWAY HOUSE WORKSHARING PROGRAM

General Statement

Group living arrangements have recently been used with different populations. College students, psychiatric residents, delinquent adolescents, and other groups have been found to function well in group homes, and achieve both short and long-term benefits from such residency. Many of these homes, however, have met with failure as a result of not having a structured system for accomplishing the proper care and housekeeping of the residence. Additionally, the lack of such a system may foster agitation, disorganization, and discontent within the setting. The development of a program that includes some motivational component to maintain housekeeping behaviors, fosters a living environment that is organized, clean, and less likely to engender negative emotions. Moreover, such a program helps develop personal responsibility within the occupants of the home. The Worksharing Program is designed to have the residents share the responsibility of housekeeping and also to evaluate the work performance of their peers.

Terminal Objective

The terminal objective is to have the residents of the Halfway House successfully complete all the housekeeping without the direct supervision of the Halfway House staff.

Purpose

1. To help develop individual responsibility
2. To help develop group responsibility and cohesiveness
3. To have residents learn appropriate work skills
4. To help improve communication skills
5. To help maintain a clean and orderly living environment
6. To help increase self-esteem

Procedure

I. General Policies
   A. All residents of the Halfway House are required to participate in the Worksharing Program.
   B. Individual programs, based on the specific needs and progress of the resident and which supersede the Worksharing Program, may be developed.
   C. Specific housekeeping duties are to be completed at the frequency specified for each chore.
   D. Jobs are to be completed by noon on Saturday.
   E. There are no jobs on Sunday.
   F. If a resident's job is not completed (Monday–Friday) by 7:45 A.M. (without a valid excuse), he/she is to be given a 20–30 minute job to be completed by 12:30 P.M.
II. Weekly Job Assignment Sheet
   A. All weekly jobs are listed on this sheet.
   B. Each resident is to complete at least one weekly job per week.
   C. Residents are to sign up for weekly jobs on Thursday evening.
   D. Residents not signing up for at least one weekly job are to be prompted to do so by the Resident Supervisor.
   E. Prompt only once per week.
   F. Place a progress note in the resident's Individual Program Book describing the incident if a prompt is necessary.

G. Residents may engage in, and complete, weekly jobs at any time during the day as long as the Resident Supervisor is present and the jobs are coordinated with him/her.
H. Jobs are chosen by the residents.
I. When using the sign-up sheet, each resident is to record his/her name on the sign-up sheet for each job chosen.
J. A new Weekly Job Assignment Sheet is to be posted each Thursday evening.
K. Weekly jobs are to be completed by 9:00 P.M. on Monday.

III. Daily Job Assignment Sheet
A. A new Daily Job Assignment Sheet is to be posted each evening by 9:00 P.M. for the following day.
B. The sheets are to be posted in the living room.
C. All daily jobs are listed on this sheet.
D. The Resident Supervisor is responsible for the posting and formulation of the Daily Job Assignment Sheets.
E. The daily jobs are to be organized into groups.
F. There are to be as many groups of jobs as there are residents present the following day.
G. Each group of jobs is to contain jobs having approximately the same amount of work time.
H. Each resident is to sign up for one group of jobs daily.
I. Residents are to sign up for a group of daily jobs by 7:00 A.M. on the day on which the jobs are to be completed.
J. Residents not signing up for a group of daily jobs are to be prompted to do so by the Resident Supervisor.
K. Whenever the Resident Supervisor needs to prompt a resident to sign up for a job, he/she is to inform a house facilitator (HF).
L. Whenever a prompt is needed, a progress note is to be written in the resident's Individual Program Book concerning the incident.
M. Daily jobs are to be evaluated from 7:30 to 8:00 A.M. (unless other arrangements have been made).
N. Residents are to complete daily jobs between 6:00 and 7:45 A.M.
O. Groups of jobs are chosen by the residents.
P. When using the sign-up sheet, each resident is to record his/her name on the sign-up sheet next to the group of daily jobs he/she has chosen.

IV. Job Description Sheet (See Table 3-2, p. 266.)
A. All jobs are described on this sheet.
B. The sheet is to be posted in the dayroom area of the house.
C. The jobs are divided into two categories:
  1. Jobs to be done on a daily basis.
  2. Jobs to be done on a weekly basis.

V. Resident Supervisor
A. A resident is to volunteer for the supervisor job for one week at a time.
B. The same resident may not be the supervisor more than once in any given, four week period.
C. The Resident Supervisor is to be responsible for (see Table 3-3, p. 268)
  1. Inspecting all completed jobs
  2. Collection of prescribed data
  3. Submitting data to HF
D. The Resident Supervisor is to ensure that all the job components, as listed on the Job Description Sheet, are appropriately completed for each job.
E. The previous Resident Supervisor is to orient and instruct the supervisor for the first two days on the job. HFs are to be available for questions.

F. A HF is to randomly choose at least 25% of the jobs inspected daily for reliability checks and 25% of the weekly jobs inspected for reliability checks (on a weekly basis).
G. Reliability checks are to consist of a HF using the same inspection sheet as the resident supervisor.
H. A resident is not required to assume the Resident Supervisor position until he/she has been residing in the Halfway House for one month.

VI. Job Inspections
A. The Resident Supervisor is to evaluate jobs using the Job Inspection Sheet. (See Figure 3-12, p. 269.)
B. Residents are to be present during the evaluation of their job(s) by the Resident Supervisor.
C. A resident may arrange special evaluation times with the Resident Supervisor if he/she cannot complete a job(s) by the prescribed deadline, and/or if he/she cannot be present during the scheduled inspection periods.
D. If a job was completed inappropriately, the Resident Supervisor is to
   1. Record the necessary data
   2. Describe to the resident responsible for the job what needs to be done for the job to pass the evaluation.
   3. Re-evaluate the job after the resident reports the completion of the suggested corrections or additions.
   4. If insufficient time remains in the job evaluation period for the resident to appropriately complete a job as described by the Resident Supervisor, arrangements are to be made with the Resident Supervisor to complete the job and have it evaluated during the next available period of time.
E. Job evaluations must meet a criterion of at least 90% for appropriateness.

Table 3-2
HALFWAY HOUSE
JOB DESCRIPTION SHEET

DAILY JOBS

Bathrooms
1. Clean sink bowl
2. Clean Toilet (outside tank, inside and outside toilet bowl, seat, lid)
3. Clean Mirror
4. Sweep floor
5. Mop floor
6. Empty trashbasket
7. Rinse out sponge and bucket
8. Return cleaning supplies to proper storage

Living and Dining Room
1. Empty ashtrays and wipe clean
2. Empty trashbaskets
3. Sweep floor
4. Vacuum rug
5. Return cleaning supplies and equipment to proper storage

Activity Room
1. Empty ashtrays and wipe clean
2. Empty trashbaskets
3. Vacuum rug
4. Return cleaning supplies and equipment to proper storage

Kitchen
1. Clean area around kitchen garbage can
2. Take out kitchen garbage
3. Sweep floor
4. Mop floor
5. Return cleaning supplies and equipment to proper storage

Hallways
1. Vacuum (or sweep) floor and dust woodwork
2. Sweep ceiling and wall cobwebs
3. Return cleaning supplies and equipment to proper storage

Laundry Room
1. Wipe off machines
2. Clean washing machine filters and dryer filter
3. Clean shelves
4. Sweep floor and woodwork
5. Mop floor
6. Empty trash
7. Return cleaning supplies and equipment to proper storage

Wash Garbage Can
1. Wash kitchen garbage can with disinfectant
2. Return cleaning supplies and equipment to proper storage

Dust and Polish Furniture
1. Dust furniture in living room
2. Polish furniture in living room
3. Dust furniture in dining room
4. Polish furniture in dining room
5. Dust furniture in activity room
6. Polish furniture in activity room
7. Return cleaning supplies and equipment to proper storage

Outside House Pick-Up
1. Pick up trash in entire yard and parking area
2. Pick up trash on front porch
3. Sweep front porch
4. Pick up trash around trash cans
5. Pick up trash on back porch
6. Sweep back porch
7. Empty trash can on front porch
8. Return cleaning supplies and equipment to proper storage

Clean Stove and Oven
1. Remove and clean each burner tray
2. Replace each burner tray
3. Wipe off front, top, and sides of stove
4. Clean oven with oven cleaner or scouring pads
5. Clean oven racks
6. Return cleaning supplies and equipment to proper storage

WEEKLY JOBS

Living and Dining Rooms
1. Dust and wash woodwork
2. Dust venetian blinds
3. Clean mirror
4. Sweep ceiling and wall cobwebs
5. Return cleaning supplies and equipment to proper storage

Activity Room
1. Dust and wash woodwork
2. Sweep ceiling and wall cobwebs
3. Dust venetian blinds
4. Return cleaning supplies and equipment to proper storage

Kitchen
1. Wipe off all counters
2. Wipe off stove
3. Wipe off cabinets
4. Clean sinks
5. Wipe off all appliances
6. Return cleaning supplies and equipment to proper storage

Showers
1. Clean shower floor with disinfectant
2. Clean shower walls
3. Clean shower curtain
4. Clean shower fixtures
5. Clean soap tray
6. Return cleaning supplies and equipment to proper storage

Refrigerator
1. Wipe off inside walls
2. Wipe off refrigerator floor
3. Wipe off any shelves that have not been assigned to a resident(s)
4. Return cleaning supplies and equipment to proper storage

Table 3-3
Duties of the Resident Supervisor

Daily jobs:
1. Prepare daily job list for next day, have it approved by an HF, and post it by 9 P.M. (Monday–Sunday).
2. Weekly jobs: Prepare weekly job list, have it approved by an HF, and post it by 9 P.M. on Thursday.
3. Evaluation of jobs: Resident Supervisor should be generally available during morning chore period. All morning chores should be completed by time specified by the government body (this includes putting away all cleaning materials). Supervisor should check to see if all chores were completed by this time, and check the chores to see that they were done properly. If some residents finish their chores before the deadline time, supervisor may check these chores at this time if he/she wishes, but only if he/she has been asked to check chore early. Supervisor should not ask if chore is finished or nag residents about finishing. It is each resident's responsibility to notify Supervisor when the chore has been completed, so that it may be checked. (This applies to extra chores also.)
4. Late jobs: In the event a job is finished late, supervisor is to inform the resident that the job was late, and then assign an extra job (this extra job should be approved by an HF before being assigned). This extra job is to be completed by a time specified by the government body (unless special arrangements need to be made), and supervisor is again to check to see that this job is finished on time and done properly. If extra job is late or done improperly, supervisor should notify an HF.
5. Weekly job evaluations: Guidelines #3 and #4 above apply. Weekly jobs to be completed by 9 P.M. Mondays.
6. If supervisor fails to post job list on time, this is to be considered the same as any other job that is completed late, and an HF is to assign an extra chore for supervisor.
7. Purchase of cleaning supplies: Each week on shopping day (or any other time if supervisor chooses to go on his/her own), supervisor is to determine what cleaning supplies, toilet paper, etc., are needed, and get the needed amount of money from the Cleaning Fund from a HF in order to buy these items during the shopping trip.
8. Other duties: By 9 P.M. Monday, supervisor is to check each resident's refrigerator shelf to make sure that shelf is clean, old food thrown out, and uncovered food is properly covered or wrapped. As with daily and weekly jobs, supervisor is to be notified by resident when resident's shelf is ready to be checked.

JOB INSPECTION SHEET

NAME: DATE: POSITION EVALUATED:		
	GOOD (COMMENTS)	**NEEDS IMPROVEMENT (COMMENTS)**
THOROUGHNESS (All requirements of job completed. Refer to Job Description Sheet)		
ABILITY TO IDENTIFY SPECIFIC CORRECTIONS NEEDED		
FOLLOW-UP ON CORRECTIONS		
General Remarks:		

Figure 3-12

HALFWAY HOUSE
AGITATION

GENERAL STATEMENT

Everyone becomes agitated from time to time. The important thing is how one deals with the agitation. Most people try to cope with problems in an objective, rational manner. Only when one's emotions are under control will an irrational approach make way for a rational-objective approach. The typical results of irrational behavior are (1) negative short-term interactions, and (2) increased negative long-term interactions. Many times irrational behavior results in emotional stress, physical injury, and/or destruction of property. Contending with such problematic behavior requires a systematic approach.

PURPOSE

1. To increase positive interactions, both short and long term
2. To develop socially acceptable means of dealing with one's agitated feelings
3. To safeguard property
4. To safeguard individuals from harm (psychological and physical)
5. To create a "cooling-off period"
6. To develop a positive self-concept

PROCEDURE

I. General Policies
   A. The agitation procedure is to be used with residents who have no individualized program(s) for such problems.
   B. An individual treatment program is to take precedence over the general Agitation Procedure.
   C. There are two types of agitation:
      1. Mild agitation
         a. Verbal threats to do bodily harm to oneself or others
         b. Verbal threats to do harm to property
         c. Screaming that can be heard at a distance of 30 feet or more
         d. Cursing, defined as words that refer to a sexual or elimination process or are religious in nature, used by themselves or in combination with other words, expressing disrespect or contempt for someone or something
         e. Verbal statements implying obstruction of another's movements
         f. Unusual and/or abrupt movements, pacing, verbal behavior (unusual is defined for each resident)
      2. Severe Agitation
         a. Causing damage to property
         b. Approaching another individual with hand(s) clenched into fist(s) or with a solid object in a raised, slashing or jabbing motion, or a combination of both
         c. Physically preventing movement of another
         d. Refusal to remove hands from another's body after being asked
         e. Damage to self or others
         f. Running away from a situation of supervision that requires physical coercion by staff to stop and/or return the resident
II. Mild Agitation Procedure
   A. First occurrence of the day
      1. Ask resident(s) to stop engaging in the behavior.
      2. Ask resident(s) to talk calmly about problem(s).
         a. If the problem involves only one resident, he/she is to discuss the issue with a staff member.

b. If the problem involves two or more residents, the issue is to be discussed by those involved.
   (1) The staff member is to serve as a moderator, observing the following guidelines:
      (a) Keep voices down
      (b) No cursing
      (c) Use positive approach to communication
      (d) Do not supply answers
c. If the residents become too excited to discuss the issue calmly, then discussion is to be postponed until everyone involved in the incident is calm and a staff member is available to discuss the problem.
3. If the resident(s) does (do) not desire to discuss the issue, tell everyone involved to stop engaging in the behavior immediately.
4. Record a progress note in the resident's Individual Program Book describing the incident (including antecedents, behavior, and consequences).
B. Second occurrence (during any given day) and subsequent occurrences
   1. Follow same procedure described above
   2. The resident(s) is (are) also to
      a. Pay a fine of $2.00
      b. Sign-up for two extra house chores (selected by staff member) for the next day
      c. Be restricted from all privileges for two days
   3. Record a progress note in the resident's Individual Program Book describing the incident
III. Severe Agitation Procedure
   A. Notify on-call psychologist as soon as possible, and police (if necessary).
   B. Subdue resident immediately, if necessary, to prevent physical injury or destruction of property.
   C. Release when calm.
   D. Follow discussion procedures as specified in Mild Agitation Procedure (Section II, above).
   E. Severe Agitation is to be dealt with on an individual basis.
   F. An emergency staffing is to be conducted within 48 hours of the incident.
   G. Record a progress note in the resident's Individual Program Book describing the incident.
IV. Data Collection
   A. Record a progress note in the resident's Individual Program Book.
   B. Record a brief note in the Halfway House Daily Log concerning the incident (e.g., date, name, behavior, "See Progress Note," house facilitator's name).
   C. Agitation Data Sheet (See Figure 3-13, p. 272.)
      1. There is to be one Agitation Data Sheet per resident.
      2. The data sheet is to be kept in the resident's Individual Program Book.
      3. Data are to be recorded by the House Facilitator (HF) observing the agitation.
      4. Data to record:
         a. Name—Record the name of the resident who engaged in the behavior.
         b. Type of agitation—Record the type of agitation engaged in (i.e., 1 = mild; 2 = severe).
         c. Discussion—Record either an *A, I,* or *N.*
            (1) Record an *A* if the resident appropriately discussed the incident following its occurrence.
            (2) Record an *I* if the resident inappropriately discussed the incident following its occurrence (inappropriate is defined as an occurrence of agitation).
            (3) Record an *N* if the resident did *not* discuss the incident after occurrence.
      4. HF—Record the initials of the HF recording the data.

HALFWAY HOUSE AGITATION DATA SHEET

NAME:											
DATE	TYPE AGITAT.	DISCUSSION	HF			DATE	TYPE AGITAT.	DISCUSSION	HF		

Figure 3-13

HALFWAY HOUSE
ELOPEMENT PROCEDURE

GENERAL STATEMENT

An effective therapeutic program requires willing participation of each resident. Elopement often indicates a lack of such willingness, and may suggest a desire to terminate treatment. Repeated elopements seriously interfere with the continuity of treatment and strongly indicate a desire to terminate treatment.

PURPOSE

1. To give the resident an opportunity to willingly participate in his/her treatment program
2. To help develop responsibility for active and willing participation in the treatment program
3. To allow each resident the opportunity to leave the program voluntarily

PROCEDURE

I. General Policies
   A. Elopement is defined as an unauthorized overnight absence from the Halfway House. (Note: Authorization for any overnight absence requires explicit written/oral permission from a staff member.)
   B. When an elopement occurs
      1. Notify the psychologist on call immediately.
      2. Write a progress note in the resident's program book concerning the incident, including any relevant events preceding the incident and a description of any actions taken.
      3. Psychology staff is to decide when or if family members and/or community agencies are to be notified.
      4. If the resident does not return within 72 hours, he/she is to be terminated from the program.
   C. When a resident returns from elopement
      1. First elopement:
         a. Check the resident to insure there are no physical/medical conditions that require attention.
         b. Offer the resident the following three alternatives and have him/her choose one:
            (1) Discharge from the program
            (2) Continued participation in the program
            (3) Possible transfer to a more restrictive program (e.g., Level III)
      2. Repeated elopements
         a. Check the resident to insure there are no physical/medical conditions that require attention.
         b. If prior elopements have occurred in the preceding 30 days, offer the resident the following choices, and have him/her choose one:
            (1) Discharge from the program.
            (2) Possible transfer to a more restrictive program.
         c. If prior elopements occurred more than 30 days before the current absence, offer the following choices, and have him/her choose one:
            (1) Discharge from the program.
            (2) Possible transfer to a more restrictive program.
            (3) Continued participation in the program, provided the psychologist concurs with this choice.
   D. Changes in the consequences of elopement for any resident may be made by the resident's treatment team.

INDEX

Agitation Procedure, 206–212, 270–273
    Incident Diary, 211
    mild agitation, 208, 270–271
    severe agitation, 208–209, 271
Aversive procedures, 8–10

Bedroom Area Preparation Procedure, 55–60
Behavior Therapy Facility Regulations, 5–11
Behavior Therapy Oversight Committee, 7–8
Behavior Therapy Unit, 1–4, 5
    physical setting, 2
    referrals, 2
    staff, 2
    treatment levels, 1–4

Canteen Procedure, 38–40
Communication Skills Program, 96–117

Daily Diary, 118–133
Daily Living Schedule, 134–150
Dental Hygiene Procedure, 67–70
Discharge Preparation Group Procedure, 218–221
Dressing Procedure, 91–95

Elopement Procedure, 215–217, 273

Florida Mental Health Institute, 24

Goal Orientation Procedure, 134–150

Halfway House
    physical setting, 4
    referrals, 4
    staff, 4, 10, 11
Halfway House Policies
    admissions, 222
    aggression, 224
    curfew, 223
    dismissal, 222
    drug/alcohol use, 223–224
    government, 222
    overnight leaves, 223
    sexual behavior, 224
    smoking, 224
    visitors, 223
    weapons, 224

Halfway House Procedures, 222–273
    Agitation, 270–273
    Elopement, 273
    Halfway House Policies, 222–224
    Individual Program Book, 230–233
    Interdisciplinary Treatment Team Conferences, 225–229
    Meals, 241–252
    Resident Payments and Rent, 259–262
    Self-Care Skills Maintenance, 234–240
    Therapeutic Community, 253–258
    Worksharing Program, 263–269
Household Financial Management Program, 151–178
    budgets, 166–168
    living accommodations, 162–166
    menu planning and budgeting, 153–162

Individual Program Book Procedure, 19–22, 230–233
Individual Treatment Agreement, 22, 233
Interdisciplinary Treatment Team, 7, 12, 225
Interdisciplinary Treatment Team Conferences Procedure, 12–18, 225–229
Interpersonal Skills, 96–117, 118–133, 134–150

Job Assignment Procedure, 182–190, 263–269

Locker Maintenance Procedure, 74–78

Meal Procedure, 86–90
Meals Procedure, 241–252
Medication Procedure, 79–85

North Carolina Mental Health, Mental Retardation and Substance Abuse Laws, 191

Outside Privileges Procedure, 191–197

Problem Solving Skills Program, 118–133
Psychiatric Unit Procedures, 1–221
    Agitation Procedure, 206–212
    Behavior Therapy Facility Regulations, 5–11
    Canteen Procedure, 38–40
    Communication Skills Program, 96–117
    Discharge Preparation Group, 218–221
    Elopement Policy, 215–217

276 INDEX

Psychiatric Unit Procedures (*cont.*)
  Goal Orientation Procedure, 134–150
  Household Financial Management Program, 151–178
  Individual Program Book Procedures, 19–22, 230–233
  Interdisciplinary Treatment Team Conferences Procedure, 12
  Job Assignment Procedure, 182–190
  Outside Privileges Procedure, 191–197
  Problem Solving Skills Program, 118–133
  Recreational-Leisure Activities Program, 179–181
  Self-Care Skills Procedure, 41–95
  Smoking Policy, 213–214
  Token Economy Program, 23–37
  Weekend Visits Procedure, 198–205

Records, 6, 7
Recreational-Leisure Activities Program, 179–181
Resident Payments and Rent Program, 259–262

Self-Care Skills Procedures, 41–95, 223, 234–240
  Bedroom Area Preparation, 55–60
  Dental Hygiene, 67–70
  Dressing, 91–95
  General, 41–54, 234–240
  Locker Maintenance, 74–78
  Meals, 86–90
  Medication, 79–85
  Shower, 71–74
  Wake-up, 61–66
Shower Procedure, 71–74
Smoking Policy, 213–214, 224

Therapeutic Community Procedure, 253–258
  administrative offices, 253–254
  by-laws, 253
  government, 222
  impeachment, 254
  voting powers, 254
Token Economy Program, 23–27
Treatment plans, 5, 10, 12–18, 19–22

Wake-Up Procedure, 61–66
Weekend Visits Procedure, 198–205
  Family's Questionnaire for Home Visits, 205
  Resident's Questionnaire for Home Visits, 204

NO LONGER THE PROPERTY
OF THE
UNIVERSITY OF R.I. LIBRARY